NEW

Total English

PRE-INTERMEDIATE

Teacher's Book with Resource Disc

Diane Naughton

Contents

Introduction   3

     What's new about *New Total English?*   3

     Course package   4

     Structure of a Students' Book unit   6

     Structure of support components   7

     Teaching approaches   8

     Students' Book contents   12

Teaching notes

     Unit by unit teaching notes   16

Class CD audioscripts   124

ActiveBook and ActiveTeach contents   135

Resource Disc

     Photocopiable class activities and teaching notes

     Photocopiable video activities and answer key

     Progress tests and answer key

     Achievement tests with answer key and teaching notes, audio and audioscripts

     Printable version of Class CD audioscripts and videoscripts

What's new about *New Total English?*

What makes *New Total English* different from – and better than – the first edition? Firstly, don't worry – we haven't thrown the baby out with the bathwater! We haven't changed everything. We've listened to what you said you liked about the first edition and have kept the most popular features. You'll certainly recognise the look, the format and some integral features from the first edition: the Lead-in pages, the easy-to-use lessons, the comprehensive Reference and Review and practice sections, the popular video clips. Changing to the new edition won't mean that you have to get to grips with a completely new course.

Real solutions to real needs

Some things <u>are</u> different, however. We've looked at every aspect of the course and tried to find solutions for some of your real needs. We've improved the flow of many of the lessons in the Students' Book, integrating more Can do statements and making sure that they all have clear 'outcomes'. We've also given more space to important aspects of language learning such as vocabulary, writing and listening. There's a free online Vocabulary Trainer with each level to help learners memorise new words and phrases; a complete Writing bank at the back of the Students' Book, covering different text types and writing sub-skills as well as new semi-authentic listening extracts to help students gain confidence in dealing with features such as redundancy, hesitation and ungrammatical speech. And, as you'd expect with a new edition, we've given the grammar, vocabulary and pronunciation syllabus a complete overhaul as well as updating much of the content.

New digital components

We've also included new digital components in the course package. The ActiveBook component features the Students' Book pages in digital format and includes integrated audio and video as well as interactive exercises for students to do in class or at home. The ActiveTeach component will help you get the most out of the course with its range of interactive whiteboard software tools and *MyTotalEnglishLab* will help students get better results with its range of interactive practice exercises, progress tests and automatic gradebook.

To sum up, we've kept all the best ingredients of the first edition, improved other features and added exciting new digital components to make *New Total English* an even better package. We hope you and your students will continue to enjoy using it.

The *New Total English* author team

Course package

Students' Book with ActiveBook and DVD

The *New Total English* Students' Books with ActiveBook and DVD are divided into 10–12 units that contain approximately 80–120 hours of teaching material. Each unit contains a balanced mix of grammar, vocabulary, pronunciation and skills:

- clear aims and objectives linked to the CEFR (Common European Framework of Reference)
- revised grammar, vocabulary and pronunciation syllabus
- new reading, listening and video material
- new Writing bank with model texts and focus on sub-skills
- revised and extended Pronunciation bank

ActiveBook:

- digital version of Students' Book with interactive activities and integrated audio and video
- video clips can be selected when you use the ActiveBook in your computer, or play it in a DVD player

Students' Book with ActiveBook, DVD and MyLab

Packaged with the *New Total English* Students' Book with ActiveBook and DVD, *MyEnglishLab* provides students with everything they need to make real progress both in class and at home:

MyEnglishLab:

- interactive exercises with feedback
- regular progress and achievement tests
- automatic marking and gradebook

Class CDs

The *New Total English* Class CDs contain all the recorded material from the Students' Books.

Workbook and Audio CD

The *New Total English* Workbooks contain further practice of language areas covered in the corresponding units of the Students' Books:

- extra grammar, vocabulary, skills and pronunciation exercises
- regular Review and Consolidation sections
- audioscripts and accompanying Audio CD
- with and without key versions available

Teacher's Book with Resource Disc

The *New Total English* Teacher's Books provide all the support teachers need to get the most out of the course:

- background notes and instructions on how to exploit each unit
- suggestions for warm-up and extension activities

Resource Disc:

- extensive bank of photocopiable and printable classroom activities
- editable and printable progress and achievement tests
- audio and video scripts

ActiveTeach and DVD

The *New Total English* Teacher's Books will be further enhanced by the ActiveTeach component which features:

- Students' Book in digital format with all the material from the ActiveBook
- all the material from the Resource Disc
- interactive whiteboard software tools
- video clips can be selected when you use the ActiveTeach in your computer, or play it in a DVD player

Vocabulary Trainer

The *New Total English* Vocabulary Trainer is a new online learning tool designed to help students revise and memorise key vocabulary from the course.
Check this exciting new component out on
www.newtotalenglish.vocabtrainer.net

Website

New Total English has its own dedicated website. In addition to background information about the course and authors, the website features teaching tips, downloadable worksheets, links to other useful websites as well as special offers and competitions. Join us online at
www.pearsonELT.com/newtotalenglish

Each unit of the *New Total English* Students' Books has the same structure:

- **Lead-in page**
  - acts as a springboard into the topic of the unit and engages learners' interest.
  - introduces essential vocabulary related to the topic so that learners start with the same basic grounding.

- **Input lessons**
  - three input lessons, thematically linked, offering interesting angles on the unit topic. Lessons are double-page at lower levels and triple-page at Intermediate and above.
  - each input lesson leads towards a Can do learning objective in line with the CEFR Can do statements.
  - each 90-minute lesson focuses on a specific grammar area and includes vocabulary and skills work.
  - each unit usually contains at least two reading texts, a substantial listening element (including semi-authentic listenings) and pronunciation work.
  - How to... boxes develop students' competence in using language, in line with the CEFR.
  - Lifelong learning boxes offer tips and strategies for developing learners' study skills.

- **Communication page**
  - revises language taught in the previous three lessons in a freer, more communicative context.
  - each communication task practises a range of skills and has a measurable goal or outcome.

- **Vocabulary page (Intermediate and above)**
  - focuses on vocabulary systems and word-building.
  - helps learners to expand and develop their vocabulary.

- **Reference page**
  - summarises the main grammar points covered in each unit and provides a list of key vocabulary.
  - helps learners to catch up if they miss lessons and is an essential revision tool.

- **Review and practice page**
  - provides a range of exercises to consolidate key grammar and vocabulary covered in the unit.
  - can be used to check progress, enabling teachers to identify areas that need further practice.

- **Writing bank**
  - provides models and tips on how to deal with different types of writing (letters, emails and so on).
  - provides guidance on different writing sub-skills such as punctuation, spelling and paragraph construction.

- **Pronunciation bank**
  - provides a list of English phonemes, guidance on sound-spelling correspondences and weak forms.
  - summarises the pronunciation points covered in each unit of the Students' Book.

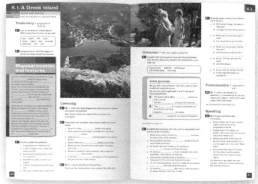

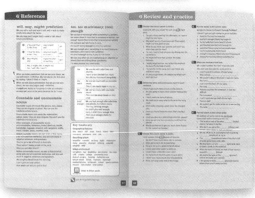

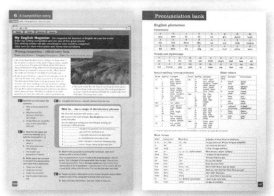

Structure of support components

A range of support components help you get the most out of each unit:

- **Students' Book with ActiveBook and DVD**
  - digital version of Students' Book with interactive activites.
  - integrated audio and video for Students' Book listening activities (including Reference pages and pronunciation activities).
  - wide variety of video clips (including drama, documentary and comedy) which can be selected when you use the ActiveBook in your computer, or play it in a DVD player.
  - interactive video activities.

- **Workbook with Audio CD**
  - consolidation of work covered in the Students' Book.
  - extensive practice of grammar, vocabulary and skills, including pronunciation.
  - regular Review and consolidation sections.
  - can be used in class or for self-study.

- **Students' Book with ActiveBook and MyEnglishLab**
  - interactive Workbook with instant feedback and automatic marking.
  - progress and achievement tests with automatic marking and gradebook.

- **Teacher's Book with Resource Disc**
  - provides step by step teaching notes including ideas for warmers and extension activities.
  - includes background notes and tips for dealing with particularly difficult language points.
  - Resource Disc features an extensive bank of photocopiable and printable classroom activities as well as editable and printable progress and achievement tests.

- **ActiveTeach**
  - digital version of the Students' Book to be used in class.
  - video clips that can be selected when you use the ActiveTeach in your computer, or play it in a DVD player.
  - all the material from the Teacher's Book Resource Disc.
  - a range of interactive whiteboard software tools.

- **Vocabulary Trainer**
  www.newtotalenglish.vocabtrainer.net
  - new online learning tool designed to help students revise and memorise key vocabulary from each unit of the course.

- **Website**
  www.pearsonELT.com/newtotalenglish
  - features background information about the course and authors as well as teaching tips, downloadable worksheets and links to other useful websites.

Teaching approaches

Grammar

New Total English places a lot of emphasis on providing learners with the grammar 'building blocks' they need to communicate confidently. It aims to give learners a thorough foundation in grammar and, at the same time, provides plenty of structured and free practice. Each unit deals with grammar in a broadly similar way:

• Clear presentation and analysis

Each lesson has a clear grammar aim which is stated at the top of the page. Lessons are double-page at lower levels and triple-page at Intermediate and above. New language items are presented in context via reading and/or listening texts and grammar rules are then analysed and explained via the Active grammar boxes, which are a key feature of each lesson. *New Total English* takes a 'guided discovery' approach to grammar and learners are actively invited to think about grammar and work out the rules for themselves.

Active grammar

Most sentences in English are active.

active subject + verb + object

1   *Americans _____ (spend) more than $110 billion on fast food every year.*

We use the passive form when …

- • who/what causes the action is unknown or not important.
- • we want to emphasise the passive subject (at the beginning of the sentence).

2   *Sixty-five million fast-food meals _____ (eat) in the US every day.*

passive subject + *am/is/are (not)* + past participle

• Varied, regular practice

Once learners have grasped the important rules, all new language is then practised in a variety of different ways so that learners are able to use the grammar with confidence. Practice activities include form-based exercises designed to help learners manipulate the new structures as well as more meaningful, personalised practice. Additional grammar practice exercises can be found in the Review and practice sections at the end of each unit as well as in the Workbooks and *MyEnglishLab*. This component, which features the Workbook exercises in digital format, also provides learners with extra guidance, tips and feedback. The Teacher's Book provides a lot of guidance on how to deal with tricky grammar points. It also contains a Resource Disc with an extensive bank of printable and photocopiable classroom grammar activities which are designed to practise the language in freer, more communicative contexts.

• Easily accessible reference material

In addition to the explanations contained in the Active grammar boxes, there is a Reference section at the end of each unit which provides a summary of the grammar rules as well as extra language notes and examples. Audio recordings of the rules and examples are available on the ActiveBook and ActiveTeach components.

Vocabulary

New Total English recognises the central role that vocabulary plays in successful communication. The emphasis is on providing learners with high-frequency, useful vocabulary which is regularly practised and revised. New vocabulary is presented and practised in a variety of different ways.

• Lead-in pages

Each unit starts with a Lead-in page which provides a springboard into the topic of each unit. Featuring a variety of attractive picture prompts and related exercises, the Lead-in pages are designed to help teachers elicit vocabulary that learners already know as well as pre-teach essential vocabulary for the rest of the unit.

• Topic-based vocabulary

Each unit focuses on useful vocabulary relating to the topic of the lessons as well as vocabulary arising from the listening and reading texts. Items are generally presented in context and practised through a variety of exercises.

Vocabulary | music

4 Complete the sentences with the singular or plural form of the words from the box.

> chorus   duet   flop   hit   lead singer
> lyrics   solo   soundtrack   theme song
> top of the charts

1   *Another Way to Die* is a _____ by Alicia Keys and Jack White.
2   Jack White is the _____ of The White Stripes.
3   All the other Bond songs are _____ – with just one singer.
4   The _____ are really good and have a strong message.
5   The first two Bond films had great _____ .
6   After *Goldfinger*, people expected a great _____ in every film.
7   Many Bond songs got to the _____ .
8   Not all Bond songs were _____ .
9   *Die Another Day* wasn't a complete _____ .
10 It had a really catchy _____ .

Additional vocabulary practice is provided in the Review and practice sections of the Students' Book and in the practice exercises in the Workbook. Photocopiable vocabulary activities are also available on the ActiveTeach and on the Resource Disc which accompanies the Teacher's Book.

• Vocabulary pages (Intermediate and above)

At the lower levels there is a lot of emphasis on building learners' knowledge of high-frequency words and phrases as well as common lexical sets. Learners are introduced to collocation work at a very early stage and from intermediate level onwards, there is a greater emphasis on vocabulary systems and word-building.

• Vocabulary Trainer

Each level of *New Total English* is accompanied by a Vocabulary Trainer. This unique online learning tool focuses on the key vocabulary in each unit and helps learners memorise new words and phrases.

Speaking

The key aim for most learners is spoken fluency. However, most learners find it difficult to talk about topics which hold no interest for them and many cannot express themselves easily without support. *New Total English* develops spoken fluency in a number of ways – by giving learners discussion topics they want to talk about; by setting up situations where they are motivated to communicate in order to complete a specific task; by providing clear models and examples of how to structure discourse and by encouraging them, wherever possible, to express their own ideas and opinions.

• Fresh angles on familiar topics

Topics in *New Total English* have been chosen for their intrinsic interest and relevance. Obscure topics, i.e. those which are only likely to appeal to a minority audience, have been avoided and discussion questions have been deliberately chosen to encourage learners to draw on their own lives and experience. Inevitably, many of the topics have been covered in other ELT coursebooks but wherever possible, we have tried to find a fresh angle on them.

• Structured speaking activities

Many of the lessons in *New Total English* culminate in a structured final speaking activity in the form of a survey, roleplay etc. Learners are given time to prepare what they are going to say and prompts to help them. The activities often involve pair and group work to maximise learners' opportunities to speak in class. Many of the structured speaking activities are linked to the CEFR Can do statements.

• How to... boxes

There are regular How to... boxes throughout the course which focus on the words and expressions learners need to carry out specific functions. e.g ordering food in a restaurant.

How to... be polite in English

Use indirect questions and polite responses	
Can you tell me if you have this jacket in medium?	1 _____
Could you tell me how much it is, please?	2 _____
Is it OK if I pay by credit card?	3 _____
Do you mind if I read it ... ?	4 _____

• Communication pages

Communication pages feature at the end of each unit and engage learners in a variety of problem-solving tasks and activities. These give learners practice in a number of different skills including speaking.

• Photocopiable class activities

The photocopiable activities on the ActiveTeach and on the Resource Disc are also specifically designed to promote speaking practice.

Pronunciation

New Total English pays particular attention to pronunciation, which is integrated into lessons which present new language. The pronunciation syllabus includes word and sentence stress, weak forms, intonation and difficult sounds. The Pronunciation bank at the back of the Students' Books provides a summary of all pronunciation points in the book as well as a list of English phonemes, guidance on sound-spelling correspondences and weak forms. The ActiveTeach includes audio to accompany the Pronunciation bank. There is additional pronunciation practice in the Workbooks and Workbook Audio CD.

Listening

Listening is one of the most difficult skills to master and *New Total English* places particular emphasis on developing learners' confidence in this area. Listening texts include short scripted dialogues as well as longer, unscripted semi-authentic listenings. There is additional listening practice in the Workbooks and the video clips on the ActiveBook and ActiveTeach components further enhance learners' confidence in understanding the spoken word.

• Scripted listening activities

Scripted listening activities include short dialogues as well as longer extracts including conversations, interviews and stories. There are lots of simple 'Listen and check your answer' exercises as well as longer, more challenging extracts where learners have to listen for specific information.

• Semi-authentic listening activities

As well as the more traditional scripted listening activities, *New Total English* also includes a range of semi-authentic listening texts, i.e. recordings of one or more people speaking in an unprepared, unscripted way, although they are aware of the relevant level and therefore have adapted their own language to a certain extent accordingly. Learners benefit from listening to a semi-authentic recording because the spontaneity of spoken English means that it is full of false starts, hesitations, redundancy and 'ungrammatical' sentences. Learners need to be aware of these features and they need to develop confidence in dealing with them in order to cope with listening in the 'real world'.

• Video clips

New Total English provides a video clip to accompany each unit of the Students' Book. The videos feature a range of authentic material from a variety of different sources including short films and clips from TV documentaries and drama. The video clips expose learners to real English and are designed to motivate learners to 'raise their game' in terms of developing their listening skills.

To make the material more accessible to learners, photocopiable activities for each video clip are available on the ActiveTeach and on the Resource Disc. There are additional interactive video exercises on the ActiveBook and ActiveTeach which students can complete in class or at home.

The video clips are available on the ActiveBook which accompanies each Students' Book and on the ActiveTeach. You can select the video clips when you use the discs in your computer, or you can play them in a DVD player.

Reading

Many learners need to be able to read texts in English – for their studies, for work or simply for pleasure – and *New Total English* recognises that reading is an extremely important skill that can have a beneficial effect on all aspects of language learning including vocabulary, spelling and writing.

New Total English encourages learners to read as much as possible – in most units there are at least two substantial reading texts – and care has been taken to introduce students to as wide a range of text types as possible, from simple forms and advertisements to short texts from newspapers and magazines.

Reading texts are accompanied by a range of activities that are designed to check comprehension as well as develop key reading skills such as reading for gist, reading for specific information, guessing the meaning of words from the context and so on.

• Choice of texts

As with the listening material in *New Total English*, texts have been chosen for their intrinsic interest as well as for their usefulness in providing a vehicle for the particular grammar and vocabulary points in focus. Many of the texts have been adapted from authentic, real-life sources such as magazines and websites, and where texts have been adapted or graded, every effort has been made to remain faithful to the orignal text type in terms of content and style.

• Exploitation of texts

Each reading text in *New Total English* is accompanied by a number of exploitation exercises that have been carefully selected to develop learners' reading skills. Activities include comprehension and vocabulary work as well as practice in dealing with different reading sub-skills such as reading for gist. There are also a number of jigsaw readings where learners work together and share information.

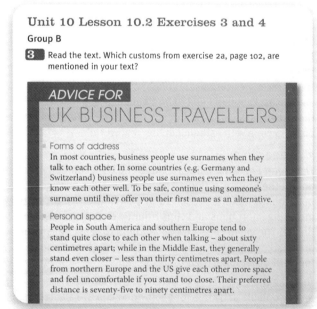

• Length and complexity

The length and complexity of the reading texts in *New Total English* get more challenging as the course progresses. At lower levels, the texts are very short and the emphasis is on training learners to read for specific information. At higher levels, learners are introduced to a a greater range and variety text types and more emphasis is placed on textual analysis.

Writing

In these days of electronic media, it is easy to forget that writing is not simply speech written down – effective writing has all sorts of conventions that differ from speech and that are necessary to learn in one's own language as well as in a foreign language.

New Total English pays particular attention to the important skill of writing. One of the most important new features of the revised edition is the Writing bank at the back of each Students' Book which contains 10 – 12 lessons that focus on different types of writing – emails, postcards, formal and informal letters and so on. Each lesson also provides additional advice and guidance on different writing sub-skills such as punctuation, spelling and paragraph construction.

• Model text types

Each Writing bank lesson has a Can do statement which refers to the written output that students complete at the end of the lesson. The lesson usually starts with a warmer that engages students in the topic. Learners then go on to focus on a model of the text type and in most cases, there is some comprehension work to ensure that students are familiar with the content before they start working on the format and related sub-skills. The lesson always finishes with a contextualised written output.

• Writing sub-skills

One of the most important aspects of the Writing bank is that it examines the sub-skills of writing in detail. This is important as it helps learners to build on and develop their writing skills, rather than simply providing practice in writing. Among the sub-skills covered are punctuation, grammatical cohesion, paragraphing and features such as varying the vocabulary used to both enhance interest and ensure lexical cohesion.

• How to... boxes

How to... boxes are a particular feature of the Writing bank. They usually focus on a particular sub-skill of writing and in some cases on written conventions, such as email or letter layout, appropriate formality of language for the text type or order of presentation of the content (such as in a review).

How to... avoid repetition

You can make your writing more interesting by avoiding repetition: by using pronouns and a range of vocabulary.

Use pronouns	1 *it* (line 6) = <u>*the sandstorm*</u>
	2 *that* (line 8) = _____
	3 *one* (line 10) = _____
	4 *he* (line 11) = _____
	5 *it* (line 26) = _____
Use a range of vocabulary	1 *beautiful* – _____
	2 *good* – _____
	3 *surprised* – _____

Learner training

New Total English places a strong emphasis on learner training and good study habits are encouraged and developed via the Lifelong learning boxes which are featured in many lessons. The Lifelong learning boxes provide useful tips and suggestions on how to continue learning outside the classroom.

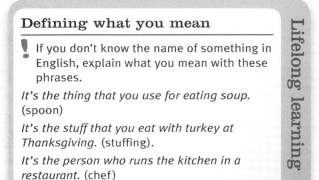

Defining what you mean

! If you don't know the name of something in English, explain what you mean with these phrases.

It's the thing that you use for eating soup. (spoon)

It's the stuff that you eat with turkey at Thanksgiving. (stuffing).

It's the person who runs the kitchen in a restaurant. (chef)

Use *thing* for countable nouns, *stuff* for uncountable nouns and *person* for people.

Revision and testing

There are plenty of opportunities for revision in *New Total English* and language is constantly recycled throughout the course. At the end of every unit, there are special Review and practice pages which take the form of mini-progress checks, enabling learners to identify areas where they might need further practice. Interactive versions of the activities on these pages are available on the ActiveBook and ActiveTeach. The Workbook and accompanying Audio CD provide further practice in grammar, vocabulary and skills covered in the corresponding Students' Book. The Workbook is available in with key and without key versions.

For learners who are really serious about making rapid progress in English, *MyTotalEnglishLab* provides the perfect solution. This exciting component features the Workbook exercises in digital format as well as tips and feedback on common errors.

Regular progress and achievement tests are provided on the ActiveTeach, Resource Disc and *MyEnglishLab*. *MyEnglishLab* also includes automatic marking and a gradebook.

New Total English and exams

The table below shows how the different levels of *New Total English* relate to the University of Cambridge ESOL main suite examinations in terms of the language taught and the topics covered.

Starter	Builds foundation for KET
Elementary	Useful for KET
Pre-Intermediate	**Useful for PET**
Intermediate	Useful for FCE
Upper Intermediate	Useful for FCE
Advanced	Useful for CAE

While *New Total English* is not an examination preparation course, a student who has, for example, completed the Upper-intermediate level would have sufficient language to attempt the Cambridge ESOL FCE (First Certificate in English) examination. Many of the exercises in the *New Total English* Students' Books and other components are similar in format to those found in the Cambridge ESOL main suite examinations but specific training is required for all EFL examinations and we would strongly recommend this.

New Total English and the CEFR

New Total English is correlated to the CEFR (Common European Framework of Reference). Please see the *New Total English* website: **www.pearsonELT.com/newtotalenglish** for details of CEFR Can do statements for each level of the course.

CEFR	
A1	Starter
A2	Elementary
B1	**Pre-intermediate**
B1+	Intermediate
B2	Upper Intermediate
C1	Advanced

Students' Book Contents

UNIT		Can do	Grammar
Welcome to New Total English p 2	Do you know...? p 8		
1 24 hours p 9–18	1.1 Are you a culture vulture?	Discuss likes and dislikes	Likes and dislikes
	1.2 Monday to Friday	Talk about how often you do things	Present Simple; adverbs of frequency
	1.3 At the same time	Talk about what you're doing now and around now	Present Continuous: now and around now
	Communication p 16 Writing bank p 135	Describe your learning needs **How to...** talk about your learning needs Write about yourself and your interests **How to...** join ideas and sentences (1)	
2 Music p 19–28	2.1 Music for 007	Describe personal events in the past	Past Simple
	2.2 Barefoot music	Talk about personal achievements and experiences	Present Perfect Simple: experience
	2.3 The Mozart effect	Ask different types of questions	Questions
	Communication p 26 Writing bank p 136	Explain why you like a piece of music Write a short biography about someone's life **How to...** plan your writing	
3 Taste p 29–38	3.1 Jamie's kitchen	Tell a friend about your future plans	*be going to*: future plans
	3.2 Let's celebrate!	Make arrangements with a friend	Present Continuous: future arrangements
	3.3 Ratatouille	Define and describe things to explain what you mean	Defining relative clauses
	Communication p 36 Writing bank p 137	Contribute to a simple discussion Write a note or message to a friend **How to...** use short forms in notes	
4 Survival p 39–48	4.1 Going to extremes	Compare people	Comparative adjectives
	4.2 Survival school	Talk about challenging events and activities	Superlative adjectives
	4.3 Surviving in English	Ask questions in everyday situations	Indirect questions
	Communication p 46 Writing bank p 138	Agree on choices with other people Write a 'thank you' email **How to...** structure a 'thank you' email	
5 Stages p 49–58	5.1 Turning eighteen	Exchange opinions with a friend	*should, have to, can*: obligation and permission
	5.2 Old friends	Talk about friends	Present Perfect Simple: *for* and *since*
	5.3 The truth about ageing	Describe yourself when you were younger	*used to*: past habits
	Communication p 56 Writing bank p 139	Tell someone's life story Complete a simple form **How to...** understand the language on forms	
6 Places p 59–68	6.1 A Greek island	Make general predictions about the future	*will, may, might*: prediction
	6.2 Mandela's garden	Describe a favourite place	Countable and uncountable nouns
	6.3 Virtual world	Give reasons for choices	*too, too much/many, (not) enough*
	Communication p 66 Writing bank p 140	Explain your preferences Write a description of a favourite place **How to...** use a range of introductory phrases	

Vocabulary	Speaking and Pronunciation	Listening and Reading
Going out	Sentence stress	R What do you like doing at the weekend?
Describing your day and lifestyle	*do/does* **How to...** respond to information	L Valentino Rossi – motorcycle champion
Time phrases		R Online chatting
		Reference p 17, **Review and Practice** p 18
Music	**How to...** refer to past times	L Music in James Bond films
Achievements	*have/has*	R Shakira – pop star and business woman
	Intonation in questions	R The Mozart effect L Music
		Reference p 27, **Review and Practice** p 28
	How to... talk about future plans Connected speech (1)	R Cook your way to a better life!
Describing food	**How to...** make arrangements	L Thanksgiving in the US
Easily-confused words	Silent letters	R *Ratatouille*
		Reference p 37, **Review and Practice** p 38
Describing people	Emphasising important words	R Going up and Going down
Survival skills		L Survival school
	How to... be polite in English Intonation in indirect questions	R One language – three cultures
		Reference p 47, **Review and Practice** p 48
	How to... exchange opinions Connected speech (2)	R Life at eighteen L The age to do things
Friendship		L Different types of friends
Habits		R How long am I going to live?
		Reference p 57, **Review and Practice** p 58
Geographical features	Contractions: *will*	L *Mamma Mia!* island
Describing a place	Diphthongs	R Garden of freedom – my favourite place
Urban environment	**How to...** talk about choices and give reasons	L *SimCity*
		Reference p 67, **Review and Practice** p 68

Students' Book Contents

UNIT		Can do	Grammar
7 Body p 69–78	7.1 Changing bodies	Talk about possible events and situations in the future	First Conditional
	7.2 Hands up	Describe someone's personality	Gerunds and infinitives
	7.3 Doctor, doctor	Discuss illnesses and give advice	*stop, try, remember*: gerunds and infinitives
	Communication p 76 Writing bank p 141	Discuss how you feel Write an apology with an explanation **How to...** use punctuation	
8 Speed p 79–88	8.1 Fast world	Discuss the use of technology	Present Simple Passive
	8.2 Married in a month	Talk about special occasions	Prepositions of time
	8.3 Fast men	Describe past actions	Past Continuous and Past Simple
	Communication p 86 Writing bank p 142	Talk for an extended period on a familiar topic **How to...** organise a presentation Write a short story describing a sequence of events **How to...** use time linkers	
9 Work p 89–98	9.1 The best job	Talk about your abilities	*can, could, be able to*: ability
	9.2 Interview horrors	Respond to simple job interview questions	Adverbs of manner
	9.3 Career criminals	Tell a story from the news	Past Simple Passive
	Communication p 96 Writing bank p 143	Take part in a simple negotiation **How to...** negotiate with other people Write a professional profile **How to...** use positive language in professional writing	
10 Travel p 99–108	10.1 Travel companions	Describe a holiday	Present Perfect Simple: *just, yet, already*
	10.2 Customs worldwide	Make generalisations about customs	Verbs with two objects
	10.3 Travel movies	Recommend a film	Past Perfect Simple
	Communication p 106 Writing bank p 144	Talk about a journey **How to...** tell a story in an engaging way Write about recent travel experiences **How to...** avoid repetition	
11 Influence p 109–118	11.1 Childhood influences	Talk about people who influenced you	*would*: past habits
	11.2 The power of advertising	Discuss adverts and their influence	Articles
	11.3 Positive thinking	Talk about decisions and plans for the future	*will* and *be going to*: decisions and plans
	Communication p 116 Writing bank p 145	Justify your opinions about people Write about your opinions of a film **How to...** join ideas and sentences (2)	
12 Money p 119–128	12.1 Honesty is the best policy	Discuss imaginary or unlikely situations	Second Conditional
	12.2 The price of success	Report what someone said to you	Reported speech
	12.3 The $1 million baseball	Describe similarities and differences	*both, either, neither*
	Communication p 126 Writing bank p 146	Ask survey questions and report the results Write a formal email/letter **How to...** structure a formal email/letter	

Communication activities p 129   **Writing bank** p 135   **Pronunciation bank** p 147

Vocabulary	Speaking and Pronunciation	Listening and Reading
Appearance	Intonation in conditional sentences	R Cover girl
Personality	Schwa /ə/ on unstressed syllables	L Hands and personality R Your skills are in your hands
Illness	**How to...** give and respond to advice	L and R Different remedies
		Reference p 77, **Review and Practice** p 78
		L The pace of life R Take your time!
Phrasal verbs: relationships	Phrasal verbs: stress	L Arranged marriage in India
Measurements	*was/were*	R Lightning Bolt!
		Reference p 87, **Review and Practice** p 88
		R Ben gets dream job
Work	Changing word stress	L Worst job interviews
Crime		R Car cleaner sent to prison
		Reference p 97, **Review and Practice** p 98
	Showing interest	R My backpacking holiday in Brazil
Greetings and gifts	**How to...** make generalisations	R Advice for UK business travellers
-ed and *-ing* adjectives	Using fillers: *anyway*	L *The Motorcycle Diaries*
		Reference p 107, **Review and Practice** p 108
Phrasal verbs		R Raised by animals
The media	Using fillers: *well*, *so* and *erm* **How to...** use persuasive language	L Advertising on television
Verb + preposition (1)		*Yes Man*
		Reference p 117, **Review and Practice** p 118
Money		R How much do you want to pay?
Money in education	**How to...** report back on discussions	L Money in education
Verb + preposition (2)	Emphasising details	R The $1 million baseball
		Reference p 127, **Review and Practice** p 128
Irregular verb table p 149	**Audioscripts** p 150	

1 | 24 hours

Overview

Lead-in	**Revision:** 24 hours
1.1	**Can do:** Discuss likes and dislikes **Grammar:** Likes and dislikes **Vocabulary:** Going out **Speaking and Pronunciation:** Sentence stress **Reading:** What do you like doing at the weekend?
1.2	**Can do:** Talk about how often you do things **Grammar:** Present Simple; adverbs of frequency **Vocabulary:** Describing your day and lifestyle **Speaking and Pronunciation:** do/does **How to...** respond to information **Listening:** Valentino Rossi – motorcycle champion
1.3	**Can do:** Talk about what you're doing now and around now **Grammar:** Present Continuous: now and around now **Vocabulary:** Time phrases **Reading:** Online chatting
Communication	Describe your learning needs **How to...** talk about your learning needs
Reference	
Review and practice	
Writing bank	Write about yourself and your interests **How to...** join ideas and sentences (1)
Extra resources	Active Teach and Active Book

CEFR Can do objectives

1.1 Discuss likes and dislikes
1.2 Talk about how often you do things
1.3 Talk about what you're doing now and around now
Communication Describe your learning needs
Writing bank Write about yourself and your interests

CEFR Portfolio ideas

a) Video your conversation with another student from Exercise 11 on page 13.
b) Write a description of something which you want to sell on eBay. Say how old it is and why you want to sell it.
c) Write an email to LangLink.co.uk. Explain why you want to learn English. Say how you like learning. Describe what you are good at doing and what you find difficult.

Lead-in

OPTIONAL WARMER

Ask the whole class to stand up. Write a statement on the board, e.g. *On Mondays I get up after 8:00 a.m.* Ss for whom this statement is true sit down. Ask a few Ss who are still standing *What time do you get up?*
Write the next statement on the board, e.g. *On Tuesdays I drive to work at about ...* (give the time).
The activity continues until only one student (the winner) is still standing.

1 ▶ Ss discuss the two questions in pairs. Get feedback from the whole class, discussing their reasons for choosing certain times of day or days of the week.

2 ▶ Put Ss in pairs to make verb phrases with the words from box A and box B. Check the answers with the whole class.

Answers	
chat on the phone	have a nap
check your emails	have a take-away
do some exercise	listen to the radio
do nothing	make breakfast/lunch/
get up early	dinner
go to bed late	read a magazine/
go shopping	newspaper
go for a swim	stay in for the evening
go for a walk	take a bus/train
have a family meal	watch TV/a DVD
have a lie-in	

▶ Ask Ss to talk in pairs about what they can and can't see in the photos, using the verb phrases from the boxes. Get feedback from various Ss.

3a ▶ Focus Ss' attention on the activities from ex. 2 and give some examples about yourself, e.g. *I chat on the phone every day.* Now tell them to work individually, writing the appropriate letter next to each activity.

b ▶ Ss compare their lists with a partner to see what they have in common. Write an example on the board, e.g. *I go to bed late at the weekend. What about you?* Remind Ss that *always/never* go before the main verb and *every day/ at the weekend* go at the end of the sentence.

EXTEND THE LEAD-IN

Ss divide the activities from ex. 2 into two columns according to whether they like doing this activity or not. Then they compare with a partner, giving their reasons. Get feedback from the whole class.

1.1 Are you a culture vulture?

A *culture vulture* is a person who loves the Arts, such as theatre, opera, painting, sculpture or literature. A *workaholic* is a person who is addicted to work (there are other expressions in English which are similar, e.g. *chocoholic*, *shopaholic*). A *couch potato* is a very lazy person. *Couch* is a synonym of *sofa*. A *party animal* is a person who loves going out and socialising with other people.

In this lesson, Ss read about what different people like doing at the weekend and talk about how they like spending their free time. Through this context they learn various ways of expressing likes and dislikes.

OPTIONAL WARMER

Write the following words on the board and elicit/teach the meanings: *party/work/couch/culture*. Now put Ss in pairs to write five words they associate with each of the four words written on the board.
Ask different Ss to read out their words at random and the rest of the class have to guess which main word it is associated with. Write the words on the board.

Reading

1a ▶ Put Ss in pairs to match the photos A–D with the descriptions 1–4. Check the answers with the whole class.

Answers
B 1
C 2
D 4

b ▶ Ss read through the text individually and decide what type of people Marek, Lola and Henry are. When Ss have finished, get feedback and ask if there are any expressions they don't understand. Elicit/teach the meaning of these expressions. Avoid going into too much detail about the various ways of expressing likes and dislikes at this point as this is covered in detail in ex. 6.

Answers
Marek – workaholic
Lola – culture vulture
Henry – couch potato

2 ▶ Ss complete the sentences in pairs. Ask different Ss to read out the completed sentences for the whole class.

Answers		3	Marek	6	Marek
1	Henry	4	Lola	7	Lola
2	Lola	5	Henry	8	Henry

3 ▶ Ss think of a person they know well and explain to a partner about that person's typical weekend, saying if he or she is more like Marek, Lola or Henry. Get feedback from a couple of Ss.

Vocabulary | going out

4 ▶ Put Ss in pairs to make verb phrases with the words from box A and box B. Elicit answers from the whole class, explaining any expressions they do not understand.

Answers
go bowling
go to the cinema
go clubbing
go to a concert
go to an exhibition
go on a guided walk/tour
go to a musical
go to the theatre

5 ▶ Put Ss in pairs to talk about which activities they normally do at the weekend. Encourage them to say why they like doing these things. Get feedback from the class.

Grammar | likes and dislikes

OPTIONAL GRAMMAR LEAD-IN

Ss close their books and work in pairs to see if they can remember any of the expressions that were used in the text to express liking or not liking. You can get them started by writing an example, e.g. *I quite like …* on the board. Get feedback and write the expressions on the board.

6 ▶ Focus on the Active grammar box and establish the fact that the faces represent different degrees of liking and not liking. Tell the Ss to work with a partner to complete the gaps by looking back at the expressions in the text on page 10. Elicit the answers from the class and write them on the board.

Active grammar

1 really like
2 'm quite keen on
3 don't mind
4 'm not very keen on
5 really hate

▶ Draw Ss' attention to the note at the bottom of the grammar box and write the following examples on the board: *I'm quite keen on + noun (I'm quite keen on art.) I'm quite keen on + verb in the -ing form (I'm quite keen on looking at art.)*

▶ Tell Ss to turn to the Reference on page 17 and ask them to underline those sentences that contain verb + noun. Ask various Ss to read them out for the whole class and then ask other Ss to read out those sentences that contain *verb + -ing*.

7 ▶ Ss work in pairs, writing sentences using the prompts. Remind them that it may be necessary to change the verb. There is also more than one possibility in some cases. Encourage the Ss to use a variety of expressions. Get feedback from the whole class.

Answers
1 I quite like musicals/I'm quite keen on musicals.
2 I really hate my job/I can't stand my job.
3 I really like guided tours.
4 I'm not very keen on going ice skating/I don't like going ice skating.
5 I don't mind doing nothing.
6 I quite like coffee/I'm quite keen on coffee.
7 I really hate chatting on the phone in English/I can't stand chatting on the phone in English.
8 I absolutely love going clubbing.

OPTIONAL EXTENSION

Write the following nouns and phrases on the board: *play football, cats, jazz, travel, chocolate, watch TV, very hot weather, chat on the Internet, cook*. Ask Ss to individually write sentences about each one, saying how much they like or dislike them. Check their work as they do this. Now take in the papers and redistribute them. Ask Ss to read out the sentences on the paper they have been given and the rest of the class try to guess who wrote it.

Pronunciation | sentence stress

8a ▶ ● 1.2 Explain to the Ss that when we speak, we stress particular types of words, namely those that are most important in conveying the meaning of what we are saying. Point out that they can find a reference for this in the Pronunciation bank on page 148.

▶ Now focus Ss' attention on the two sentences in ex. 8a and tell them they are going to listen to the sentences and underline six words that are stressed in each one. Point out that the first stressed word, *really*, is already underlined. First, allow them to guess in pairs which words are going to be stressed. Now play the recording and ask students to underline the words. Have them check with a partner and then play the recording again. Check the answers with the whole class.

Answers
1 I <u>really</u> <u>like</u> watching <u>television</u> and I <u>absolutely</u> <u>love</u> going to the <u>cinema</u>.
2 He <u>quite</u> <u>likes</u> going for a <u>walk</u>, but he <u>really</u> <u>hates</u> going to the <u>gym</u>.

b ▶ Ss tick the types of words which are stressed in ex. 8a. Elicit the answer from the class.

Answers
a ✓
b ✗

9 ▶ Ss rewrite the sentences in ex. 7 so that they are true for themselves. Then they work in pairs, saying the sentences with the correct sentence stress. Have some of the Ss read out their sentences for the rest of the class.

Speaking

10 ▶ Put the Ss in pairs (A and B). Tell student A to look at the questions on page 11 and student B to look at the questions on page 129. Student A asks his/her questions to student B, making a note of the answers. Then student B asks his/her questions to student A and notes the answers.

11 ▶ Tell the Ss to look back at the descriptions in ex. 1a and decide which one best fits their partner. They tell each other and see if they agree.

OPTIONAL EXTENSION

Write the following question on the board: *What do you like doing … at Christmas/in the summer holidays/when you're tired/with your friends/on your own?* Ask Ss to write their answers to the question on a piece of paper. Now ask them to stand up and mingle with other Ss. They must try and find somebody who has written the same answer as them. At the end, get feedback from the whole class to see what Ss have got in common.

1.2 Monday to Friday

Valentino Rossi, nicknamed 'The Doctor', was born in 1979 in Urbino, Italy, but now lives in London. He was only 17 when he started racing in 1996, and he became the youngest rider ever to win the 125cc World Championship the following year at the age of 18. He is now thought to be one of the most successful motorcycle racers of all time, with 9 Grand Prix World Championships to his name. Rossi is currently number 9 in the ranking of the highest earning sports personalities in the world, earning $16 million a year just from his contract with Yamaha alone.

In this lesson, Ss listen to a man and a woman talking about the professional motorbike racer, Valentino Rossi, and the things he does on a typical day. Ss then talk about their own daily routines and lifestyles and through this context revise the form and use of the Present Simple and learn adverbs of frequency.

OPTIONAL WARMER

Write *famous sportspeople* on the board and brainstorm the names of ten people. Then put Ss in pairs to talk about what they know about two or three of them. Encourage them to talk about what they think the sportsman or woman might do on a normal day when they are not competing. Get feedback from the class.

Listening

1a ▶ Put Ss in pairs to predict the answer to the question, using the photos and/or what they might already know. Don't ask for feedback at this point.

b ▶ 🔘 1.3 Tell Ss they are going to listen to a dialogue between a man and a woman talking about Rossi in order to check their answer to ex. 1a and complete the fact file. Play the recording and elicit the answers.

Answers
Nationality: Italian
Job: Motorbike racer
Number of world championships: 9 ✓

2a ▶ Focus Ss' attention on the expressions in the box and check they understand them all. Now put them in pairs to suggest possible answers to questions 1 and 2. Get feedback from the class but don't confirm any answers.

b ▶ 🔘 1.4 Play the second part of the dialogue so that Ss can check their answers to questions 1 and 2. Tell them that they won't hear all the expressions shown in the box. Let them compare with a partner and then elicit the answers.

Answers
1   On a race day, Rossi gets up early and prepares for the race.
2   On a normal day, Rossi gets up late, goes to the gym, goes out in the evening and goes to bed late.

3 ▶ Read through questions 1–8 with the whole class and check they understand them. Now play the recording again so that the Ss can make a note of the answers. Allow them to talk to a partner first and then elicit the answers from the whole class.

Answers
1   He gets up at about six or seven o'clock.
2   He gets up at eleven o'clock.
3   No, he doesn't.
4   He goes to the gym between twelve and two in the afternoon.
5   He often listens to music and plays computer games. He sometimes watches a film.
6   He goes to parties and clubs with friends.
7   He usually goes to bed about three or four in the morning.
8   No, he doesn't.

4 ▶ Put Ss in pairs to discuss the questions and then get feedback from the whole class.

Vocabulary | describing your day and lifestyle

5 ▶ Ask Ss to try to complete the sentences with the adjectives from the box. Let them compare with a partner and then check the answers with the whole class.

Answers
1   boring
2   busy
3   stressful
4   relaxing
5   lazy
6   fun
7   unusual

6 ▶ Read through the questions with the Ss and check they understand them. Now put them in pairs to ask and answer the questions. Encourage them to give details. Go around the class monitoring their conversations and then ask some of the Ss to report their discussions to the rest of the class.

Grammar | Present Simple; adverbs of frequency

OPTIONAL GRAMMAR LEAD-IN

Write the following question on the board.
How often do you … go out in the evening/go to bed early or late/go to the gym/get up early or late/talk to your family or friends?
Ask Ss to answer the questions in pairs or small groups and then ask various Ss to answer for the whole class. Write any adverbs of frequency they use on the board and at the end elicit/teach that these words are called *adverbs of frequency*. Then elicit from the Ss the name of the tense they have been using (Present Simple) and explain that this is the grammar point they are going to study next.

7a ▶ Focus Ss' attention on part A of the Active grammar box and the instructions 1 and 2. Put Ss in pairs to complete the rule and the example sentences. Copy the first part of the Active grammar box on the board and elicit the answers from the class to complete it.

Active grammar

A   habits
–   don't
?   does
?   do

---

b ▶ Now focus Ss' attention on part B and read through the adverbs of frequency that are given, pointing out that they are in order of most to least frequent. Tell the Ss that *never* and *hardly ever* can only be used in affirmative sentences as we don't have double negatives in English.

▶ Put Ss in pairs to read through the rules, choosing the correct alternative. Elicit answers from the class and then draw their attention to the Reference on page 17.

Active grammar

1   before   2   after   3   end

---

8 ▶ Put Ss in pairs to find and correct the mistakes. Elicit answers from the class.

Answers
1   A: <u>Do</u> you get up early?
    B: Yes, I do. I <u>always</u> get up early because I start work at 8.30.
2   A: <u>Does</u> your brother go to the gym?
    B: Yes, he <u>does</u>. He usually goes to the gym three times a week.
3   A: <u>Do</u> you go clubbing at the weekends?
    B: No, I <u>don't</u>. I hardly ever go clubbing.
4   A: <u>Does</u> your sister go out after work?
    B: No, she doesn't. But she <u>sometimes</u> phones her friends.

OPTIONAL EXTENSION

Dictate the following sentences to the Ss. As they write them down, they add an adverb of frequency in the correct position so that the sentences are true for them. Ask them to compare with a partner and then get feedback from a number of Ss.
I eat meat. I sleep for eight hours. I am busy. I go to the cinema. I do my English homework.

Pronunciation | *do/does*

9 ▶ 🌐 1.5 Tell the Ss that there are two different ways of pronouncing *do* and *does*. Explain that in question forms the pronunciation is weak and in short answers it is strong. Play the recording and get the Ss to repeat the sentences as a class. Now have them practise in pairs. Ask a couple of Ss to say the sentences for the whole class. Draw Ss' attention to the Pronunciation bank on page 148.

Speaking

10a ▶ 🌐 1.6 Focus the Ss' attention on the topics in the box. Tell them they are going to listen to a dialogue between a man and a woman who are talking about their habits. Tell them to tick the topics they hear mentioned. Play the recording and then elicit answers from the class.

Answers   getting up   going out
               exercise/sport   work

---

b ▶ Focus the Ss on the *How to…* box and read through the different functions and examples with the whole class, checking they understand them. Now tell them to listen to the recording again and number the phrases in the order they hear them. Play the recording again and then elicit the answers from the class.

Answers
3   Do you?!
1   Six o'clock!
2   Are you serious?!
5   Really? Me too!
6   Yes, that's the same as me!
4   Really? I don't.

11a ▶ Put Ss in pairs to write five questions about a person's habits. Tell them they can use the ideas in ex. 10, or ideas of their own.

b ▶ Now move the Ss around so that each person is with a different partner. Tell them to ask and answer each other's questions using the phrases from the *How to…* box. Get feedback from the class to find out if they have anything in common with their partners.

OPTIONAL EXTENSION

Ss change partners again and tell another person about the habits of the first person they interviewed.

1.3 At the same time

Social networking sites such as Facebook or Twitter are becoming increasingly popular with people of all ages. They allow you to create a profile of yourself, contact friends or people you knew in the past and make new friends. People can upload photos, make comments on each other's news and photos and chat to each other in real time through a messenger service. Facebook always implies a two-way relationship as you cannot follow another person's life unless they accept you as a friend. With Twitter, however, the relationship can be one way and you can follow the life of people who don't even know you exist. MSN is a messenger service where people can communicate in real time and it's also a search engine. eBay is a website where people buy and sell things.

In this lesson, Ss read a text from a social networking site. Through this context they consider the use and form of the Present Continuous and practise time phrases.

OPTIONAL WARMER

Put Ss in pairs and write *Facebook* on the board. Tell Ss they have two minutes to write as many words as they can related in some way to this social networking site. After two minutes, stop them and ask the pairs how many words they have written. The pair with the highest number read out their words. If the words are all acceptable, they win. If not, the pair with the next highest number reads out theirs.

Reading

1 ▶ Put Ss in small groups to answer the questions. Before they begin, explain the meaning of the word *bid* (offer an amount of money to buy something; other people can then offer more and you lose the chance to buy the item unless you offer to pay a higher amount). Get feedback from the class.

2 ▶ Ss read the text quickly to find out what Joe is looking for on eBay. Elicit the answers from the whole class.

Answers
A guitar and a pair of ice skates

3 ▶ Tell Ss to read the text again and answer the questions with a partner. Get feedback from the whole class.

Answers
1 Because he is/he's having guitar lesson at the moment.
2 Someone he works with.
3 50 euros
4 He's at work.
5 He decides his top price is 70 euros.
6 150 euros

▶ Ask Ss if there are any other words or phrases in the text that they don't understand. Encourage other Ss to explain them before explaining them yourself.

4 ▶ Put Ss in groups and ask them to discuss the questions. Get feedback from the whole class. Make a list on the board of good things and bad things about social networking sites and have a class vote to decide if they are mainly good or bad.

Grammar | Present Continuous: now and around now

OPTIONAL GRAMMAR LEAD-IN

Ask Ss *Why did Joe say 'I'm having guitar lessons.' and not 'I have guitar lessons.'*? Allow the Ss time to talk about the question with a partner and then get feedback from the whole class. Try to elicit the difference between the Present Simple and the Present Continuous.

5a ▶ Focus the Ss on the Active grammar box and tell them to fill in the gaps A and B with the headings in ex. 5a. Elicit the answers from the class.

Active grammar
A 2
B 1

▶ Give the Ss some more examples by asking the following question: *What are you doing now?* Elicit *studying English*, *listening to the teacher* or *speaking in English* as examples of actions happening 'now'. Now tell them about a book you are reading at the moment as an example of things happening 'around now'. Ask: *What book are you reading at the moment?* Ask various Ss to answer.

▶ Read through the rules in the second half of the Active grammar box with the Ss and check they understand them. Contrast state verbs with other verbs such as *speak*, *dance* or *play* in order to explain the meaning of state. Explain that these verbs are not usually used in the Continuous tense. Have Ss look at the Reference on page 17 and read through the other examples of state verbs.

b ▶ Ss look back at the text on page 14 with a partner and find more examples for each heading in the Active grammar box. Elicit examples from the class.

Answers
A (Temporary actions happening around now):
I'm working all the time ...
Where are you having lessons?
I'm having lessons from someone I work with.
B (Actions happening at this moment):
I'm doing two things at once ...
I'm writing a report and trying to buy a guitar ...
I'm making my first bid now.
Someone else is bidding €70.
It's all happening very quickly now.
I'm bidding €95 now ... .
You don't see what you're buying ... how much you're paying.

▶ Remind the Ss they have reference to this grammar point on page 17.

6 ▶ Ask the pairs to complete the sentences. Elicit the answers from the whole class.

Answers
1   go
2   buy/don't like
3   do you usually do/go
4   isn't studying/'s travelling
5   Do you know/'m learning
6   are you doing/'m working

OPTIONAL EXTENSION

Put the Ss in small groups and have one student from each group come to the front of the class. Give them a sentence that they have to mime to the rest of their group. The Ss go back to their group and mime the sentence. The person who guesses then comes to the front of the class to get the next sentence to mime.
Possible sentences: *You're making a cake. You're doing an exam. You're eating spaghetti. You're climbing a mountain. You're repairing a bicycle*, etc.

Vocabulary | time phrases

7 ▶ Put Ss in pairs to match the phrases from the box with the phrases in sentences 1–3. Elicit the answers from the class. Note that *at once* can also mean *immediately*.

Answers
1   24 hours a day
2   Each time
3   at the same time

8 ▶ Ss choose the correct options. Let them compare with a partner and then elicit the answers from various Ss.

Answers
1   at the same time
2   Every time
3   at once
4   all the time
5   Each time
6   at the moment
7   24 hours a day

9 ▶ Put Ss in pairs to answer the questions. Encourage them to give extra information or justify an answer where possible. Get feedback from various Ss.

Speaking

10a ▶ Ss write down an example of the five things given. Tell them they have to imagine these things are related to their lives at the moment, e.g. if they have written *London*, they are now living in London.

b ▶ Put Ss in pairs to talk about their imaginary new lives. They have to imagine they haven't seen each other for six years. Encourage Ss to ask follow-up questions where possible, e.g. *Do you like living here?*, and to give extra information where possible.

OPTIONAL VARIATION

Ask Ss to make a list of some of the important things that have changed in their lives in the last six years, e.g. passing their driving test or getting a (new) job. Now put them in small groups to talk about what they are doing now that they weren't doing six years ago. Point out that they are only using the Present Continuous so they don't need to talk about what they were doing previously.

1 Communication

In this lesson, Ss talk about reasons for learning a language and what is difficult and easy when learning a language. They then listen to two people discussing the same thing. Finally, they think about ways of improving their English.

OPTIONAL WARMER

Divide the class into two teams and tell them you are going to have a language 'competition'. Each team takes it in turns to ask the question *What language do they speak in ...* (name of country)*?* The other team scores a point if they get the answer correct (with the correct pronunciation). The team with the most points at the end wins.

1 ▶ Put Ss in groups to discuss the questions. Get feedback from the whole class.

2a ▶ 🔊 1.7 Read through the questions with the whole class and check they understand them. Play the recording and get the Ss to take notes. Let them compare with a partner and then play the recording again before eliciting the answers from the whole class.

Answers
Stig
1 Japanese; because his wife's parents don't speak English
2 speaking; listening
3 reading and writing
4 reading and writing

Tessie
1 Spanish; because she dreams of living in Latin America
2 understanding what people say; reading
3 expressing herself
4 speaking skills/fluency

b ▶ Focus Ss on the *How to...* box. Play the recording again and have Ss write S or T to indicate who says each phrase. Elicit the answers from the class.

Answers
I'm quite good at speaking. *S*
My listening's not bad. *S*
I'm quite good at understanding what people say. *T*
I'm pretty good at reading. *T*
The most difficult thing is learning to read and write. *S*
I'm finding it (rather) difficult to express myself. *T*
I really want to improve my reading and writing. *S*
I would really like to improve my speaking skills. *T*
Communication is the most important thing. *T*

3 ▶ Put the Ss in pairs to ask and answer questions 1–4. Encourage them to use language from the *How to...* box. Get class feedback from some of the Ss.

4 ▶ Focus the Ss on the Lifelong learning box. Ask them to talk in pairs about how often they do each of these things and then think of another tip on how to improve each aspect of their English.

5 ▶ Put Ss in small groups to discuss the ideas they had for ex. 4. They have to decide on the three best learning tips. Get feedback from the whole class and write all the suggested best learning tips on the board. Have a class vote to see which are the most popular (Ss can only vote for three).

OPTIONAL VARIATION

Draw three columns on the board with the headings: *I already do*; *I'm going to do*; *I'm not going to do*. Put Ss in groups to talk about the different tips using these expressions. Encourage them to give reasons for why they are going to do something or not.

1 Review and practice

1 ▶

Answers
1 I'm <u>quite</u> keen on watching football.
2 I <u>can't</u> stand science fiction films.
3 I <u>really</u> like sending text messages.
4 I really <u>hate</u> the winter.
5 I quite <u>like</u> pizza.
6 I absolutely <u>love</u> going to the beach.
7 I <u>don't</u> mind getting up early.
8 I <u>am ('m)</u> not very keen on dancing.

2 ▶

Answers
1   I usually get up
2   do you start
3   I go to bed
4   Do you go to bed
5   I usually watch a DVD
6   Do you have a snack
7   I have dinner
8   Does he swim
9   He always gets up
10 swims
11 he goes
12 does he go
13 He doesn't often go

3 ▶

Answers
1   am ('m) sitting
2   am ('m) having
3   Is Jack watching
4   is ('s) checking
5   Is John doing
6   is ('s) walking
7   is ('s) going

4 ▶

Answers
1   is he speaking
2   doesn't rain
3   're working
4   Do you prefer
5   'm staying
6   does she want
7   Are you studying
8   's working

5 ▶

Answers					
1 go	3	listen	6	has	
2 moment	4	same	7	guided	
	5	catch	8	these	

Writing bank

1 ▶ Ss read the text quickly and match the headings with the paragraphs.

Answers
1   b
2   d
3   a
4   c

2 ▶ Ss read the text again and answer the questions.

Answers
1   To help travellers find places to stay and meet people in the places they are travelling to
2   To make friends, have a good time and improve his English
3   He's an architect.
4   Taking people to famous places, restaurants and nightclubs / clubbing and dancing / running / cycling / going to the gym

3a ▶ Ss complete the *How to...* box with words from the box.

Answers
1   and
2   but
3   because
4   so
5   or
6   when

b ▶ Ss find another example of these words in the text.
4 ▶ Ss choose the correct word.

Answers
1   and
2   or
3   so
4   but
5   when
6   because

5a ▶ Ss make notes for their profile about their aims, personal description and interests.

b ▶ Ss write their profile, using linkers to join ideas and sentences.

Overview

Lead-in	**Revision:** Music
2.1	**Can do:** Describe personal events in the past **Grammar:** Past simple **Vocabulary:** Music **Speaking** **How to...** refer to past times **Listening:** Music in James Bond films
2.2	**Can do:** Talk about personal achievements and experiences **Grammar:** Present Perfect Simple: experience **Vocabulary:** Achievements **Speaking and Pronunciation:** have/has **Reading:** Shakira – pop star and business woman
2.3	**Can do:** Ask different types of questions **Grammar:** Questions **Speaking and Pronunciation:** Intonation in questions **Reading:** The Mozart effect **Listening:** Music
Communication	Explain why you like a piece of music
Reference	
Review and practice	
Writing bank	Write a short biography about someone's life **How to...** plan your writing
Extra resources	Active Teach and Active Book

CEFR Can do objectives

2.1 Describe personal events in the past
2.2 Talk about personal achievements and experiences
2.3 Ask different types of questions
Communication Explain why you like a piece of music
Writing bank Write a short biography about someone's life

CEFR Portfolio ideas

a) Video your talk from Exercise 11 on page 23.
b) Write a short biography about a famous person. Mention his/her background, preferences and achievements. Do NOT include his/her name. Can your friends guess who it is?
c) Recording: Talk about your 3 favourite possessions and say why you like them.
d) Choose your favourite single/album. Write a short biography of the artist/composer.

Lead-in

OPTIONAL WARMER

Write the word *music* on the board. Ss brainstorm words related to music, in pairs. Give Ss a few minutes to do this, then ask each pair how many words they have. Have the pair with the fewest words read out their list and write the words on the board. Now ask other Ss to add more words. Ask Ss to think of complete sentences using words from the list, e.g. *Beyoncé is a singer*. Have different Ss read out one sentence each.

---

1 ▶ Tell Ss to look at the photos and say what musical instruments they can see in pairs. Then ask them to make a list of other musical instruments they know. Get feedback from the whole class and write the words on the board.

Answers
Main photo: saxophone   Bottom photo: double
Top photo: violin   bass, saxophone
Middle photo: drums, guitar

2a ▶ 🔘 1.8 Ss listen to the recording and match each extract with a type of music from the box. Let Ss compare in pairs and then get feedback.

Answers
1	jazz	3	classical	6	pop
2	reggae	4	heavy metal	7	country
		5	opera	8	Latin

---

b ▶ Ask Ss to talk in pairs or small groups about what kind of music they prefer. Remind Ss that they can use the language they learned for expressing likes and dislikes in lesson 1.1. Ask them if it depends on what they are doing and where they are, e.g. when they are studying/working/doing exercise/relaxing/going out.

3a ▶ Focus on the words and phrases in the box and ask Ss if they understand all of them. Explain any they don't understand (*a single* is one song chosen from an album to be promoted). Ss complete the sentences with the correct expression. Check in pairs and then with the whole class.

Answers
1	read music	3	download	5	composer
2	single/album	4	artist	6	concert

---

b ▶ Ss write sentences about themselves using the words in the box. Then they tell a partner. Finally, get feedback from the whole class.

EXTEND THE LEAD-IN

Ss, in small groups, brainstorm song titles in English, checking the meaning with you or each other. Ss, paired from different groups, play hangman with those titles. Alternatively, Ss draw pictures on the board as clues to the titles. The rest of the class can guess the title.

2.1 Music for 007

It is estimated that about half of the world's population have seen James Bond films and the James Bond theme tune is possibly the best known tune in film history. The James Bond series started in 1962 with the film *Dr No*. Of eight Oscar nominations, four were for film scoring or the title songs (*Live and Let Die* – best original song; *The Spy who Loved Me* – best musical scoring, best original song; and *For Your Eyes Only* – best original song).

In this lesson, Ss listen to a radio programme about James Bond films and the music in them. Then they look at the grammar of the Past Simple and talk about their early life.

OPTIONAL WARMER

Write *James Bond* on the board and put Ss in pairs to say what they know about these films. Get feedback from the whole class. Now write the following artists' names on the board: *Carly Simon, Duran Duran, Jack White, Alicia Keys, Madonna, Paul McCartney, Shirley Bassey*. Ask Ss to discuss what they know about the artists and what they think they have in common. Get feedback from the whole class (They have all sung 'Bond' songs).

Listening

1a ▶ Put Ss in pairs to try to answer questions 1–4. Don't get feedback at this stage.

b ▶ ● 1.9 Play the recording and ask Ss to check their answers to the questions in ex. 1a. Let them compare with a partner and then elicit the answers from the whole class.

Answers
1   Ian Fleming
2   He is a spy who works for the British Secret Service.
3   Sean Connery
4   *Quantum of Solace*

2a ▶ ● 1.10 Play the recording and ask Ss to match the artists (a–f) to the songs. Elicit the answers from the class.

Answers
Goldfinger – Shirley Bassey (f)
Diamonds Are Forever – Shirley Bassey (f)
Moonraker – Shirley Bassey (f)
A View to a Kill – Duran Duran (d)
Live and Let Die – Paul McCartney and Wings (c)
Nobody Does It Better – Carly Simon (a)
Die Another Day – Madonna (e)

b ▶ Give Ss time to read through the sentences to check they understand them and then play the recording again. Ss complete the sentences. Allow them to compare with a partner and then elicit the answers from the whole class.

Answers
1   2008
2   *Goldfinger*
3   three
4   1971
5   *A View to a Kill*
6   1970s
7   *Die Another Day*

3 ▶ Put Ss in small groups to discuss the questions. Get feedback from the whole class.

Vocabulary | music

4 ▶ Ss complete the sentences with words from the box. Let them compare with a partner and then elicit the answers from the whole class, checking that they understand all the meanings (a *flop* is when something has no success at all; *catchy* means easy to remember).

Answers
1   duet
2   lead singer
3   solos
4   lyrics
5   soundtracks
6   theme song
7   top of the charts
8   hits
9   flop
10 chorus

5 ▶ Put Ss in groups to discuss the questions. Get feedback from the whole class.

Grammar | Past Simple

OPTIONAL GRAMMAR LEAD-IN

Write the following three sentences on the board but with the words in the wrong order, e.g.
1 *very saw week good last I film a.* (I saw a very good film last week.)
2 *like the I film didn't the in the music.* (I didn't like the music in the film.)
3 *go cinema Who you the did with to.* (Who did you go to the cinema with?)
Ss put the words in the correct order in pairs. Elicit the answers and ask: *What tense is this?* (Past Simple)

6a ▶ Put the Ss in pairs to complete the Active grammar box. Elicit the answers and explain that they can use the complete form *did not* or the contracted form *didn't* (more common in spoken English). Remind Ss that we use this tense to refer to finished actions in the past.

Active grammar

+   That song started Shirley Bassey's career in 1964.
  She became an international star immediately.
  People expected a great theme song in every film.
−   The first two films did not (didn't) have a theme song.
  Moonraker was not (wasn't) a very successful film.
?   How many Bond songs did she sing?
  When was the first famous theme song?

b ▶ In their pairs, Ss identify the regular and irregular verbs. Elicit the answers.

Answers
Regular: start, expect
Irregular: become, have, be, sing

▶ Draw Ss' attention to the Reference on page 27 and the Irregular verb table on page 149.

Put Ss in pairs and have one S in each pair look at the irregular verbs on page 149. Tell them to read out the infinitives of ten verbs they know. Their partner must say the past form. Then they change roles.

7 ▶ Ss complete the paragraph. Let them compare with a partner and then elicit the answers from various Ss.

Answers
1 grew up
2 didn't have
3 separated
4 appeared
5 began
6 went
7 started
8 didn't finish
9 left
10 made

8a ▶ Ss write the questions. Let them compare with a partner and then elicit the answers from various Ss.

Answers
1 Did she have any brothers and sisters?
2 When did she begin playing a musical instrument?
3 What did she do when she was twelve?
4 How long did she spend at university?
5 When did she make her first album?

b ▶ Tell the Ss to cover the text from ex. 7 and put them in pairs to ask and answer the questions.

OPTIONAL EXTENSION

Put Ss in small groups to write music quiz questions in the past, e.g. *When did Michael Jackson die?* (2009). Tell them they must know the answers. Now each group takes turns to ask the questions to the other groups, who have to write down the answers. The team with most correct answers in the end wins.

Speaking

9 ▶ Focus the Ss on the *How to...* box and ask them to complete it in pairs, using audioscript 1.10 on page 150 and the underlined phrases. Elicit the answers.

Answers
1 in
2 in the
3 when
4 that
5 later

10a ▶ Ss use the prompts to write questions. Elicit the correct forms from the whole class.

Answers
• When/Where were you born?
• Where did you grow up?
• What did you like/dislike about school?
• What job did you want to do?
• What hobbies/sports did you do as a teenager?
• What did you do when you left school?

b ▶ Put the Ss in pairs to ask and answer the questions. Tell them to use the *How to...* box when giving their answers. Encourage them to ask follow-up questions and to give as much detail as possible. Tell the student who is asking the questions to take notes of the answers.

▶ Now rearrange the pairs and ask them to tell each other what they found out about their original partner.

OPTIONAL VARIATION

Tell Ss to secretly write two numbers between 1 and 8 on a piece of paper. Then in pairs, student A interviews student B with the questions from ex. 10a. Student B must answer truthfully, except when the question corresponds to the numbers on his/her paper. In this case, student B lies. Student A must guess which two answers are false. Then they change roles.

OPTIONAL EXTENSION

Play twenty questions. Write down the name of a famous dead person. Ss can ask up to a maximum of twenty questions in the Past Simple to guess who the person was. You can only answer 'yes', 'no', 'maybe', e.g. *Was the person a man? Did he make films?* Then the Ss play the game in groups.

2.2 Barefoot music

Shakira was born in Barranquilla, Colombia, in 1977. Her father is American of Lebanese descent and her mother is Colombian of Catalan–Italian descent. Her name is Arabic and can be translated as 'woman full of grace'. She showed great artistic talent from a very early age, writing poetry from the age of four and songs from the age of eight. At ten, she began winning local and national talent competitions. Her first album *Magia* (Magic), featuring the songs she wrote between the ages of eight and thirteen, was recorded by Sony Music when she was only fifteen. At nineteen she briefly turned to acting and appeared in the Colombian soap opera *The Oasis*. She admits herself, though that she wasn't very good at acting and she decided to concentrate on her musical career, going on to achieve international fame and recognition by the age of twenty-five. She speaks five languages – Spanish, English, Arabic, Portuguese and Italian – fluently and is a talented dancer and record producer. She has also set up her own charity and is a Goodwill Ambassador for UNICEF.

In this lesson, Ss read a text about Shakira and then look at the grammar of the Present Perfect Simple and vocabulary related to achievement before talking about their own achievements.

OPTIONAL WARMER

Put Ss in pairs to make a list of ten pop stars and pop groups. Then put two sets of pairs together and tell them to take it in turns to explain who the people on their list are without saying the name. The other pair has to guess the names on the list. When they have finished, ask them to talk in their groups about what they think of all the stars they have mentioned: *Do they like their music? Do they think they are nice people? Do these stars do anything to help others in the world?*

Reading

1 ▶ Focus Ss on the photos of Shakira and put them in pairs to talk about what they know about her. Get feedback from the class. Now ask them to look again at the photo on the top left and ask what they think is the connection between Shakira and the child.

▶ Ss read the text and check their ideas. Explain any words from the text that Ss don't understand.

Answers
The child is at an event organised by Shakira's charity. The child may be a student at a school built by Shakira's charity.

2a ▶ Ss A read the text on page 129 and answer the questions and Ss B read the text on page 133 and answer the questions.

Answers
Student A
1 Her father is American and her mother is Colombian.
2 She was four.
3 Her father's business failed and he lost a lot of money.
4 To show her that her life wasn't so bad.
5 At the age of thirteen.
6 She bought her parents a car.
Student B
1 She released more albums.
2 She won a star on the Hollywood Walk of Fame.
3 Live Earth
4 five
5 They are both important to her. One thing feeds the other one.
6 She wants it to reach the 300 million children in the world who don't go to school.

b ▶ Student A tells student B about what they read, using the answers to their questions as a guide and then student B does the same. Encourage them to add as much extra information as possible.

3 ▶ Put the Ss in groups to discuss the questions. Get feedback from the whole class.

Grammar | Present Perfect Simple: experience

OPTIONAL GRAMMAR LEAD-IN

Write the following questions on the board: *Have you ever met a famous person? What groups or singers have you seen? Have you ever played a musical instrument?* Put Ss in pairs to answer the questions and then ask a few Ss to answer for the whole class. Encourage them to give complete answers, modelling if necessary. Ask Ss if they know which tense you are using and write *Present Perfect Simple* on the board.

4a ▶ Ss look at the underlined verb phrases in the text from ex. 1 and identify the tenses with a partner, saying if they know when each action happened.

Answers
she's sold – Present Perfect Simple – We don't know when this happened.
she started – Past Simple – We do know when this happened.

b ▶ Ss complete the rules with a partner. Elicit the answers from the class and write them on the board, illustrating each one with an example (see answers).

Answers
- We use the Past Simple to talk about an action or experience at a specific time in the past (e.g. *I went to the cinema last night*).
- We use the Present Perfect Simple to talk about an action or experience at some time in the past up until now. The specific time is not important or not known (e.g. *I have been to Paris twice*).

5a ▶ Put Ss in pairs to complete the Active grammar box. Elicit answers from various Ss. Point out the use of *ever* and *never* when used with the Present Perfect Simple.

> **Active Grammar**
> + She <u>has</u> given millions of dollars to charity.
> – He <u>hasn't</u> seen the film.
> ? <u>Have</u> you ever been on TV?
>   I <u>gave</u> a speech to 150 people last year.

▶ Read through the rules about the use of *ever* and *never* when used with the Present Perfect Simple. Ask the class some questions with *ever* to practise this: *Have you ever eaten Indian food? Have you ever run a marathon? Have you ever been to England?* When a student says 'no', encourage them to give a full answer with *never*, e.g. *No, I've never eaten Indian food.*

b ▶ In pairs, Ss look back at the texts in ex. 1 and on page 133 (there aren't any examples in the text on page 129) to find other examples of the Present Perfect Simple. Elicit examples from the Ss. Draw the Ss' attention to the Reference on page 27.

Answers
Text (page 22): she's done
Text (page 133): she has earned; Shakira has done; She has also given; has now paid for

6 ▶ Ss complete the text individually. Let them compare with a partner and then elicit the answers from various Ss.

Answers
1 has ('s) had
2 have not (haven't) met
3 have not (haven't) paid
4 have ('ve) learned
5 have ('ve) downloaded
6 have ('ve) bought
7 have not (haven't) had

7 ▶ Ss complete the exchanges in pairs. Go around the class checking the Ss' work and discussing reasons for mistaken tenses. Elicit the answers from various Ss.

Answers
1 Have you ever won
2 have
3 won
4 Has he ever met
5 has
6 's met
7 Have you ever played
8 have
9 was
10 Have you ever
11 haven't
12 saw

Pronunciation | *have/has*

8 ▶ 🔘 1.11 Tell the Ss that *have* and *has* can be pronounced in two different ways depending on whether they are used in a question or in a short answer. Play the recording and get the class to repeat as a group. Now ask individual Ss to say the sentences, checking that they are pronouncing the *have* or *has* in the correct way.

9 ▶ Put Ss in pairs to ask and answer the questions from ex. 7. Go around the class, monitoring the Ss' work and checking for good pronunciation. Ask a few Ss to ask and answer the questions for the whole class.

Vocabulary | achievements

10a ▶ Working in pairs, Ss match the verbs with the noun phrases and then check with the texts in ex. 1 and 2a. Point out that there is sometimes more than one way to match the verbs and the phrases but that you want the combinations that appear in the text. Elicit the answers from the whole class.

Answers
2 f   4 a   7 e
3 d   5 c   8 b
        6 h

b ▶ Tell the Ss to cover the table in ex. 10a before they choose the correct options in pairs. Elicit the answers from the whole class.

Answers
1 gave
2 won
3 speak
4 got
5 does
6 started
7 earned
8 passed

Speaking

11 ▶ Read through all the questions with the whole class and then tell Ss to choose one topic that they would like to talk about. Give the Ss five minutes to make notes and ask you for any vocabulary that they need.

12 ▶ Put the Ss in small groups to talk about the questions they have prepared. Each student talks for one minute. When they have finished, the others ask three follow-up questions, using the Past Simple. At the end, ask the Ss if they were surprised about anything they heard from their classmates.

> **OPTIONAL EXTENSION**
> Put Ss in small groups to talk about the list of things in ex. 10a. Ask them to answer the following questions: *Which of these things have you done? Which haven't you done? Which would you like to do?* Encourage them to give as much information as possible.

2.3 The Mozart effect

The Mozart Effect® is the name of a book by Don Campbell, first published in 1997. It talks about the positive effects that different types of music can have on the mental and physical health of families and communities, helping everybody from children with learning disorders to adults with depression. Research on music therapy, carried out in France in the 1960s and later in the US, has shown that Mozart is particularly effective because it is structural and not over-emotional.

In this lesson, Ss read about 'The Mozart Effect®' and listen to two people talking about music. They then look at the grammar of question formation.

OPTIONAL WARMER

Tell Ss you are thinking of a famous person (Mozart) and they have to guess who it is by asking questions. You can only answer *yes/no/I don't know*. Give Ss a few minutes to think of possible questions in pairs before you begin. Ss ask questions until somebody guesses. If they ask all twenty questions and nobody guesses, give them clues by telling them some of the information below.
(Mozart, born in Austria in 1756, was both a musician and a composer. He was a child prodigy and started composing at the age of five. He married Constanze Weber, with whom he had six children and they lived in various countries. He was particularly influential in the music of the Germanic world, although he had a great impact on the whole world. His most well-known works are *The Magic Flute*, *Requiem* and *Don Giovanni*. He died in Vienna in 1791, at the age of just 35.)

Reading

1 ▶ 🌐 1.12 Focus on the adjectives in the box. Ask a few Ss to read them aloud and check that everybody understands them all. Play the recording and Ss tell a partner how each piece makes them feel. Get feedback from the class.

2 ▶ Read through the headings (a–c) with the whole class, checking that everybody understands. Ss read through the text quickly and choose a heading for each paragraph. Tell them not to worry about any words they don't understand at the moment. Ss check their answers with a partner, then check with the whole class.

Answers	
1	b
2	a
3	c

3 ▶ Ask various Ss to read the statements aloud and check that everybody understands. Ss read the text again more carefully and decide if the statements are true (T) or false (F), or if the information isn't given (NG). Ss check their answers with a partner, then with the whole class.

Answers	
1	NG
2	F
3	T
4	NG
5	F
6	F
7	NG
8	T

▶ Ask Ss if there any words in the text which they don't understand. Encourage other Ss to explain them, but if nobody can, explain them yourself. Point out the difference between *affect* (verb) and *effect* (noun).

4 ▶ Ss discuss the questions in pairs and then compare answers with another pair. Get feedback from the class.

Listening

5 ▶ 🌐 1.13 Read through the sentences with the whole class and check they understand them. Play the recording and Ss mark the sentences true (T) or false (F). Elicit the answers from the whole class.

Answers	
1	T
2	F
3	T
4	T

6 ▶ Get different Ss to read out the questions and check everybody understands. Now play the recording a second time and Ss tick the questions they hear. Let them compare with a partner and then check with the whole class.

Answers
1, 3, 5, 6 and 9

7 ▶ Play the recording again. Ss listen and make notes about what the woman says in response to the questions they ticked in ex. 6. Let them compare with a partner and then check the answers with the whole class.

Answers	
1	She thinks yes, but maybe it depends on what kind of person you are and what kind of music you like.
3	She listens to music every day.
5	Yes, she has the radio on in the car.
6	She loves all kinds of music, but her favourite is probably rock.
9	ages/years ago

Grammar | questions

> **OPTIONAL GRAMMAR LEAD-IN**
>
> Write the following sentences on the board: *I'm a teacher. I live in the country. I go to the cinema twice a week. I can play the guitar. I finished university last year.* Put Ss in pairs to write possible questions for these answers. Get feedback from the whole class.

8 ▶ Focus Ss on the Active grammar box and read through the information about the two different types of questions with the whole class. Now Ss complete the second part of the Active grammar box with *before* or *after*. Allow Ss to check with a partner and then get feedback from the whole class. After you've checked the answers, draw the Ss' attention to the Reference on page 27.

> **Active grammar**
>
> A before
> B before
> C before

9 ▶ Ss individually correct the mistakes in eight of the questions. Go around the class monitoring their work and answering any questions they have. Let them compare with a partner and then get feedback from the whole class.

> **Answers**
> 1 What kind of music <u>do</u> you like?
> 2 <u>Can you</u> play the piano?
> 3 ✓
> 4 Would <u>you</u> like to be a professional musician?
> 5 <u>Have</u> you ever downloaded music from the internet?
> 6 Who <u>is</u> your favourite singer or group?
> 7 What music <u>do</u> you listen to in the morning?
> 8 ✓
> 9 Did you <u>take</u> music exams when you were a child?
> 10 <u>Are you</u> listening to music at the moment?

Pronunciation | intonation in questions

10 ▶ ● 1.14 Explain to the class that our intonation changes depending on what kind of questions we ask. When the questions have a *yes*/*no* answer, our voice goes up at the end. When it is a *Wh-* question, our voice goes up and then down. Play the recording and get the whole class to repeat together. Then have the Ss practise in pairs. Ask a few Ss to demonstrate for the whole class. Draw the Ss' attention to the Pronunciation bank on page 148.

Speaking

11a ▶ Put Ss in pairs to write six questions for a music survey. Tell them they can use the ideas from ex. 6 and 9, but encourage them to be as original as possible. Monitor the Ss' work as they do this, correcting any grammatical mistakes in the questions.

b ▶ Now put the Ss in small groups of four (excluding their original partner) and Ss ask their questions to the other four in the group. If you have a small class, get Ss to write the questions individually and do the survey in pairs. Get feedback from the class.

> **OPTIONAL EXTENSION**
>
> Put the following topics on the board: *eating and cooking, sports and hobbies, cinema and theatre, reading, going out.* In pairs, Ss choose one of the topics and write five questions they could ask to do a survey about that topic. Then they interview other members of the class and either give an oral or written presentation about what they found out.

2 Communication

This lesson is based on an idea taken from one of the longest-running BBC radio programmes, called *Desert Island Discs*. It first started in 1942 and interviews famous people who say what eight pieces of music they would take if they were stranded alone on a desert island.

In this lesson, Ss listen to a radio programme in which somebody chooses their top three records. They then choose their own top three and discuss their choices.

OPTIONAL WARMER

Write *desert island* on the board and give Ss two minutes in pairs to make a list of words they would associate with it. Ask the pair with the most words to read them out. If they are all associated, the pair wins. If not, ask the pair with the second longest list.

1a ▶ Focus on the photo and ask Ss to discuss in pairs what they think the radio programme is about. Get feedback from the whole class.

b ▶ 🔘 1.15 Play the recording and ask Ss to check their predictions (somebody has to choose three pieces of music they would want to have with them if they were alone on a desert island).

2a ▶ 🔘 1.16 Play the recording and ask Ss to complete the table with three pieces of music and three artists.

b ▶ Ss compare their answers in pairs and then check the answers with the whole class.

Answers
Feelin' so good – Jennifer Lopez
Symphony number 5 – Mahler
Imagine – John Lennon

3 ▶ Ss discuss the questions in small groups. Get feedback from the whole class.

4a ▶ Ss complete the sentences with the words from the box.

b ▶ 🔘 1.17 Ss listen and check. Have different Ss read out the sentences for the whole class. Check that they understand all the words, especially the difference between *remember* and *remind* (make someone *remember* something).

Answers
1 reminds
2 happy
3 memories
4 cry
5 reminds
6 remember

c ▶ Focus Ss on the Lifelong learning box and read through the tip with the whole class. Now ask Ss to record the other words from ex. 4a in the same way. When they've finished, ask them to compare their definitions and example sentences with a partner. Ask various Ss to read their definitions and examples for the whole class.

5 ▶ Ss work individually to make a note of three pieces of music, the artist and why they like each piece. Go around the class helping Ss with any vocabulary they might need.

6a ▶ In groups of three, Ss talk about their choices using their notes and the words from ex. 4a.

b ▶ Get feedback from the different groups to see if their musical taste is similar or different.

OPTIONAL VARIATION

Rather than making notes in ex. 5, ask Ss to write a full account of their choices and reasons. Then take in the accounts and redistribute them so that each student has another student's paper. In turn, the Ss read out the accounts and the rest of the class has to guess whose it is.

Review and practice

1 ▶

Answers
1	sold; bought	4	ate; drank
2	fell; broke	5	were; took
3	lived; walked	6	went; saw

2 ▶

Answers
1	met	4	didn't like	8	Did you like
2	went	5	said	9	didn't like
3	thought	6	were you	10	hated
		7	lived	11	stopped

3 ▶

Answers
1. have not (haven't) heard
2. Have you ever run
3. have ('ve) been
4. Have you ever broken
5. has not (hasn't) ridden
6. Have you done
7. have ('ve) worked
8. Have you ever downloaded

4 ▶

Answers
1	Have you done	5	Were you
2	have	6	wasn't
3	've had	7	was
4	worked	8	's had

5 ▶

Answers
1. What do you like eating for breakfast?
2. Where do you usually go for your holidays?
3. What (musical instrument) did she play when she was a child?
4. What did you buy yesterday?
5. What can your mother do really well?
6. When did you go to see Beyoncé in concert?
7. How many times were they late for school last week?

6 ▶

Answers
1. I find it difficult to understand the lyrics of English songs.
2. The film had great music. I really want to buy the soundtrack.
3. My sister won lots of prizes for singing when she was young.
4. I never buy CDs from shops. I always download music from the internet.
5. I was nervous about giving a speech to over 200 people.
6. She was pleased when she passed her piano exam with distinction.
7. I'd like to listen to more classical music.

Writing bank

1a ▶ Ss number the topics in order.

b ▶ Ss read the biography and check their answers. Get feedback from the class.

Answers
a	3
b	1
c	4
d	5
e	2

2 ▶ Ss read the text again and complete the sentences. Elicit the answers from the class.

Answers
1. Jamaica
2. England
3. father died
4. nineteen
5. solo singer
6. thirty-six
7. *One Love*

3a ▶ Ss complete the *How to...* box with the headings (a–c). Check the answers with the whole class.

Answers
1. a
2. c
3. b

b ▶ In pairs, Ss organise the information about Paul McCartney in terms of the three paragraphs in part 3 of the *How to...* box. Check the answers with the whole class.

Answers
Paragraph 1 – a, c, g
Paragraph 2 – b, e, h
Paragraph 3 – d, f, i

4a ▶ Ss make notes about the person they have chosen. Help them with vocabulary at this stage. If you have time, let them talk to a partner to see if they can offer them any helpful advice.

b ▶ Ss write the biography.

Overview

Lead-in	Revision: Taste
3.1	**Can do:** Tell a friend about your future plans
	Grammar: *be going to*: future plans
	Speaking and Pronunciation:
	How to... talk about future plans
	Connected speech (1)
	Reading: Cook your way to a better life!
3.2	**Can do:** Make arrangements with a friend
	Grammar: Present Continuous: future arrangements
	Vocabulary: Describing food
	Speaking:
	How to... make arrangements
	Listening: Thanksgiving in the US
3.3	**Can do:** Define and describe things to explain what you mean
	Grammar: Defining relative clauses
	Vocabulary: Easily-confused words
	Speaking and Pronunciation: Silent letters
	Reading: *Ratatouille*
Communication	Contribute to a simple discussion
Reference	
Review and practice	
Writing bank	Write a note or message to a friend
	How to... use short forms in notes and messages
Extra resources	Active Teach and Active Book

CEFR Can do objectives
3.1 Tell a friend about your future plans
3.2 Make arrangements with a friend
3.3 Define and describe things to explain what you mean
Communication Contribute to a simple discussion
Writing bank Write a note or message to a friend

CEFR Portfolio ideas
a) Choose a photograph of a local celebration. Write a short text saying what you do at the celebration and describe any special things you eat.
b) Write an email to one of your friends. Ask your friend if he/she wants to go out for a pizza on Tuesday evening. Suggest a time and place where you can meet.
c) Prepare a website for the restaurant you planned on page 36. Use ideas from exercise 1.

Lead-in

OPTIONAL WARMER
Introduce Ss to the topic of taste by asking the following questions: *What does* taste *mean?* (It's a sense which we use to distinguish the flavour or quality of something, e.g. *It tastes sweet.*) Write on the board: *Taste is a sense. We taste with our mouths. What other senses do we have? Which parts of the body do we use?* (Sight. We see with our eyes; Sound. We hear with our ears; Smell. We smell with our nose; Touch. We feel/touch with our hands.)

1 ▶ Ask Ss to put the words from the box into three different categories. At the same time, they identify these things in the photos. Get feedback from the whole class.

Answers
a food and drink: aubergine, bread, mineral water, olive oil, plum
b people: chef, customer, waiter/waitress
c kitchen equipment: cooker, saucepan

▶ Now, in pairs, give Ss a few minutes to think of more words for each category. Write the categories on the board and have Ss tell you their ideas to complete each one.

2a ▶ Focus on the words in the box and check to see if Ss understand them. Allow them to use dictionaries if they have them. Give a clue for a word or phrase and have Ss guess which one it is, e.g. *What can you do if you feel fat? What is the name of a person who cooks for a job? What do we call a list of instructions for cooking?*

▶ Have Ss complete the sentences with the words and phrases and check them with the whole class. Pay special attention to the pronunciation of recipe /resəpi/.

Answers			
2	vegetarian	5	diets
3	traditional dish	6	chefs
4	main course	7	allergic
		8	menu

b ▶ 🔘 1.18 Tell Ss they are going to listen to the answers to the questions from ex. 2a (including the example). Ss have to write the letter of the correct answer next to the appropriate question. Play the recording and then let Ss compare with a partner. Now play the recording again for the Ss to check. Elicit the answers from the whole class.

Answers					
1	H	3	F	6	G
2	C	4	A	7	D
		5	B	8	E

3 ▶ Ss ask and answer the questions in pairs. Get feedback from the whole class about their answers.

3.1 Jamie's kitchen

In recent years, celebrity chefs and TV cooking programmes have become increasingly popular in Britain. Jamie Oliver became an overnight success when he appeared on a documentary about the restaurant where he was working in London. The next morning he was called by five different TV production companies, who wanted him to work for them. He chose one and made the incredibly popular series *The Naked Chef*. He's made over 16 other TV programmes in the last ten years, written numerous books, and started projects to help the unemployed and encourage people to eat more healthily.

In this lesson, Ss read about Jamie's restaurant Fifteen, which trains unemployed young people to be chefs, and his other ventures which have tried to encourage adults and children alike to eat and cook more healthily. Through this context, Ss analyse the grammar of *be going to* and learn to talk about future plans.

OPTIONAL WARMER

Ask Ss questions about cooking programmes (if there are no celebrity chefs in their country, ask them to imagine the answers to the last two questions). *Do you watch cooking programmes? Why or why not? What time are cooking programmes normally on the TV? Who do you think usually watches them? What are celebrity chefs normally like? Are they usually men or women? Do these chefs do anything else apart from making cooking programmes?*

Reading

1 ▶ Tell the Ss to look at the photos and read the first paragraph. They then talk to a partner about who Jamie Oliver is and what he has achieved. Get feedback from the class.

Answers
Jamie Oliver is a celebrity chef. He has a chain of restaurants, he's made many TV series and he's written cookery books.

2 ▶ Read out sentences a–e with the whole class and check they understand. Now Ss read the rest of the text and talk to a partner about the areas in which Jamie has made a difference to people's lives. Tell them not to worry about any words they don't understand at this point. Get feedback from the class.

Answers
Jamie has made a difference in a, d and e.

3 ▶ Ss read the text again and complete the sentences. Let them compare with a partner and then elicit the answers.

Answers
1 pub
2 unemployed
3 chef
4 recipe
5 menus

4 ▶ In pairs, Ss look back at the text and try to work out the meaning of the phrases from the context given. Get feedback from the class.

Suggested Answers
1 his love for/his great interest in
2 they haven't done this job before
3 very good chefs
4 someone or something that is successful
5 food that people don't have to spend a lot of money on
6 what they usually cook most days

▶ Ask Ss if there are any other words in the text that they don't understand. Write them on the board and encourage other Ss to explain, using the context around each word to help them. Help with any words they can't explain, again showing how context can assist understanding.

5 ▶ Ss work in groups to discuss the questions. Get feedback from the whole class.

Grammar | *be going to*: future plans

OPTIONAL GRAMMAR LEAD-IN

Tell the Ss one of your plans for next weekend, e.g. *Next weekend I'm going to go to the beach*. Write on the board the stem: *Next weekend/tomorrow/tonight I'm going to ...* . Tell the Ss to complete the sentence with a true plan of their own, and then chain around the classroom with each student saying his or her sentence and asking the next student about theirs (*What are you going to do next weekend?*). Alternatively, have Ss stand up and mingle, asking and answering this question.

6a ▶ Ss complete the Active grammar box individually, checking their answers in the last paragraph of the text. Write the sentences on the board and elicit the answers from the Ss.

Active grammar
+ My children <u>are going</u> to eat their vegetables.
– I'm <u>not going</u> to miss it!
? What's <u>Jamie going</u> to do next?

b ▶ Ss find three more *be going to* examples from the text. Get different Ss to give you the examples.

> **Answers**
> ... he is going to teach people to cook professionally.
> ... I'm not going to eat fast food anymore.
> I'm going to cook for my friends ... .

▶ Point out that the verb *be* can take either its full form or the contracted form (the second is more common in spoken English). Remind Ss that *be going to* is used for future plans and intentions that the speaker has thought about before speaking and draw their attention to the Reference on page 37.

7 ▶ Ss write complete sentences. Elicit the answers from various students.

> **Answers**
> 1 I'm going to start making my own bread.
> 2 Rachel isn't going to use a recipe for her cake.
> 3 Are we going to have pizza or pasta tonight?
> 4 They're not (aren't) going to eat fast food anymore.
> 5 What are you going to have for the main course?
> 6 He's going to book the restaurant for 8 o'clock.
> 7 Are you going to try that new dish she made?
> 8 Where are you going to do your cookery course?

Speaking

8 ▶ Focus Ss on the *How to...* box and tell the Ss to read the example sentences and complete the box with the heading (a–d). Let Ss compare with a partner and then elicit the answers. Get various Ss to read out the examples too and check that everybody understands them.

> **Answers**
> 1 d
> 2 a
> 3 c
> 4 b

Pronunciation | connected speech (1)

9a ▶ 🔘 1.19 Write the example sentence: *What are your plans for the next two years?* on the board and explain to Ss that in natural speech the first two words are linked because *what* finishes in a consonant sound and *are* starts with a vowel sound. Play the recording and ask the whole class to repeat the question. Now let Ss practise in pairs. Get one or two Ss to demonstrate for the whole class.

b ▶ 🔘 1.20 In pairs, Ss look at the *How to...* box again and mark the parts of the sentences where they think the words will be linked. Point out that when a word ends in 'consonant + e' it also finishes with a consonant sound, e.g. *because*.

▶ Play the recording. Ss listen, check and repeat. Then let Ss practise in pairs. Get various Ss to demonstrate for the whole class.

> **Answers**
> 1 What are you going to do this year?
> 2 I want to work in a restaurant as a chef.
> 3 I'm going to get a job as a waiter in October.
> 4 I'd like to speak English better because I want to work abroad.
> 5 I'm going to get a place at college to learn about hotel management.

10a ▶ Focus on the topics in the box and tell Ss to make notes about their plans for the next two years. Tell them to think about describing the plans, giving time references if known and giving reasons. Give an example of your own that they can use as a model, e.g. *Next year I'm going to travel to England because my best friend is going to get married.* Help them with any vocabulary they need at this stage.

b ▶ Put Ss in small groups to talk about their plans. Get feedback to see if the Ss in each group have similar or different plans.

> **OPTIONAL VARIATION**
>
> Ask Ss to choose one of the topics and to write a question related to that topic, e.g. *Are you going to study English next year? Are you going to change your job soon?* Monitor the Ss' work as they do this and then have the Ss stand up and mingle, asking and answering each other's questions. Walk around the class monitoring their conversations as they do this.

> **OPTIONAL EXTENSION**
>
> Tell Ss you are going to tell them three plans for this week, one of which is false. Talk about your plans to the class. Ss then discuss with a partner and guess which one is false. Encourage them to ask follow-up questions in order to get extra information upon which to base their decision, e.g. *'I'm going to go to the cinema.' 'What are you going to see?'* Get feedback from the whole class and reveal the correct answers.
> Tell the Ss to write three sentences about their plans for this week, one of which is false. Put them in small groups and get them to tell their sentences to the others, who must guess which one is false. Again, encourage them to ask follow-up questions.

3.2 Let's celebrate!

Thanksgiving Day is a national holiday in the US (fourth Thursday in November) and Canada (second Monday in October). The festival commemorates the harvest feast shared by the English Pilgrim settlers and members of the Wampanoag people at Plymouth in 1621. The Pilgrims wanted to thank the Native Americans for looking after them in their first, difficult year. Nowadays, people express gratitude to God for his blessings and give thanks to dear ones for their love and support. Eating a big, special meal with family is an important part of Thanksgiving Day celebrations. If you live in New York, you can go to Macy's Thanksgiving Day Parade; if not, you can watch it on TV (more than 44 million watch it each year). Macy's is a chain of department stores and has organised the parade since 1924. It takes place in Manhattan and has a six-mile route. The parade is made up of massive balloons of cartoon characters, marching bands, floats, live music and other performances.

In this lesson, Ss listen to a conversation about a typical Thanksgiving Day meal. Through this context they analyse the use of the Present Continuous for arrangements.

OPTIONAL WARMER

Write the title *Let's celebrate!* and ask Ss to think of as many occasions as possible in which people celebrate (e.g. Christmas, Eid, Thanksgiving, birthdays, weddings, new babies, new jobs, passing an exam, passing a driving test). Get feedback from the class and write the occasions on the board. Now ask Ss in small groups to choose two or three of these occasions and talk about what people usually do to celebrate them. Get feedback from different groups.

Listening

1 ▶ In groups, Ss look at the photo and discuss the questions (it's the United States; the festival is Thanksgiving Day). Get feedback from the whole class.

2a ▶ Tell Ss they are going to listen to Tarin and Marcos talking about Thanksgiving Day. First, focus on the box and ask Ss, in pairs, to label the pictures (A–E) with the types of food. Elicit the answers from the whole class.

Answers
A turkey and stuffing
B sweet potatoes
C maple syrup
D cranberry sauce
E apple pie

b ▶ 1.21 Play the recording and Ss number the words from ex. 2a in the order they hear them. Let them check with a partner and then elicit the answers from the class.

Answers
6 apple pie
4 cranberry sauce
3 maple syrup
5 stuffing
2 sweet potatoes
1 turkey

3 ▶ Get various Ss to read out the questions and check everybody understands them. Play the recording again and Ss take notes. Let them compare with a partner before checking the answers with the whole class.

Answers
1 At her house.
2 Some people go out for a walk, but most people sit around and watch TV together.
3 No, they don't. It isn't commercial.
4 They have maple syrup or fresh fruit like apples, oranges and pears.
5 The main ingredients of stuffing are bread and meat, usually sausages.
6 No, they don't. Some people have pumpkin pie or pie made of pecan nuts.
7 It starts at about two o'clock in the afternoon (although Marcos is invited to go at midday for drinks).

4 ▶ Focus on the photo of Macy's Parade and ask the Ss what they can see. Give them some more information about the parade (see the introduction to this lesson). Now ask the Ss to talk about the two questions in pairs. Get feedback from the whole class.

Vocabulary | describing food

5 ▶ In pairs Ss try to answer the questions using vocabulary from the box. Allow them to use dictionaries if they have them. Elicit answers from the class.

Answers
1 baked, boiled, fried, grilled, roast
2 savoury, spicy, sweet
3 *Roast* means cooking with dry heat and basting with oil or fat. It is normally used for meat (although we do sometimes use it for potatoes or other vegetables). *Baked* is usually used when we mix together different ingredients (often using flour) to produce something else, e.g. bread or cake, but it can also be used for potatoes or apples when they are cooked in their skins.
4 *Fresh* means the food is recently picked or prepared. *Raw* means the food is not cooked.

OPTIONAL EXTENSION

In pairs or small groups, Ss think of two types of food that are normally used with each adjective. Get feedback from the class.

6 ▶ Put Ss in pairs to find and correct the mistakes in seven of the ten sentences. Ask various Ss to read out the sentences with corrections.

> **Answers**
> 1 ... eat cakes and other <u>sweet</u> things.
> 2 ✓
> 3 ... I had <u>grilled</u> sausages
> 4 ... the freshly <u>baked</u> bread
> 5 ✓
> 6 the <u>roast</u> chicken because it was in the oven for too long.
> 7 ... a take-away of <u>spicy</u> Indian curry
> 8 ✓
> 9 ... something <u>savoury</u> like nuts or cheese.
> 10 ... delicious <u>raw</u> fish; it wasn't cooked at all.

7 ▶ Put Ss in small groups to discuss the questions. Get feedback from the whole class.

Grammar | Present Continuous: future arrangements

> **OPTIONAL GRAMMAR LEAD-IN**
>
> Tell the Ss what you are doing after class (invent it if you like). Say: *After class I'm having a meeting with the head teacher. What are you doing after class?* Chain around the class, eliciting answers. Don't worry if Ss use a mixture of Present Continuous and *be going to*.

8 ▶ 🔊 1.22 Focus on the Active grammar box and play the beginning of the recording (up to ' ... I'd really love you to come') so that Ss can complete the sentences. Let them compare with a partner before eliciting the answers from the class.

> **Active grammar**
>
> + My brother is staying with friends next week. I'm having a meal at my house to celebrate Thanksgiving.
> − I'm not doing anything.
> ? What are you doing next Thursday?

▶ Point out that the Present Continuous is used to talk about future arrangements (a plan that has been agreed with somebody else and certain details like time and place have been fixed). Remind them that in Lesson 1.3 they used the Present Continuous to refer to things happening now or around now. Explain that this tense has both functions.

▶ Write two example sentences on the board:
1 *Tonight I'm meeting Sue in a Mexican restaurant.*
2 *Next year I'm going to learn to drive.*

Ask Ss: *Which sentence refers to a general plan or intention?* (2) *What tense do we use?* (be going to + infinitive) *Which sentence tells us where and when the action is going to happen?* (1) *Which tense do we use?* (Present Continuous: *be* + verb + *-ing*). Draw the Ss' attention to the Reference on page 37.

9 ▶ Ss choose the correct options in pairs. Elicit the answers from the class. In instances where the Present Continuous is used, the *going to* option is not incorrect, but the Present Continuous is more common.

> **Answers**
> 1 are coming
> 2 is going to celebrate
> 3 'm meeting
> 4 is taking part
> 5 'm going to learn
> 6 is leaving

Speaking

10 ▶ 🔊 1.23 Focus on the *How to...* box and get various Ss to read out the examples for each of the four functions. Play the recording while Ss read audioscript 1.23 on page 152. Then they add one more phrase to each section with a partner. Elicit the answers from the class.

> **Answers**
> Make a suggestion: (1) I'm having a meal at my house to celebrate Thanksgiving and I'd really like you to come.
> Accept or reject: (2) Oh, thanks, I'd love to! That's very kind of you.
> Arrange to meet: (3) Why don't you come at about midday for some drinks first?
> Confirm: (4) Perfect! See you then.

11a ▶ Ss make notes individually about the meal they would like to have, including information about where and when it will be.

b ▶ Get the Ss to mingle, trying to make arrangements with as many people as possible. Tell them that they should only accept the ones they think they would enjoy and obviously they can't accept more than one arrangement at the same time.

> **OPTIONAL EXTENSION**
>
> Put Ss in groups and tell them to choose a date in the near future that they are going to celebrate, e.g. somebody's birthday, a local holiday, etc. Then they must make plans for that day, including a meal and other activities. Tell them to decide on the menu, how things will be cooked, the time of the meal and the other activities they are going to arrange. When they've finished, each group gives a short presentation of the celebration for the rest of the class. After all the groups have explained their plans, the class can vote which one (not their own) they would like to go to. The group that gets the most 'guests' wins.

3.3 *Ratatouille*

Ratatouille is a 2007 computer-animated Disney film. The title refers to a French dish of cooked vegetables (which is made towards the end of the film), but it is also a play on words because the main character is a rat called Remy, whose dream is to become a great chef. The plot follows Remy as he seeks to realise his dream by forming an alliance with Linguini, a boy who washes the dishes in a famous Parisian restaurant. When *Ratatouille* was released in the United States in 2007, it met with both critical acclaim and box office success, and later won the Academy Award for Best Animated Feature.

In this lesson, Ss read about the film *Ratatouille* and through this context look at the use of defining relative clauses.

OPTIONAL WARMER

Play a game of Hangman with a number of animated film titles, e.g. *Batman, The Incredibles, Toy Story, Shrek, The Lion King* on the board. Then put Ss in pairs to say what they know about each film. Get feedback from the class.

Reading

1a ▶ Ask one of the Ss to read out the definition and check that everybody understands all the words. Now tell them to look at the photo and discuss the questions in pairs. Get feedback from the class.

b ▶ Ss read the text quickly to check their answers. Tell them not to worry about any words they don't understand at this stage. Elicit the answers from the class.

Answers
1   Because the main character is a rat and the film is about cooking. Ratatouille is a typical French dish.
2   Remy and his brother Emile.
3   They are brothers and cooking partners.
4   Remy living his dream of becoming a master chef.

2 ▶ Ss read the text again and complete the notes in pairs. Elicit the answers from the class.

Answers
2   It's set in modern-day France.
3   It's about a rat called Remy and Linguini, a boy who works in the kitchen of a restaurant in Paris.
4   The problem is that the new cook makes boring food and the restaurant is losing customers. The restaurant has also had a bad review.
5   The plan is for Remy and Linguini to make more interesting food together.

3 ▶ Ss think of a film they like and make notes using the headings from ex. 2. In pairs, Ss talk about the film.

OPTIONAL VARIATION

Divide the class into two teams or more, depending on the size of your class. Have each team choose five films. They then write information about the films using headings 2 and 3 from ex. 2. Instead of using headings 4 and 5, write the following prompts on the board: *4 The plot/story; 5 What happens in the end*. Now play a game of guessing the films. Each team reads out the information about their films without saying the title. The other teams listen and write the name of the film on a piece of paper. When all the teams have finished, check the answers and the team with the most correct answers wins.

Grammar | defining relative clauses

OPTIONAL GRAMMAR LEAD-IN

Dictate the following stem sentences to the Ss: *Chef Skinner is a man who … ; Linguini wants to make food which … ; Remy arrives at a restaurant where … .* Tell the Ss to work in pairs to complete the sentences in some way. Get feedback to find out how many ways of completing the sentences Ss have found. Ask the class: *What is the grammatical name of this type of sentence?* (defining relative clause)

4 ▶ Focus on the Active grammar box and tell Ss to complete it, referring to the underlined sentences in the text *Ratatouille*. Get feedback and write the answers on the board.

Active grammar
A   We use <u>who</u> for people.
B   We use <u>which</u> for things.
C   We use <u>where</u> to say what happens in a place.

▶ Explain to the Ss that these clauses give extra information that is necessary for us to understand the noun. Write on the board *I saw the boy* and ask the Ss: *Do we know which boy?* (No) Finish the sentence on the board so that it reads *I saw the boy who lives next door.* Ask: *Do we know which boy?* (Yes)

▶ Point out the position of the relative pronouns, the absence of commas and the fact that *who* or *which* can be replaced with *that* in informal language. Tell the Ss that there is a complete explanation in the Reference on page 37.

5a ▶ Ss complete the sentences. Ask various Ss to read out the answers.

Answers
1   where
2   who
3   which
4   where
5   who
6   which
7   who
8   where

b ▶ Ss decide in which sentences we can use *that*. Elicit the answers.

> **Answers**
> Sentences 2, 3, 5, 6 and 7

6 ▶ Read through the Lifelong learning box with the Ss. Explain how important it is to be able to communicate when you only have a limited vocabulary. Point out the use of *thing*, *stuff* and *person* and ask the Ss: *Which would you use with the following words?*
doctor (person), *a sweet* (thing), *coffee* (stuff), *teacher* (person), *orange juice* (stuff), *vegetables* (things)

▶ Put the Ss in pairs. Student A looks at page 129 and student B looks at page 134. Tell them not to look at each other's book. Each student takes it in turn to describe each of their words, using a defining relative clause.

Pronunciation | silent letters

7a ▶ Focus the Ss on the extract from the dictionary, and tell them to pronounce the word with a partner. Ask: *Which letter is silent?* (the second *o*) Ss repeat the word after you.

b ▶ 🌐 1.24 Ss look at the words in the box and identify the silent letter. Now play the recording and Ss check their answers. Chain around the class, with different Ss pronouncing the words.

> **Answers**
>
> | calm | island | spaghetti |
> |---|---|---|
> | comfortable | knife | vegetable |
> | hour | lamb | Wednesday |
> | | receipt | yoghurt |

8 ▶ 🌐 1.25 Play the recording. Ss listen and repeat the sentences in pairs. Ss then practise saying the sentences. Go around the class checking pronunciation. Explain that *hour* takes the article *an* not *a* because of its silent letter.

▶ Ask the Ss, in pairs, to brainstorm some more words with silent letters. Then ask them to either write the words on the board or spell them out so that you can write them on the board. Tell the rest of the class to copy the words and circle the silent letters. Get feedback from the class and practise pronouncing the words. Possible words: *knock*, *know*, *climb*, *science*, *autumn*, *psychology*, *exhibition*, *business*, *write*.

▶ Get Ss to turn to the Pronunciation bank on page 147 and look at the Reference on silent letters. In pairs, get them to pronounce the words and to discuss the meanings. Get various Ss to read out the words for the whole class and elicit/teach the meanings.

Vocabulary | easily-confused words

9a ▶ Ss discuss the difference in meaning between the paired words.

b ▶ Put the Ss in groups so that they can compare their ideas. Get feedback from the class.

> **Answers**
> - *Argument* means that people are angry and disagreeing. *Discussion* is a debate about something and the people are not angry.
> - *Chef* is a person who cooks, usually professionally. *Chief* is a high position in an organisation, e.g. the chief of police.
> - *Cook* here is a noun (although it is also a verb) and it means a person who cooks (more frequent than *chef* for non-professional situations) and *cooker* is the machine.
> - *Educated* means that a person has had schooling. *Polite* refers to a person with good manners.
> - *Now* is at the moment and *actually* means really.
> - *Plate* is the object where we put the food and *dish* is the food itself.
> - *Recipe* is the instructions for cooking and *receipt* is a piece of paper you get when you have bought something.
> - *Sensible* is a person who acts logically and practically and *sensitive* is a person who feels deeply the things that happen around him/her.

10a ▶ Ss choose the correct option. Elicit the answers.

> **Answers**
>
> | | | | | | |
> |---|---|---|---|---|---|
> | 1 | chief | 3 | dish | 6 | polite |
> | 2 | recipe | 4 | actually | 7 | sensitive |
> | | | 5 | argument | | |

b ▶ Ss write sentences with the other words. Go around the class monitoring their work and then get some Ss to read out their sentences.

> **OPTIONAL VARIATION**
>
> Ask the Ss to write questions that they can ask of other members of the class, using any of the words from ex. 10a, e.g. *Are you a good cook? Do you usually keep your receipts?* Monitor their work as they do this and then get the class to stand up and mingle, asking and answering each other's questions. Walk around the class and monitor their conversations as they do this.

Speaking

11a ▶ Read through the topics with the whole class and then tell the Ss to choose one and make notes about it.

b ▶ Put Ss in groups of three to talk about their topics. Try to arrange them so that the three Ss in each group have chosen different topics. As each student talks, get the others to think of one question they would like to ask when they've finished. At the end, Ss ask this question.

> **OPTIONAL EXTENSION**
>
> Write the following sentences on the board: *A good restaurant is a place where … . A polite person is someone who … . A good dish is one which … .* Ask Ss to discuss in pairs how they would finish these sentences. Get feedback from the whole class.

3 Communication

In this lesson, Ss talk about their favourite restaurant. They listen to a woman talking about her plans for a new restaurant and then, in groups, design their own restaurant.

OPTIONAL WARMER

Write *starters, main courses, desserts* on the board and check the Ss understand. Now put Ss in pairs to brainstorm dishes that are normally in each category. Get feedback and write the dishes on the board. Then Ss talk in pairs about which dishes they like and don't like.

1 ▶ Tell Ss they are going to talk about one of their favourite restaurants. Read through the different points they should cover, giving examples in relation to one of your favourite restaurants, e.g. type and quality of food – *In my favourite restaurant they serve top quality fish and salads.*

▶ Give the Ss a little time to think about their own favourite restaurants, making a few notes. Help with any difficult vocabulary and then put them in small groups so they can share their ideas.

2a ▶ 🔘 1.26 Ask various Ss to read out the questions before they listen and check everybody understands them. Play the recording and Ss answer the questions. Let them compare with a partner.

b ▶ Focus on the menu and explain any words Ss do not know. Now play the recording again for Ss to check their answers from ex. 2a and complete the menu. Elicit the answers from the class.

Answers
1   On the ground floor of a big building in the centre of town near the school.
2   Anita's
3   No, she's going to serve European food, too (Italian and modern French food).
4   No, it isn't. It's going to be affordable.
5   nine (three starters, three main courses and three desserts)
6   waiter service
7   She's going to have music to create a young, lively atmosphere and paintings by local artists on the walls.

MENU
Tomato soup
Roast chicken with potatoes
Apple pie with cream

3a ▶ Ss work in small groups of three to design their own restaurant. Ask one member of each group to take notes. Encourage them to pay attention to details mentioned in ex. 1. Go around the class helping with any difficult vocabulary.

b ▶ Each group presents their ideas and at the end. The whole class votes for the restaurant they think is most likely to succeed.

OPTIONAL EXTENSION

Put Ss in groups to discuss some of the best and worst restaurants they have been to, using the points from ex. 1. Get feedback from the whole class.

Review and practice

1 ▶

Answers
1 No, I'm going to have something later.
2 No, I'm going to take him/her after dinner.
3 No, I'm going to buy it at the weekend.
4 No, I'm going to paint it on Tuesday.
5 No, I'm going to clean it in the morning.

2 ▶

Answers
1 When are you going to give up?
2 Are you going to buy her a present?
3 Where are you going to put it?
4 Are you going to wash the car?

3 ▶

Answers
1 The waiter who brought us our food was very friendly.
2 This is the restaurant where John asked me to marry him.
3 The train which goes to the airport runs every twenty minutes.
4 The men who robbed the post office escaped in a black BMW.
5 This is the corner of the road where the accident happened.

4 ▶

Answers
A: Hi Tim! What <u>are you doing</u> this evening?
B: Not a lot. Actually, <u>I'm having</u> a quiet evening at home alone.
A: Why don't you come round to my house? <u>I'm</u> inviting a few friends over for dinner.
B: I'm not sure. I'm quite tired.
A: How about tomorrow night?
B: I'm <u>going</u> to the cinema with my brother. Why don't you come, too?

5 ▶

Answers
1 She's going to the dentist's on Monday morning/at 11:00 a.m.
2 She's having lunch with Jenny at 2:00 p.m.
3 She's going to Italian class in the evening/at 6:30 p.m.
4 On Tuesday she's giving a presentation in the morning/at 10:00 a.m.
5 She's having a meeting with the Marketing Director in the afternoon/at 3:00 p.m.
6 She's phoning the US office at 6:00 p.m.
7 She's going to the cinema with Nathan in the evening/at 8:00 pm.

6 ▶

Answers	2 sweet	4 recipe
1 receipt	3 cooker	5 raw

Writing bank

1 ▶ Ss read the notes and messages and match them with the reasons for writing.

Answers	1	A	3	B
	2	C	4	D

2 ▶ Ss read the notes and messages again and say if the statements are true (T) or false (F).

Answers	1 F	2 T	3 T

3a ▶ Ss complete part A of the *How to...* box with the headings. Check the answers with the whole class.

Answers	1 c	2 b	3 a

b ▶ Ss write the abbreviations in part B of the *How to...* box.

Answers	1	Fri	4	4
	2	a.m.	5	c
	3	cos	6	pls

c ▶ Ss find five more abbreviations in the notes and messages from ex. 1.

Answers
Sat = Saturday
u = you
2 = to
thanx = thanks

4a ▶ Ss rewrite the notes.

Suggested Answers
1 Want to meet for breakfast at café on corner on Sunday? Could meet at 10:00?
2 Yes. Would like you to drive me to airport this afternoon. See you at 4:30. Thanks.
3 Could get you a magazine after work today because I go past shop. Want me to get you one?

b ▶ Ss rewrite the text messages.

Suggested Answers
1 Will meet u at station. Can u buy sandwich 4 me? C u later.
2 Want 2 come 4 dinner Fri? Haven't seen u 4 ages. Pls come.
3 Thanx 4 inviting me 2 your party. Love 2 come.

5a ▶ Ss choose one of the reasons for writing from ex. 1 and think about what they want to say.

b ▶ Ss write a note or a text message.

Overview

Lead-in	Revision: Survival
4.1	**Can do:** Compare people **Grammar:** Comparative adjectives **Vocabulary:** Describing people **Speaking and Pronunciation:** Emphasising important words **Reading:** Going up. Going down
4.2	**Can do:** Talk about challenging events and activities **Grammar:** Superlative adjectives **Vocabulary:** Survival skills **Listening:** Survival school
4.3	**Can do:** Ask questions in everyday situations **Grammar:** Indirect questions **Speaking and Pronunciation:** **How to...** be polite in English Intonation in indirect questions **Reading:** One language – three cultures
Communication	Agree on choices with other people
Reference	
Review and practice	
Writing bank	Write a 'thank you' email **How to...** structure a 'thank you' email
Extra resources	Active Teach and Active Book

CEFR Can do objectives

4.1 Compare people
4.2 Talk about challenging events and activities
4.3 Ask questions in everyday situations
Communication Agree on choices with other people
Writing bank Write a 'thank you' email

CEFR Portfolio ideas

a) Recording: record your sentences from Exercise 11 on page 41.
b) Write a *thank you* note to your British friend who sent you some flowers/chocolate for your birthday.
c) Write a description of a dangerous/wild place in your country. Explain what you must do/take to be safe in this place.

Lead-in

OPTIONAL WARMER

Introduce Ss to the topic of survival. *What does survival mean?* (Survival is when someone or something continues to live or exist after being in a dangerous situation.) *What is the verb? What do we call the person who survives?* (*Survive* and *survivor*) *Which famous survivors can you think of?* (Robinson Crusoe, Gulliver and many others from literature.) *What songs or TV shows do you associate with survival?* (*I Will Survive* by Gloria Gaynor, *I'm a Survivor* by Destiny's Child.)

---

1 ▶ Focus Ss on the photos. Ask Ss, in pairs, to write three words for each photo. Then ask them to describe the photos using those words. Elicit the words that Ss have chosen and write them on the board. Then ask four different Ss to talk about each photo.

Suggested Answers
Main photo: desert: hot, dry, lonely
Top photo: river: rafting, water, fast, wet, to drown
Middle photo: mountain: to climb, cold, snow, skis
Bottom photo: jungle: hot, humid, trees, car, lost, directions
Example description of top photo: A group of people are rafting down a river. The water and the boat are moving very fast. The people are getting wet. It looks exciting, but also dangerous.

2a ▶ 🔵 1.27 Read through the different situations with the whole class and check they understand them. Play the recording and Ss number the situations in the order they hear them. Make sure they know that one situation is not used. Let them check in pairs.

Answers
a	4	c	3	f	2
b	1	e	5		Extra situation = d

---

b ▶ Play the recording again, pausing after each speaker. Tell Ss, in pairs, to choose a phrase from the box which they have heard the speaker say and encourage them to talk about what the person has said and how they used the word. Elicit the answers from the whole class.

Answers
f	a challenge	b	control your fear
e	achieve your goal	a	physical/mental strength
		c	rely on

---

c ▶ In pairs, Ss match the phrases from the box with the definitions. Elicit the answers from the class.

Answers
		3	a challenge
1	control your fear	4	rely on
2	achieve your goal	5	physical/mental strength

---

3 ▶ Ss discuss the questions in pairs or small groups. Get feedback from the whole class.

4.1 Going to extremes

In modern-day society many people seem to enjoy setting themselves dangerous and challenging goals, which according to psychologists may be a result of the lack of risk in everyday life. As our daily routines can often be a little boring, thousands are turning to extreme sports from bungee-jumping to sky diving in order to get that 'adrenalin rush'. This refers to a physical reaction to a situation of risk in which the body releases adrenalin to help us cope with that situation. This makes people feel very excited. People who like doing extreme sports are sometimes referred to as 'adrenalin junkies'.

In this lesson, Ss read about two mountaineers and a diver who successfully achieved their goals, despite pushing themselves to the limits. Through this context, Ss consider adjectives for describing personality and the grammar of comparatives.

OPTIONAL WARMER

Write *going to extremes* on the board. Ask Ss: *What do you think this means? What type of people go to extremes? Why do they do it?*
Get feedback from the class and then ask them to brainstorm activities/hobbies/sports in which they think people push themselves to the limit. If Ss don't know the name of the sport, they can just describe it. Get feedback and write the activities on the board. If they don't mention some of the more recent sports listed below, add them to the list. Possible answers: *rock climbing, white-water rafting, trekking, racing-car driving, snow boarding, bungee-jumping, hang gliding.*
Ask Ss: *Have you ever done any of these activities? Would you like to do one of them?*

Reading

1 ▶ Ss look at the photos and article headings in pairs and discuss the question. Get feedback from various Ss.

▶ Ss read the texts quickly to check their ideas. Tell them not to worry about anything they don't understand at this stage. Get feedback about what the people achieved.

Answers
- Habeler and Messner were the first people to climb Mount Everest without bottled oxygen.
- Sara Campbell became the world free-diving champion in 2009.

2 ▶ Read through the statements with the whole class and check they understand. Ss read the text again and decide if the sentences are true (T) or false (F). Let them check their answers with a partner before getting feedback from various Ss.

Answers
1 F
2 F
3 T
4 F
5 F
6 T
7 T
8 T

▶ Ask the Ss if there are any words or phrases in the texts that they don't understand. Encourage Ss to answer each other's questions before explaining them yourself.

3 ▶ Ss discuss the questions with a partner. Get feedback from the whole class.

Vocabulary | describing people

4a ▶ Focus Ss on the adjectives in the box and tell them to turn to page 130. Ss read the descriptions and match an adjective to each one. Elicit the answers from the class.

Answers
1 generous
2 confident
3 funny
4 intelligent
5 reliable
6 motivated
7 determined
8 fit
9 talented

b ▶ Ss rewrite the descriptions in pairs. Check the answers with various Ss.

Answers
1 My aunt is generous. She gave me £200 at Christmas!
2 Jane is confident that she will pass her end-of-year exams.
3 Mick is funny. He's very good at telling jokes.
4 Sarah is intelligent. She's got lots of qualifications.
5 Petra is reliable. She won't be late.
6 Flora is motivated. She studies hard and gets good results.
7 My dad is determined. He's decided to run a marathon and I'm sure he'll do it.
8 Penny is fit. She exercises at least five times a week.
9 Sam is talented as a writer. She won a short story competition in June.

5 ▶ Ss use appropriate adjectives from ex. 4a to describe Sara Campbell, and Habeler and Messner. They can also add any more adjectives that they feel will match the descriptions. Get feedback from the whole class.

OPTIONAL EXTENSION

Ask Ss to write the name of a person they know or know of who they would describe by using each of the nine adjectives. Then put them in small groups to talk about these people, explaining why they have chosen to describe them with this adjective. Give them an example, e.g. *My brother is very generous. He always pays for everybody when we go out for a meal.*

Grammar | comparative adjectives

OPTIONAL GRAMMAR LEAD-IN

Ask Ss to close their books. Write *cat*, *horse* and *big* on the board. Ask the Ss to make a sentence to compare them. Elicit or model *A horse is bigger than a cat*. Do the same with *pencil*, *table* and *small*. Now write *car*, *bike* and *expensive* on the board. Ask the Ss to make a sentence to compare them. Elicit or model *A car is more expensive than a bike*. Do the same with *mountaineering*, *swimming* and *dangerous*. Elicit rules for making comparatives.

6a ▶ Ss complete the table in the Active grammar box in pairs and then check their answers with the texts from ex. 1. Go through the answers with the class, making reference to the rules for the different categories.

Active Grammar

deep	deeper than
fit	fitter than
happy	happier than
dangerous	more dangerous than
bad	worse than
far	further (farther) than

▶ Focus Ss on *fit–fitter than* and elicit/teach the reason why the *t* is doubled in the comparative form (when an adjective ends in vowel + consonant, we double the consonant).

▶ Ask Ss: *What do you think the comparative form of brave is?* Elicit/teach *braver* and point out that when an adjective already ends in *-e*, we only add *r*.

▶ Point out that *far* has two possible comparative forms. Both have exactly the same meaning and are used interchangeably.

b ▶ Focus on parts A and B of the Active grammar box. Ask Ss to discuss in pairs the difference in meaning between the phrases. Get feedback from the class.

Answers
1 *as ... as* means two things are the same; *not as ... as* means two things are different.
2 *a bit* means there is a small difference; *much* means there is a big difference.

▶ Draw the Ss' attention to the Reference on page 47.

7a ▶ Focus on the information given in the box and read through the example with the whole class. Tell Ss to work in pairs to make sentences comparing Louisa and Carla. Encourage them to use modifiers and the two forms of comparative sentences shown in the Active grammar box.

b ▶ 🔘 1.28 Play the recording for Ss to listen and check their answers.

Answers
• Louisa is a bit fitter than Carla./Carla isn't as fit as Louisa.
• Louisa is a bit more determined than Carla./Carla isn't as determined as Louisa.
• Carla is much braver than Louisa./Louisa isn't as brave as Carla.

Pronunciation | emphasising important words

8 ▶ 🔘 1.29 Explain to Ss that we often stress certain words in a sentence to emphasise what we think is important. Point out that they have reference to this in the Pronunciation bank on page 148. Now play the recording so that Ss can notice the stress. Let them practise saying the sentences with a partner.

Speaking

9 ▶ Divide the class into two groups, A and B. Ss A look at page 41 and Ss B look at page 130. Tell the Ss to read through the questions and match each one with an adjective from ex. 4a on page 41. Go around the class helping them with any difficult vocabulary as they do this. Elicit the answers from the groups.

Answers
A
1 motivated
2 funny
3 reliable
4 confident

B
1 fit
2 intelligent or talented
3 generous
4 determined

10 ▶ Reorganise the class so that a student A is working with a student B. They take it in turns to ask and answer each other's questions, making a note of the answers.

11 ▶ Ask the Ss to use their notes to make sentences comparing themselves with their partners. Put each student with a different partner so that they can tell each other about their original partner. Encourage them to give reasons, as in the example.

4.2 Survival school

In recent years there has been a growing interest in how to survive in the wild. Game shows, documentaries and now survival schools cater to this new trend. These schools offer short courses in how to survive in the wilderness without any modern comforts.

In this lesson, Ss listen to the chief instructor of Hillside Survival School describing the courses that are on offer. Through this context, Ss learn superlative adjectives and vocabulary associated with survival skills and challenging activities.

OPTIONAL WARMER

Write *the wilderness* on the board and explain the meaning to the Ss (a wild and uncultivated region, as of forest or desert, uninhabited or inhabited only by wild animals). Ask Ss to talk in pairs about times they have been in the wilderness, or what they know about it if they haven't been. Ss can ask the following: *When was the last time you went to a wild place? Why did you go there? What did you do there? Did you enjoy yourself? Would you like to go (again) to a place like this? What kind of wild places have you seen on the TV, in films or heard about? Would you like to visit them?*

Vocabulary | survival skills

1 ▶ Focus on the words/phrases in the box and read through the example question. Give Ss two or three minutes to match these words/phrases to the underlined phrases in the sentences. Check Ss' answers as a class.

Answers
1 survival skills
2 build a shelter
3 challenge
4 push yourself
5 cope with

2 ▶ Give Ss about five minutes to ask and answer the questions in pairs. Get feedback from various Ss.

Listening

3 ▶ 🔘 1.30 In pairs, Ss look at the photos and talk to a partner about what they can see. Get feedback from a few Ss and tell the whole class that they are going to listen to David Johnson from the Hillside Survival School. Read through the three questions with the whole class and play the recording. Let Ss compare their answers with a partner and then check with the whole class.

Answers
1 He started the school and he's the chief instructor there.
2 He's talking to a group of colleagues/people who work together and he's explaining the types of courses the school organises and why people do them.
3 He's at the company where these people work.

4 ▶ Read through the notes with the whole class and then play the recording again so that the Ss can complete them. Let them compare with a partner and then elicit the answers from various Ss.

Answers
1 in the army and in other well-known survival schools
2 to help people to work together as a team
3 groups of friends
4 a weekend
5 throughout the year
6 £175
7 between November and February
8 £195
9 to find it and cook it over an open fire
10 to build it and then sleep in it

5 ▶ Put the Ss in small groups to discuss the questions. Get feedback from various Ss.

Grammar | superlative adjectives

OPTIONAL GRAMMAR LEAD-IN

Write the following sentences on the board with the words in the wrong order:
1 *The the course survival basic is most popular.* (The basic survival course is the most popular.)
2 *January year is coldest the of the month in England.* (January is the coldest month of the year in England.)
Give Ss a few minutes to try to arrange the words in the correct order in pairs. Tell them the first and the last words are in the correct place already. Elicit the answers and write the sentences on the board, underlining *most popular* and *coldest*. Ask Ss: *What is the name of these types of adjectives?* (superlative)

6a ▶ Ss complete the Active grammar box in pairs. Tell them to check their answers with audioscript 1.30 on page 152. Elicit the answers from the whole class.

Active grammar

cold	the coldest
wet	the wettest
popular	the most popular
comfortable	the most comfortable
good	the best

▶ Talk through the different categories with the Ss, drawing a parallel with the grammar of comparatives, which they studied in the last lesson. Pay particular attention to the following:

• two-syllable adjectives ending in -y, use -est; the -y changes to -i (e.g. the noisiest);

• when a one-syllable adjective ends in -e, simply add -st (e.g. the nicest, the largest); when a one-syllable adjective ends in a vowel and a consonant, double the consonant (e.g. wettest, fittest).

b ▶ Focus on part A of the Active grammar box and read through the grammar rule with the whole class. Write two more examples on the board to illustrate the difference between using the or a possessive adjective, e.g. July and August are the hottest months in England; History is her worst school subject.

▶ Now ask the Ss to read through part B and complete the examples with the prepositions. Have two Ss read out the example sentences and check the prepositions.

Active grammar

1 in
2 of

▶ Give Ss two more examples, e.g. Sunday is the most relaxing day of the week; The art gallery is the most modern building in the town. Draw Ss' attention to the Reference on page 47.

7 ▶ Put Ss in pairs to read the sentences and correct the mistakes. Elicit the answers from various Ss.

Answers
1 That is the hardest I've ever pushed myself at work.
2 This is the biggest challenge of the day.
3 Could you survive in the hottest place in the world?
4 Building a shelter was the most difficult thing we did.
5 Lara is the best in the class at coping with new situations.
6 Simon is the most experienced person in our office.
7 My sister is the bravest person in our family.
8 That course was the worst experience of my life.

8 ▶ Focus on the email and note and tell Ss they were written by two people who went on a course at Hillside Survival School. Ss read and complete them using eight of the ten words from the box. Elicit the answers from various Ss.

Answers
1 difficult
2 most
3 worst
4 exciting
5 of
6 best
7 noisiest
8 in

▶ Ask the Ss if the people who wrote these feel positive or negative about the experience (positive).

Speaking

9 ▶ Focus on the example and read it aloud for the whole class. Now Ss write complete questions. Elicit the answers from various Ss.

Answers
1 What is the most dangerous thing that/which has ever happened to you?
2 Who is the most determined person in your family or class?
3 What is the most challenging job (that) you've ever done?
4 What is the most difficult exam (that) you've ever taken?

10 ▶ Put Ss in small groups to discuss the questions from ex. 9.

▶ Get one student from each group to report back to the rest of the class about the most interesting thing they have found out.

OPTIONAL VARIATION

Before doing the discussion, ask Ss to choose two of the questions from ex. 9 and write a follow-up question they could ask about each one. Get them to ask their follow-up questions in the discussion.

OPTIONAL EXTENSION

Write the following on the board: The worst problem in our city/town. The best film of the last year. The most dangerous animal in the world. The fittest person in the class. The most beautiful holiday destination in your country. Put Ss in groups to decide one thing for each category. Encourage them to give reasons for their choices. Rearrange the class so that Ss are in different groups and ask them to compare their answers to see if they were the same. Where they are different, ask them to try and convince each other.

4.3 Surviving in English

Although the British, the Americans and the Australians share a common language, English, it is not a universal language and there are many differences in pronunciation, vocabulary and grammar. There are also many cultural differences and as a learner of English it has become increasingly important to understand these differences in order to communicate successfully.

In this lesson, Ss read about cultural and linguistic differences between the British, the Americans and the Australians and through this context they consider the use of indirect questions to express politeness.

OPTIONAL WARMER

Write the following question on the board: *Which countries can you name where English is the most important language*? Let Ss make a list in pairs and then elicit the countries and write them on the board, e.g. *England*, *Scotland*, *Wales*, *Ireland*, *the US*, *Canada* (official language with French), *Australia*, *South Africa*, *New Zealand*. There are many other countries, e.g. India, the Philippines, Ghana, etc., where English is an official language but it is not the one most predominantly used as a means of communication. Ask Ss to discuss in small groups anything they know about these countries. Get feedback from the whole class.

Reading

1a ▶ Focus on the three photos and the title of the text. Ask Ss to answer the questions in pairs. Get feedback from various Ss.

Answers
1   Photo 1: United Kingdom (London)
    Photo 2: US (New York)
    Photo 3: Australia (Sydney)
2   The title means that although they speak English in the three countries, their cultures are different.

b ▶ Ss read through the text quickly and match the headings (a–c) with the paragraphs. Elicit the answers from various Ss.

Answers
1   a
2   c
3   b

2 ▶ Have various Ss read out the questions and check everybody understands. Now Ss read the text again and answer the questions with a partner. Tell them not to worry about any words or phrases they don't understand at this stage, unless it prevents them from answering the questions. Elicit the answers from various Ss.

Answers
1   stand in line
2   they say 'sorry'
3   G'day!
4   the US
5   the US
6   Can I have the check, please?
7   the left side
8   on the sidewalk

▶ Ask Ss if there are any words or phrases in the text that they still don't understand. Encourage other Ss to explain them before doing so yourself.

3 ▶ Ss discuss the questions in small groups. Get feedback from the whole class.

4 ▶ Focus on the Lifelong learning box and read through the tip with the whole class. In pairs, Ss look at the American words and say if they know the British equivalent. Get feedback from the whole class, writing the British words on the board.

Answers
apartment – flat
cell phone – mobile phone
chips – crisps
cookie – biscuit
elevator – lift
gas – petrol
pants – trousers
purse – handbag
restroom – toilets
vacation – holiday

Listening

5 ▶ ⦿ 1.31 Focus on the three situations and ask Ss to suggest in pairs sentences they might hear in each one. Get feedback from the whole class. Now play the recording and Ss match dialogues (1–3) with the situations (a–c). Elicit the answers from the class.

Answers
a   3
b   1
c   2

6 ▶ Play the recording again and Ss answer the questions. Elicit the answers from the class.

Answers
1   5.45 p.m.
2   the newspaper
3   Yes, they do.

Grammar | indirect questions

> **OPTIONAL GRAMMAR LEAD-IN**
>
> Write the following stems on the board: *Do you know ...* ; *Could you tell me ...*; Tell the Ss to imagine they are in London and they are lost. They want to go to Trafalgar Square. In pairs, Ss discuss how they would complete the stem sentences. Get feedback and elicit/teach the correct form (*Do you know/Could you tell me where Trafalgar Square is*?) Do the same with the following situation. You phone the theatre and you want to know what time the show starts. Elicit the correct answer (*Do you know/ Could you tell me what time the show starts*?)

7 ▶ 🌐 1.31 Read through the questions with the whole class. Then play the recording again and Ss tick the questions they hear. Elicit the answers from the class.

> **Answers**
> 1 b
> 2 a
> 3 a

8a ▶ Read through the first part of the Active grammar box with the whole class, explaining that to ask a direct question in English can be seen as impolite if we don't know a person very well, and that we use an indirect form to be more polite. Read through the example beginnings of indirect questions and point out that these types of questions can be divided into three categories (A, B and C). Ask the Ss to read this information in pairs and to match the question pairs from ex. 7 to the question types A, B or C. Elicit the answers from the class and draw Ss' attention to the Reference on page 47.

> **Active grammar**
> A 3
> B 1
> C 2

b ▶ Ss look at ex. 7 again and decide which question in each pair is direct or indirect. Elicit the answers and write the examples on the board next to the appropriate structure.

> **Active grammar**
> 1a – direct
> 1b – indirect
> 2a – indirect
> 2b – direct
> 3a – indirect
> 3b – direct

9 ▶ Focus on the example and then put Ss in pairs to rewrite the direct questions as indirect questions, using the words in brackets. Get various Ss to read out the questions.

> **Answers**
> 1 Can you tell me what time it is, please?
> 2 Do you mind if I borrow your pen for a minute?
> 3 Could you tell me if you have any 1st class stamps?
> 4 Can you tell me if there's a post office near here?
> 5 Do you know where I can get an application form, please?

Pronunciation | intonation in indirect questions

10a ▶ 🌐 1.32 Explain that when we use indirect questions our tone of voice changes to make them sound more polite. Ask the Ss to listen to the recording and repeat the question, copying the intonation. Draw Ss' attention to the Pronunciation bank on page 148.

b ▶ 🌐 1.33 Ss practise asking the other indirect questions from ex. 9 with appropriate intonation. Then play the recording so that they can check and repeat.

Speaking

11 ▶ 🌐 1.34 Focus on the *How to...* box and read through the questions with the whole class. Now play the recording and Ss write the responses. Let them compare with a partner and then check with the whole class.

> **Answers**
> 1 Yes, certainly ... I'll just have a look for you.
> 2 Yes, of course. It's fifty-five dollars.
> 3 Yes, that's fine.
> 4 No, that's fine. Go ahead.

12 ▶ Tell the Ss to look at audioscript 1.31 on page 153. Ask them to choose one of the dialogues and practise it with a partner. Encourage them to change parts and extend and elaborate the dialogue. Have some pairs of Ss act it out for the rest of the class.

> **OPTIONAL EXTENSION**
>
> Put Ss in groups and ask them to imagine they are from a different country from the one they are living in at the moment. They are planning to visit the country (where they are living at the moment) and would like to know about the customs, food, etc. Get them to write five indirect questions they would like to ask, e.g. *Could you tell me what the food is like?* Monitor their work and then reorganise groups so Ss can ask and answer each other's questions.

4 Communication

In this lesson, Ss listen to a conversation about a survival course. They look at language for expressing opinions, making suggestions and comparisons and then work with other Ss to agree on choices.

1a ▶ Focus Ss on the words in the box and tell them to work with a partner to label the things they can see in the photo. Get feedback from various Ss, eliciting/explaining the meaning of problematic words with the whole class, e.g. *We use a torch at night to see in the dark.*

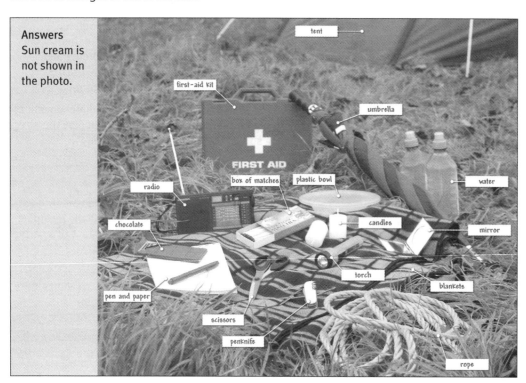

Answers
Sun cream is not shown in the photo.

tent
first-aid kit
umbrella
water
radio
box of matches
plastic bowl
candles
mirror
chocolate
torch
blankets
pen and paper
scissors
penknife
rope

b ▶ Put Ss in different pairs to take turns at covering the photo: one student looks, while the other one remembers the items. See which student can remember the most.

OPTIONAL VARIATION

Put Ss in pairs. One student looks at the photo and gives clues for two or three items for the other S to guess, e.g. *It's sweet and you can eat it.* Then they swap roles.

---

2 ▶ 🌐 1.35 Read through the questions with the whole class and then play the recording. Ss listen and note down their answers. Allow them to compare with a partner and then get feedback from several Ss.

Answers
1   a group of colleagues
2   blankets, penknife, matches, tent and chocolate

---

3 ▶ Tell Ss to look at audioscript 1.35 on page 153 while you play the recording again. As they listen, tell them to underline ways of expressing opinion, making suggestions and making comparisons. Get feedback from various Ss, writing the expressions on the board.

Answers
1   Expressing opinions: I'm sure we're all going to have ... ; I suppose it's good ... ; I think we should take ... ; In my opinion ... ; I'm not sure ... ; I think it's going to be difficult.
2   Making suggestions: Shall we ... ; How about ... ; Couldn't we make ... ; Why don't we have ... ?
3   Making comparisons: Which of them ... is the most important? Do you think they're more important than ... ?

4a ▶ Ss work in pairs to make a list of the five things from ex. 1a that they think they should take, discussing their reasons for choosing these things. Help Ss with any vocabulary they need at this stage.

b ▶ Organise the Ss into groups of four so that they can compare their lists. Tell them they must come to an agreement about which five things to take, so each pair must try to persuade the other. Encourage them to use the language from ex. 3. Get feedback from the whole class.

OPTIONAL EXTENSION

In pairs, Ss think of one other item that is not in the photo that would be useful to take. They then present their idea to the rest of the class, explaining why they think this item is useful. The class votes for their favourite item.

Review and practice

1 ▶

Answers		
1 quieter	3	worse
2 more exciting	4	happier
	5	further/farther

2 ▶

Answers
1 The gold watch is more expensive than the silver watch.
   The silver watch isn't as expensive as the gold watch.
2 The Brighton train leaves later than the London train.
   The London train doesn't leave as late as the Brighton train.
3 Health is more important to me than money.
   Money isn't as important to me as health.
4 Brown bread tastes better than white bread.
   White bread doesn't taste as good as brown bread.

3 ▶

Answers		
1 the most expensive	3	the tallest
2 the hottest	4	the fastest
	5	the friendliest

4 ▶

Answers
1 Today was the hottest day of the year.
2 You are much braver than me.
3 Harry is the most intelligent boy in his school.
4 These jeans are a bit more expensive than those ones.
5 This is the oldest house in the town.
6 She seems a bit happier than yesterday.
7 It was the worst shock of my life.
8 Greece is much hotter than England at the moment.

5 ▶

Answers
1 <u>Do</u> you know why he isn't home yet?
2 Do you know <u>if</u> I can pay by credit card?
3 Can you tell me <u>where</u> I can find a garage?
4 Can you tell <u>me</u> whose car this is, please?
5 Do you know <u>what</u> time the next train for Manchester leaves?

6 ▶

Answers
1 Do you know where I can find a cheap hotel?
2 Can you tell me if there's an internet café near here?
3 Do you mind if we share a taxi to the airport?
4 Is it OK if I borrow your phone?
5 Could you tell me if I need a visa to go to Ireland?

7 ▶

Answers				
1 cope	2	generous	4	fit
	3	fear	5	rely

Writing bank

1a ▶ Ss think of four reasons for writing a 'thank you' email and say which one(s) they have written recently.

b ▶ Ss read the emails and say why each one was written.

Answers
The first is to say thank you for a wedding present.
The second is to say thank you for having her to stay.

2 ▶ Ss read the emails again and answer the questions.

Answers
1 Yes, they had a brilliant time.
2 She went to some interesting places and met some of Giovanna's friends.

3a ▶ Ss complete the *How to…* box.

Answers	
1	Hi
2	to say thanks
3	Thank you for
4	really good to
5	see you again
6	Lots of

b ▶ Ss complete the sentences with the words in the box.

Answers	
1	soon
2	having
3	thanks
4	seeing
5	sends
6	much

4a ▶ Ss make notes about the four questions in preparation for writing a 'thank you' email.

b ▶ Ss write the email, using their notes.

5 Stages

Overview

Lead-in	Revision: Stages
5.1	**Can do:** Exchange opinions with a friend
	Grammar: *should, have to, can*: obligation and permission
	Speaking and Pronunciation:
	How to... exchange opinions
	Connected speech (2)
	Reading: Life at eighteen
	Listening: The age to do things
5.2	**Can do:** Talk about friends
	Grammar: Present Perfect Simple: *for* and *since*
	Vocabulary: Friendship
	Listening: Different types of friends
5.3	**Can do:** Describe yourself when you were younger
	Grammar: *used to*: past habits
	Vocabulary: Habits
	Reading: How long am I going to live?
Communication	Tell someone's life story
Reference	
Review and practice	
Writing bank	Complete a simple form
	How to... understand the language on forms
Extra resources	Active Teach and Active Book

CEFR Can do objectives

5.1 Exchange opinions with a friend
5.2 Talk about friends
5.3 Describe yourself when you were younger
Communication Tell someone's life story
Writing bank Complete a simple form

CEFR Portfolio ideas

a) Write a 'To Do' list of things you have to do next week. Write a sentence for each item explaining why you have to do it.
b) Make an album of photographs from your childhood. Write a caption for each picture giving your age, the place and your activity. Show your album to your classmates.
c) Write a list of news headlines reporting important events in the world during your life. Write the date of each event, explain the event and your reaction to the event at the time.
d) Show your albums of photographs to another student. Record a conversation in which your partner asks about the pictures.

Lead-in

OPTIONAL WARMER

Write *stage* on the blackboard and ask the Ss if they know what it means. Elicit/tell Ss that it's a step, level or period in the development or process of something, e.g. when you are doing the washing, the first stage is to put the clothes in the washing machine. Ask Ss to practise this by describing the stages for other things, e.g. making a cup of coffee.

▶ Write the following ages on the board: *1, 15, 30, 50, 65* and *80*. Ask the Ss to brainstorm one or two things normally associated with each stage of a person's life. Give the following example: *When you are one, you can't speak and you sleep a lot*. Get feedback from the whole class.

1 ▶ Write *early/late/mid-twenties* on the board. Ask Ss which one they would use for a person who is 21, and for a person who is 25 or 28. Tell them to look at the photos and discuss with a partner what the people are doing and how old Ss think they are. Ss share their ideas with the rest of the class.

2a ▶ Check that Ss understand the words in the box, e.g. *When you are six months old, what are you?* (a baby) *When you are two years old, what are you?* (a toddler).

▶ Tell the Ss to write an age range for each word individually.

b ▶ Have Ss compare with a partner to see if they agree or disagree with each other and then discuss each concept with the whole class. These age ranges are not strictly defined and are to some extent culturally subjective. However, the following ranges could be suggested as a guideline: adolescent (11–16); (young) adult (18 +); baby (0–12 months); child (3–16); middle-aged person (40–60); old/elderly person (60+); retired person (60+); teenager (13–19); toddler (1–3 years).

3 ▶ Ss work in small groups to discuss the age at which people in their country normally do the activities in the box. If your class is of mixed nationality, it might be a good idea to group Ss according to their country of origin, as far as possible. Have Ss share their ideas with the whole class.

4 ▶ Read the example to the Ss and tell them they have to talk about themselves or somebody they know well in a similar way. Give Ss a few minutes to think and make brief notes. Have them work with a partner to tell their stories.

Get some feedback by asking individual Ss to tell you about what their partner told them.

EXTEND THE LEAD-IN

Put the Ss in small groups and tell them to look back at the words or phrases in ex. 3 and choose four of them. Ask them to talk about the age at which people did these things 50 years ago. Do they think that it was better in the past or do they prefer the way things are now?

5.1 Turning eighteen

In many countries worldwide, a person's eighteenth birthday is of great importance, as it marks the age at which a teenager is generally recognised to have become a legal adult. In many countries in Europe, including Britain, Spain, Portugal, Germany and Denmark among others, you can't vote or get married without your parents' consent until you are eighteen. Other rights are often acquired at this age too. In Europe, on the whole, you have to be eighteen to hold a full driving licence, although in Britain this right is given to people at the age of seventeen.

In this lesson, Ss read about three young people, from different cultural backgrounds, commenting on life at eighteen. Through this context they analyse the grammar of *should(n't)*, *(don't) have to* and *can/can't*.

OPTIONAL WARMER

Write a number of dates on the board, e.g. *August 2010, December 2008, 2001, 1998*. Ask Ss to think about these dates and to tell their partner what they remember or know about their life at that point. Get feedback from various Ss.

Reading

1 ▶ Ss discuss the questions in pairs. Encourage them to give reasons for their answers. Get feedback from various Ss.

2 ▶ Ss read text 1 and answer the questions in pairs. Check the answers with the class.

Answers
1   eighteen-year-olds
2   send comments to say what life is like for them

3a ▶ Focus on the box and make sure the Ss know that *career* refers to your professional life. Put Ss into three groups, A, B and C. Ss in group A read text 2 on page 50, Ss in group B read the text on page 130 and Ss in group C read the text on page 134. They work individually at this stage, ticking the subjects mentioned by the person they are reading about.

b ▶ Rearrange the class so that there is one student from group A, one from B and one from group C together. Ss take it in turns to tell the others about the text they have read. Encourage Ss to use their own words as much as possible. The other Ss listen and complete the rest of the table. Finally, check the answers with the whole class.

Answers
Gregor: the army, education, free time, family and money (he says it would be expensive to get a place of his own)
Miguel: education (he's just left school), free time, career, money and family
Fei: education, career, money and family

4 ▶ Read through the questions with the whole class. Ss work in the same groups as in ex. 3b, discussing their answers. Get feedback from various Ss.

Grammar | *should, have to, can*: obligation and permission

OPTIONAL GRAMMAR LEAD-IN

Write the following sentences on the board:
You should speak in English in class; *You can eat in class*; *You have to be a good swimmer to study English.*
Ss work in pairs to say if the sentences are true or false, correcting the verb form of the false sentences to make them true. Elicit feedback from the whole class.

5 ▶ Ss underline examples of *should, shouldn't, have to, don't have to, can* and *can't* in the text about Gregor in ex. 3. Elicit the example sentences and write them on the board in this order. (There are three examples of *can*. Don't use *when you can be a student* as it is a question.)

Answers
… it should be optional … .
… military service shouldn't be compulsory.
… they usually have to go into the army … .
… I don't have to do military service … .
… I can do a lot of things … .
… I can't go out every night … .

▶ Now focus on the Active grammar box and ask Ss to complete the rules in pairs. Get various Ss to read out the completed rules so that you can check their answers.

Active grammar

A   We use <u>have to</u> to say when something is necessary and there is no choice.
B   We use <u>don't have to</u> to say when something is not necessary and there is a choice.
C   We use <u>should</u> to say something is the right thing to do in your opinion.
D   We use <u>shouldn't</u> to say something is not the right thing to do in your opinion.
E   We use <u>can</u> to say when something is permitted.
F   We use <u>can't</u> to say when something is not permitted.

▶ Tell Ss to look back at the sentences they underlined in the Gregor text and ask: *How is* have *grammatically different from* should *and* can?

Ss discuss the question in pairs. Elicit/teach the answers (*have* takes the full infinitive and the auxiliary verb, *should* and *can* take the infinitive without *to* and no auxiliary verb). Point out that Ss can consult the Reference on page 57.

6 ▶ Ss choose the correct word. Elicit answers from various Ss.

> **Answers**
> 1 have to
> 2 can
> 3 should
> 4 don't have to
> 5 shouldn't

7 ▶ Ss complete the sentences. Let them compare with a partner and then elicit the answers from various Ss.

> **Answers**
> 1 should
> 2 have to
> 3 don't have to
> 4 shouldn't
> 5 can't

Pronunciation | connected speech (2)

8a ▶ 🔘 1.36 Explain that when two consonants are next to each other, one of them is often not pronounced. Focus on the two sentences and play the recording. Tell Ss to circle one consonant that they think is not pronounced in each sentence. Elicit the answers, explaining that the *t* at the end of *can' t* and *shouldn' t* is not pronounced because the next word begins with a consonant.

> **Answers**
> You shouldn't sit around doing nothing.
> You can't go out every night.

b ▶ Ss listen again to check and then repeat the sentences.

▶ For extra practise ask Ss to look back at the sentences in ex. 6 and ex. 7 which contain *can't* and *shouldn't* and practise saying them, in pairs, with good pronunciation.

Listening and speaking

9a ▶ 🔘 1.37 Get various Ss to read out the sentences and check that everybody understands them. Tell the Ss to listen to three dialogues and to match them with the topics (a–e). Point out that two of the topics are not mentioned. Play the recording and allow Ss to compare with a partner before eliciting the answers.

> **Answers**
> a 1
> c 3
> e 2

b ▶ Check the Ss understand the questions and play the recording again. Ss take notes and then compare with a partner. Elicit the answers from various Ss.

> **Answers**
> 1 You change/develop.
> 2 A kind of civil service where you work in hospitals or on farms.
> 3 To do well at school so you can go to university and get a good career.

10a ▶ Ss complete the *How to...* box with the headings (a–c). Get various Ss to read out the headings and the examples for the whole class.

> **Answers**
> 1 c
> 2 b
> 3 a

b ▶ Put the Ss in small groups to discuss one of the topics from ex. 9a. Get feedback from the whole class.

> **OPTIONAL VARIATION**
> Write the following on the board.
> *agree strongly* ✓✓
> *agree* ✓
> *neither agree or disagree* ?
> *disagree* ✗
> *disagree strongly* ✗✗
> Ask Ss to read the sentences in ex. 9a again and indicate their opinion with the symbols shown above. Give them time to think about their reasons and then put them in groups to discuss the different topics.

> **OPTIONAL EXTENSION**
> Write the following statements on the board:
> *All school children should wear uniforms. Young people shouldn't be allowed to drive until they are twenty-one. Children should be allowed to work at fourteen.*
> Divide the class into two groups, A and B. Tell group A that they have to think of arguments to support all three of the statements and group B that they have to think of arguments against those statements.
> Ss work together for five to ten minutes. Reorganise the class so that one student from group A is with a student from group B. Using the *How to...* box as a guide, they discuss the statements from the position they have been given.
> Alternatively, have a whole class debate on the issues. After the arguments for and against have been presented, you could allow Ss to vote, expressing their own personal point of view.

5.2 Old friends

The Internet has transformed means of communication over the last decade and staying in touch with people is now easier than ever. Websites such as Facebook, MySpace and Twitter allow you to create your own profile, upload photos, get in contact with old school friends, workmates, people from university and old neighbours and meet new people at the same time. They also allow you to play games, set up businesses and exchange presents. More and more people are incorporating visits to these kinds of sites into their everyday life.

In this lesson, Ss read the profile of a woman who belongs to a social networking website and through this context consider the use of the Present Perfect Simple with *for* and *since* and vocabulary related to friendship.

OPTIONAL WARMER

Tell the Ss to write down the name of a friend from primary or secondary school who they no longer see. They then work in pairs to talk about their memories of that person. After a few minutes, ask the Ss: *Would you like to meet this person again? Have you any idea what this person is doing now?*

Grammar | Present Perfect Simple: *for* and *since*

OPTIONAL GRAMMAR LEAD-IN

Refresh Ss' memory of the Present Perfect Simple as compared with the Past Simple (Lesson 2.2) by asking the following questions and eliciting answers from the Ss: *Have you ever been to Paris? What did you do last night?* Write the two questions on the board and ask Ss what tense they are. Elicit rules for when we use each tense. If they don't remember, tell them to look back at the Reference on page 27.
Ask Ss to write one more question in the Present Perfect Simple and one in the Past Simple. Ss mingle, asking and answering each other's questions.

1 ▶ Focus Ss on the extract from the website and tell them to read through the text quickly, without worrying at this stage about things they don't understand. Ask them what the purpose of the extract is (to give information about what Tina Armstrong is doing now and to allow her old friends to get in touch with her).

2 ▶ Focus Ss on the part of the text that is underlined and tell them to answer the questions, with a partner. Check the answers with the whole class.

Answers
1   two years ago
2   Yes, she does.

3 ▶ Focus Ss on the Active grammar box and read through the rule that explains this use of the Present Perfect Simple with the whole class. Read out the examples and add a couple of your own, e.g. *We've been in class for ... minutes. I've been a teacher since ... .*

▶ Contrast the two uses of the Present Perfect Simple that Ss have studied so far, writing the following example sentences on the board: *I have been in hospital twice* (an action in the general past – we don't know when it happened). *I have been in hospital for three days/since Tuesday* (an action that started in the past and continues now).

▶ Ss complete sentences A and B with *for* and *since*. Write the sentences on the board and elicit the answers to complete them.

Active grammar
A   We use <u>for</u> when we give the length of the time.
B   We use <u>since</u> when we give the beginning of the time.

▶ Go through the common time expressions with the whole class, checking Ss understand them. If Ss are not clear about *for* and *since*, do some extra practice. Dictate the following prompts and tell Ss, working with a partner, to write them down using *for* or *since*; *last week* (since); *ten years* (for); *two hours* (for); *four o' clock* (since); *I was a child* (since); *a long time* (for); *primary school* (since).

▶ Now ask a few questions of various Ss to check they understand how to use time expressions with the Present Perfect Simple. Indicate whether you want them to answer with *for* or *since*, e.g. *How long have you been in class? How long have you been an English student? How long have you known ...* (name of another student in the class)? *How long have you lived here?*

▶ Focus again on the Active grammar box and explain the contrast with the Past Simple. Draw Ss' attention to the Reference on page 57 and the list of irregular verbs on page 149.

OPTIONAL VARIATION

Put Ss in pairs and have one student look at the irregular verb list on page 149 and test their partner on the past participles by saying the infinitives of ten verbs. They then change roles.

4 ▶ Ss read and complete the dialogue in pairs. Have two of the more confident Ss read it out to check the answers.

Answers
1   since
2   for
3   since
4   for

5 ▶ Ss correct five of the six sentences in pairs. Elicit the answers from various Ss.

> **Answers**
> 1 I have (I've) worked … .
> 2 He bought … .
> 3 … she has (she's) been … .
> 4 We lived … .
> 5 ✓
> 6 I have (I've) met … .

6 ▶ Focus on the box and read out the example sentences. Now tell Ss to choose three people or things and explain to a partner how long they have known or had them. Encourage them to give extra information in their descriptions and encourage the partner who is listening to ask follow-up questions. Get a few Ss to give examples for the whole class.

Vocabulary | friendship

7 ▶ Ss work with a partner to match the phrasal verbs with the definitions. Check the answers with the whole class, asking Ss read out the full definitions.

> **Answers**
> 1 f
> 2 d
> 3 b
> 4 h
> 5 a
> 6 c
> 7 e
> 8 g

8 ▶ Ss complete the story. Tell them to make any necessary changes to verb forms. Let them compare their answers with a partner and then check the answers with the whole class, reading through the text and eliciting a phrase for each gap.

> **Answers**
> 1 got on
> 2 went out
> 3 lost touch (split up would also be acceptable here)
> 4 got in touch
> 5 catch up
> 6 split up
> 7 fall out
> 8 keep in touch

Listening

9a ▶ 🔊 1.38 Focus on the photo and tell Ss to listen to a conversation between Tina and Martin and make a note of who Alison, Jake and Melanie are. Let them compare with a partner and elicit the answers from the class. (They are Tina's closest friends.)

b ▶ Read through the questions with the whole class and play the recording again. Ss make a note of their answers and then compare with a partner. Elicit the answers from the whole class.

> **Answers**
> 1 for years/since primary school/since they were four and a half
> 2 about once a month
> 3 at work
> 4 He's always encouraging and motivating her.
> 5 for about ten years
> 6 She doesn't give advice, she listens.

Speaking

10 ▶ Ss complete the diagram with the names of three close friends and a word or a phrase about each one.

11a ▶ In pairs, Ss look at each other's diagrams and write two questions they can ask about each person. Encourage them to use some of the vocabulary from ex. 7. Go around the class, monitoring their work.

b ▶ Ss ask and answer the questions about their friends in pairs. Encourage them to ask more follow-up questions.

> **OPTIONAL EXTENSION**
> Write: *social networking sites: good or bad?* on the board. Put Ss in small groups to discuss this statement. Get feedback from the whole class.

5.3 The truth about ageing

Although life expectancy around the world has generally risen, there is still a great difference between countries. The highest life expectancy can be found in countries such as Japan, Australia and many European countries, where many people live to be over 80. The lowest is in countries such as Sierra Leone, Zambia or Afghanistan (35–45). Life expectancy also varies according to sex, with women usually outliving men. There is much scientific debate about the factors that influence life expectancy in developed countries. On the one hand, genetics seem to play a part and on the other hand, diet and lifestyle could be influential. In developing countries, poverty and war are undoubtedly important factors.

In this lesson, Ss read a text about ageing and through this context analyse the grammar of *used to* for past habits and situations.

OPTIONAL WARMER

Write the following lists of countries and numbers on the board: *US, India, Zimbabwe, Japan, Argentina, Morocco* and *82.6, 78.2, 75.3, 71.2, 64.7* and *43.5*. Tell the Ss that the numbers represent the life expectancy in these countries. In pairs, they match a country with a number, giving their reasons for the order they choose. Get feedback from the whole class

(Answers: Japan – 82.6; USA – 78.2; Argentina – 75.3; Morocco – 71.2; India – 64.7; Zimbabwe – 43.5)

Reading

1a ▶ Read the statements with the whole class and check they understand them. Put the Ss in pairs to discuss how true they think they are. Encourage them to give reasons for their opinions. Get feedback from the whole class.

b ▶ Ss read the text quickly and match the statements from ex. 1a with the paragraphs (A–C). Tell them not to worry about any words they don't understand at this stage. Elicit the answers from the class.

Answers
A 1
B 3
C 2

2 ▶ Get various Ss to read out the statements and check everybody understands them. Ss read the text again, marking the statements true (T) or false (F). Let them compare with a partner and then elicit the answers from the class.

Answers
1 T
2 F
3 F
4 T
5 F
6 T

▶ Ask Ss if there are any words or phrases in the text that they don't understand. Encourage other Ss to explain them before explaining them yourself.

3 ▶ Put Ss in small groups to discuss the question. Get feedback from the whole class.

Vocabulary | habits

4 ▶ Refer Ss to the underlined parts of the text and the two vocabulary boxes. In pairs, Ss make verb phrases with the words from A and B. Elicit the answers from the class.

Answers
be mentally active
do physical exercise
eat healthily
eat junk food
think positively
worry about things

5 ▶ Put Ss in groups to discuss the questions. Get feedback from the whole class.

Grammar | *used to*: past habits

OPTIONAL GRAMMAR LEAD-IN

Write the following sentences on the board with the words in the wrong order:
eat John to of lot chocolate a used. (John used to eat a lot of chocolate.)
to do exercise didn' t use any He. (He didn't use to do any exercise.)
use he about Did his to lifestyle worry? (Did he use to worry about his lifestyle?)
Put Ss in pairs to put the words in order. Elicit the answers and write them on the board. Ask Ss: *Does this tense refer to the present, past or future*? (past)

6a ▶ Focus on the Active grammar box and tell Ss to complete the example sentences with *use* or *used*. Copy the sentences on the board and elicit the answers to complete them.

Active grammar
+ Jeanne Calment <u>used</u> to ride a bicycle until she was 100.
– She didn't <u>use</u> to worry about things.
? Did she <u>use</u> to have good lifestyle habits?

▶ Read through the rule at the top of the box with the Ss and ask: *Does* Jeanne Calment used to ride a bicycle *refer to a habit or a situation*? (habit)

▶ Write an example of a situation on the board, e.g. *I used to live in a big house.* Ask Ss to turn to the Reference on page 57 and ask: *Does the form of* used to *change with* he *or* she? (No)

b ▶ Ss scan the text for three more examples of this structure. Ask various Ss to tell you the examples and write them on the board.

Answers
... she used to be a heavy smoker ... .
... she didn't use to eat very healthily ... .
... she used to eat more than two pounds of chocolate ... .

▶ Point out to Ss that this structure only exists in the past. If we want to say something similar about our habits in the present, we use the adverb of frequency *usually*. Write the following examples on the board: *I used to eat a lot of chocolate (past). I usually eat a lot of chocolate (present).*

7 ▶ Ss complete the sentences. Let them compare with a partner and then check the answers with the whole class.

Answers
1   I used to eat a lot of junk food, but now I don't.
2   I didn't use to worry about things, but I do now.
3   Did you use to do regular physical exercise when you were a child?
4   My father used to do a lot of physical exercise, but he stopped in 2005 after an accident.
5   Did people use to be more mentally active 100 years ago?
6   My sister didn't use to like healthy food, but now she loves it.

8 ▶ Ss choose the correct words. Let them compare with a partner and then check the answers with the whole class.

Answers
1   used to walk
2   went
3   usually cook
4   didn't finish
5   used to play
6   didn't use to do

9a ▶ Focus on the Lifelong learning box and read through the tips with the whole class, checking they understand them. Then ask them to answer the questions. Get feedback from the whole class and encourage them to adopt any good learning habits they don't already have.

b ▶ In pairs, Ss think of three more good learning habits. Get feedback from various Ss, asking them to explain why they think what they suggest is a good idea.

OPTIONAL VARIATION

Ask Ss to individually write one more tip. Monitor their work as they do this. Now ask Ss to mingle, asking the other Ss if they usually do this and trying to convince them to do it if the answer is 'no'.

Speaking

10 ▶ 🔘 1.39 Focus on the topics in the box and tell Ss to listen to a man talking about his childhood. Play the recording and get them to answer the questions. Let them compare with a partner and then elicit the answers from the class.

Answers
1   He mentions holidays, pets and playing with friends (a sport, football, is also mentioned in the context of playing with friends, but this is not the main topic).
2   The story about the dog is false.

▶ Play the recording again and ask the Ss to note down any extra information the man gives about the three topics and the questions the woman asks at the end to discover the false story. Let them compare with a partner and then get feedback from the whole class.

11 ▶ Give the Ss a little time to think about their statements and then put them in pairs to tell each other the three things. The listener has to guess which one is false. Encourage them to ask each other questions, as in the listening, to guess the false statement.

OPTIONAL VARIATION

Put the Ss in groups of three and tell them that each one has to prepare a short story, using *used to*, about their childhood. In each group, two Ss should tell a true story and one a false one. Give them time to prepare this and to decide whose story will be false, and help with any vocabulary. Each group then tells their three stories to the rest of the class. The other groups can ask questions and must finally guess which student is lying.

OPTIONAL EXTENSION

Divide the class into five groups and give one of the following categories to each group: *pets, food, holidays, sports, school.* Each group has to think of two questions for their category, e.g. Pets: *Did you use to have a dog? Did you use to have a cat?* Food: *Did you use to like vegetables? Did you use to eat in restaurants?*
When they have written their questions, Ss mingle and interview the other Ss in the class. Then they go back to their original group, compare results and present the final results to the rest of the class, e.g. *Four Ss used to have a cat, three Ss used to have a dog and seven Ss didn't use to have a pet.*

5 Communication

This lesson is based on an idea taken from a popular TV programme called *This is Your Life* that was first shown in the US in the 1950s and then in Great Britain (1955–2003). On this programme celebrities were surprised by a presentation of their past life in the form of a narrative and reminiscences by relatives and friends.

In this lesson, Ss listen to a radio programme called *This is Your Life*, which presents the life of Michelle Obama. Then they talk about the life of somebody they know.

1 ▶ Focus Ss on the photos and, in pairs, ask them to talk about what they know about each person. Get feedback from the whole class.

Suggested Answers
Photo 1: Penélope Cruz. She's a Spanish actress, born in Madrid in 1974. She's made many Spanish language films, notably with the director Pedro Almodóvar, and has also been a great success in Hollywood. She became the first Spanish actress to win an Oscar in 2009 for the Woody Allen film *Vicky Cristina Barcelona*. She has been romantically linked to Tom Cruise, Matthew McConaughey and is now married to Javier Bardem.
Photo 2: Maria Sharapova. She's a Russian tennis player who was ranked 14th in the world in 2010. She was born in 1987 and moved to the USA in 1994. Apart from playing tennis, she is known for her beauty and has taken on many modelling assignments.
Photo 3: Michelle Obama (see audioscript 1.40, page 00)

2a ▶ ● 1.40 Play the recording and Ss identify the woman, giving reasons for their choice. Get feedback from various Ss.

Answer
Michelle Obama

b ▶ Read through the phrases with the whole class and then play the recording again. Ss put the phrases in the order they hear them. Check the order with the whole class.

Answers
a 6
b 3
c 5
d 2
e 4
f 1

3 ▶ Individually, Ss complete the fact file about a family member or a famous person. If you have access to the Internet, they could look for information in order to complete this for a famous person.

4a ▶ Ss make notes about what they want to say. Remind them to include phrases from ex. 2b.

b ▶ Ss take turns to talk to the class about the person they have chosen. Alternatively, put Ss in small groups to do this. Tell the Ss not to mention the name. The other Ss wait until the end of the presentation and then guess who the person is.

OPTIONAL EXTENSION
Play 'Names on your back'. Give each student a small piece of paper, preferably a small Post-it note. They secretly write the name of an internationally famous person on their paper and then stick it on the back of another student. Tell the Ss they have to guess 'who they are' by asking *yes/no* questions, e.g. *Am I a man? Am I American? Do I make films?* etc. Ss get up and mingle with each other. Tell them they can ask one question to each student at a time and then they must move on to somebody else. When they think they know who they are, they consult you. If they are right, they take off the name and have won the game. Continue playing, however, until you have somebody for second and third place.

5

Review and practice

1 ▶

> **Answers**
> 1 In the UK, you have to wear seatbelts in the back of a car.
> 2 My brother can watch TV for a maximum of two hours a day.
> 3 You should go to Germany to improve your German.
> 4 You have to show your student card to get a reduction.
> 5 You don't have to drive me to the airport. I'll get a taxi.
> 6 You shouldn't drink coffee just before you go to bed.
> 7 You can't play loud music between 11 p.m. and 7 a.m.

2 ▶

> **Answers**
> 1 You can't enter without a ticket.
> 2 Does he <u>have to</u> work this weekend?
> 3 ✓
> 4 They <u>don't</u> have to wear school uniform.
> 5 <u>Should you</u> take a coat with you?
> 6 ✓
> 7 Are you sure you have to take all your certificates to the interview?

3 ▶

> **Answers**
> 1 for   2 for   3 since   4 since   5 for

4 ▶

> **Answers**
> 1 I have played the guitar since I was a child.
> 2 My parents have lived in Bristol since April.
> 3 He hasn't worked for ten years./He hasn't worked since his accident ten years ago.
> 4 I have had a dog for two years.
> 5 I have known Jack since October.
> 6 She hasn't played tennis since she was fifteen.
> 7 I have studied English for three years.
> 8 He hasn't seen Angie for five years.

5 ▶

> **Answers**
> 1 ✓
> 2 Did you use <u>to</u> play football at school?
> 3 She didn't <u>use</u> to get good marks at school.
> 4 Where <u>did</u> you use to live before you came here?
> 5 ✓
> 6 I used <u>to</u> like my job more than I do now.
> 7 Did you <u>use</u> to eat a lot of junk food?
> 8 My parents didn't use <u>to</u> have a television.

6 ▶

> **Answers**
> 1 do   2 got   3 in   4 lost   5 up   6 place   7 active

Writing bank

1 ▶ Ss read the types of forms and say what type forms A and B are.

> **Answers**
> A a landing card
> B a homestay application form

2 ▶ Ss read the forms again and answer the questions.

> **Answers**
> 1 No, only in form A.
> 2 Form A: Write in block capitals.
>   Form B: Type or use black ink.
> 3 Jayne Jenkins (she doesn't use block capitals).

3 ▶ Ss look at the *How to…* box and match the words or phrases from column A with the words or phrases from column B.

> **Answers**
> 1 f
> 2 e
> 3 d
> 4 h
> 5 i
> 6 b
> 7 c
> 8 a
> 9 g

4 ▶ Ss complete the form.

Overview

Lead-in	Revision: Places
6.1	**Can do:** Make general predictions about the future **Grammar:** *will, may, might*: prediction **Vocabulary:** Geographical features **Speaking and Pronunciation:** Contractions: *will* **Listening:** *Mamma Mia!* island
6.2	**Can do:** Describe a favourite place **Grammar:** Countable and uncountable nouns **Vocabulary:** Describing a place **Speaking and Pronunciation:** Diphthongs **Reading:** Garden of freedom – my favourite place
6.3	**Can do:** Give reasons for choices **Grammar:** *too, too much/many, (not) enough* **Vocabulary:** Urban environment **Speaking and Pronunciation:** **How to...** talk about choices and give reasons **Listening:** *SimCity*
Communication	
Reference	
Review and practice	
Writing bank	Write a description of a favourite place **How to...** use a range of introductory phrases
Extra resources	Active Teach and Active Book

CEFR Can do objectives
6.1 Make general predictions about the future
6.2 Describe a favourite place
6.3 Give reasons for choices
Communication Explain your preferences
Writing bank Write a description of a favourite place

CEFR Portfolio ideas
a) Choose a place in your country which has changed in the past 100 years. Explain how it has changed and why it has changed. Has the change made this place better or worse? Write a magazine article about this place including your opinion about the change.
b) Pairwork recording: record your conversation from Exercise 11b on page 65.
c) Make a video for a tourist who will visit your country (or a country you know well). Talk about the weather in different parts of the country and different times of the year. Use a map of your country to help you explain what you are talking about.

Lead-in

OPTIONAL WARMER
Write *places* on the board and the example *beach*. Give Ss a couple of minutes to brainstorm, in pairs, names of places, e.g. *village, town, city, mountain, countryside, desert, forest,* etc. Ss may also suggest more specific places such as *school, shop, restaurant,* etc. Get feedback from the Ss, writing the places on the board.
Give Ss a clue to one of these places, e.g. *There are many of these in the city centre. You can buy things in this place (shop).* Ask the Ss to do the same in pairs: one student gives a clue for a place written on the board and the other one guesses the place name.

1a ▶ Focus Ss' attention on the photos and tell them to work in pairs to suggest which continent they associate each photo with. Encourage them to give reasons for their choice. Elicit answers from different Ss and see if all the class agree.

Answers
Main photo: Asia
Top photo: Europe
Middle photo: South America
Bottom photo: Africa

---

b ▶ Ss work in pairs to answer the questions. Elicit answers from various Ss.

Suggested Answers
1   Spain, any country in South America except Brazil
2   Italy, Spain, France, Croatia, Greece, Turkey, Lebanon, Egypt, Morocco, Algeria, etc.
3   Denmark, Norway, Sweden, Finland, Latvia, Lithuania, Estonia
4   United Kingdom, Ireland, Australia, New Zealand, Malta, South Africa, Kenya, India, Pakistan, Japan, etc.
5   Ecuador, Colombia, Brazil, Republic of The Congo, Uganda, Kenya, Somalia, Maldives, Indonesia
6   any country in the Southern hemisphere

---

c ▶ Ss talk in pairs about the countries they have visited and those they would like to visit and why. Ask some Ss to share their opinions with the class.

2 ▶ In pairs, Ss talk about the meaning of the underlined words or phrases. Ask various Ss to explain them for the whole class.

▶ Now Ss ask and answer the questions in pairs. Elicit the answers from various Ss.

Answers
1   Canberra
2   Istanbul
3   Athens
4–8 Open answers

6.1 A Greek island

Greece, officially the Hellenic Republic, is a country in southern Europe. It has borders with Albania, Macedonia, Bulgaria and Turkey. The Mediterranean Sea lies to the south of mainland Greece, the Aegean Sea to the east and the Ionian Sea to the west. Greece has the tenth longest coastline in the world and many islands (approximately 3000, of which 140 are inhabited). Eighty percent of Greece consists of mountains, the highest of which is Mount Olympus. Modern Greece has its roots in the ancient Greek civilisations, which are generally believed to be the beginning of Western civilisation. Nowadays, a large percentage of Greek income comes from tourism.

In this lesson, Ss are introduced to geography vocabulary and listen to a radio programme about tourism in Greece. Through this context, they consider the grammar of making predictions.

OPTIONAL WARMER

Write the following words on the board: *Kilimanjaro*; *Loch Ness*; *Copacabana*; *Majorca*; *the Mediterranean*; *the Atlantic*; *the Thames*; *the Amazon*; *the Sahara*. Ask Ss: *What are these things and where can you find them?* Get feedback from the whole class. Teach the words Ss don't know.
(Kilimanjaro is a mountain in Tanzania; Loch Ness is a lake in Scotland (*loch* means lake); Copacabana is a beach in Brazil; Majorca is an island off the coast of Spain; the Mediterranean is the sea found between Southern Europe, the Levant and Northern Africa; the Atlantic is an ocean found between America and Europe/Africa; the Thames is a river in London; the Amazon is a river or rain forest in South America and the Sahara is a desert in Africa.)

Vocabulary | geographical features

1 ▶ Focus Ss on the words in the box and ask them if they understand them all. Elicit/teach the meaning of any words that Ss don't understand.

▶ In pairs, Ss say which things they can see in the photo. Get feedback from the class.

Answers
bay, beach, cliff, coast, forest, sea

2 ▶ Ss complete the text with the singular or plural form of the words from ex. 1. Let them compare with a partner and then read out the text, eliciting the words from various Ss.

Answers
1 peninsula
2 sea
3 islands
4 coast
5 beaches
6 cliffs
7 bays
8 mountain
9 river
10 forest
11 lakes

▶ Ask the Ss if there are any other words in the text that they don't understand. Encourage other Ss to explain the meaning of these words before explaining them yourself.

3 ▶ Put Ss in pairs to answer the questions. Get feedback from the class.

Listening

4 ▶ 🌐 1.41 Read out the question for the class and put Ss in pairs to predict the answer. Get feedback from the whole class.

▶ Play the recording and Ss make a note of their answer. Let them compare in pairs and then elicit the answer from the class.

Answer
Tourism will be good for business but the island will not be as peaceful.

5 ▶ Give the Ss a little time to read through the sentences and check that everybody understands them. Play the recording again and Ss complete the sentences. (Point out that the sentences are not direct quotes from the radio programme.) Let them compare with a partner and then get various Ss to read them out for the whole class.

Answers
1 popular
2 tourist
3 (very) small
4 musical
5 pine forests
6 (about) twenty-five
7 wedding

▶ Ask the Ss if they have seen the film *Mamma Mia!* and what they thought of it.

6 ▶ Put the Ss in groups to discuss the question. Get feedback from the whole class.

OPTIONAL VARIATION

Write *tourism: good or bad?* on the board. Divide the class into two groups: in one group they have to make a list of the advantages of tourism and in the other group they make a list of the disadvantages. If the Ss' country of origin is a tourist destination, tell them to concentrate on their own country. If not, tell them to think of tourism in a general sense. Have a class debate or put the Ss in small groups to present their arguments.

Grammar | *will, may, might*: prediction

OPTIONAL GRAMMAR LEAD-IN

Write the following sentences on the board: *People will go on holiday to the moon in the future. Holidays may get cheaper in the next ten years. I might travel to another country soon.* Ask the Ss to look at the parts of the sentences which are underlined and answer the question: *Is it certain that this thing is going to happen?* (*will* – yes, *may/might* – no) Now get the Ss to talk in pairs about whether they think those sentences are true or not. Encourage them to give reasons. Get feedback from the whole class.

7 ▶ Focus Ss on the Active grammar box and read through the rule at the top with the whole class. Explain that we use *will* when we are more certain about our predictions. Tell them that we often use this with *I think* to show it is our opinion or with *I'm sure/I'm certain* when we think we are certain. Write a couple of examples on the board: *I think it will rain tomorrow, I'm certain it won't snow.* Now read the second rule and explain that *may* and *might* have the same meaning and are used when we are not sure about our predictions, e.g. *It may rain next week.*

▶ Ss complete the sentences in pairs and then check their answers with audioscript 1.41 on page 154. Write the sentences on the board and elicit answers from the Ss to complete them.

Active grammar

+ The *Mamma Mia!* effect will increase tourism on other islands.
  The film might be very good for business.
− They may not keep the peaceful atmosphere of the island completely.
  Skopelos won't stay the same.
? Will the film bring success for the island of Skopelos?

▶ Refer Ss to the Reference on page 67 and ask them to read through the information. Now ask:
What's the short form of saying I will go? (I'll go) *What's the short form of saying* I will not go? (I won't go) *Does the verb form of* will, may *and* might *change with* he, she *or* it? (no) *What do you use with will if you are not very sure about the prediction?* (I don't think) *What verb can we use if we would like something to happen, but we're not sure?* (I hope …)

8 ▶ Ss complete the sentences in pairs. Elicit the answers from various Ss.

Answers	
1 will ('ll) come	4 will ('ll) have
2 may/might build	5 may/might disappear
3 will not (won't) go	6 may/might not find
	7 will ('ll) be

9 ▶ Ss put the words in the correct order and then check with a partner. Ask various Ss to read out the answers.

Answers
1 Yes, I think it will change it a lot.
2 I think I will live by the coast.
3 I think they will go to Greece.
4 Yes, I think I will.
5 It is possible he might not get the job.

Pronunciation | contractions: *will*

10 ▶ ⬤ 1.42 Ask Ss to look back at the answers to questions 1–4 from ex. 9. Tell them to decide in pairs if you can contract the subject + *will* in each case. Elicit the answer.

Answer
In questions 1–3 it is possible, in 4 it is not.

▶ Ask the Ss why they think it is not possible in 4 (because it is a short answer and there is no verb after *will*). Draw the Ss' attention to the Pronunciation bank on page 148.

▶ Play the recording and ask Ss to repeat, pronouncing the contraction in the correct way. Then allow them time to practise the sentences in pairs. Ask various Ss to read out the sentences for the whole class.

Speaking

11 ▶ Ask the Ss to read the instructions in pairs. If you have Ss from different countries or regions, try to pair them so that those from the same country/region are together. If the Ss are all from the same place, tell them they can choose a place they know or have visited. Tell them to draw the map and discuss the questions, making notes about their answers.

▶ Put Ss into small groups. Tell them to show each other their maps and explain about the places they chose and the future of tourism in that area. Get feedback from the whole class.

OPTIONAL EXTENSION

Write the following phrases on the board: *have (more) children, get married, start my own business, take a year off to travel, move house, live abroad, be famous, appear on TV.* Put Ss in small groups to make predictions about themselves using *will, might* and *may* with regard to these things. Encourage them to give reasons for their predictions where possible. Get feedback from various Ss.

6.2 Mandela's garden

Nelson Mandela was born in 1918 in South Africa. He studied to be a lawyer and joined the African National Congress in the early 1940s in order to fight against the laws of apartheid and for the freedom of the black people of South Africa. During years of anti-apartheid struggle, he was arrested many times and spent decades in prison. He was finally released in 1990 and served as president of South Africa from 1994–1999. Mandela is a firm believer in democracy and has constantly fought for equality. He was given the Nobel Peace Prize in 1993 and in 2009, the United Nations declared that 18 July, Mandela's birthday, would be celebrated as 'Nelson Mandela International Day' to honour his contribution to world freedom.

In this lesson, Ss read about the garden Mandela looked after during his years in prison and through this context, look at the grammar of countable and uncountable nouns.

OPTIONAL WARMER

Ask the Ss to think about people who are in prison for a very long time. Tell them to brainstorm with a partner the things that prisoners might do to keep themselves occupied. Get feedback from the class (e.g. some prisoners have studied degree courses, written books, etc.).

Reading

1 ▶ Ss write down the information they know about Nelson Mandela and then compare with a partner. Get feedback from the whole class.

2a ▶ Ask Ss to look at the pictures and answer the question in pairs. Get feedback from various Ss.

b ▶ Ss read the text quickly and check their answers. Tell them not to worry about any words or phrases they don't understand at this stage. Ask various Ss to tell you what the text is about in their own words.

Answers
Nelson Mandela created a garden whilst he was in prison.

3 ▶ Ask different Ss to read each question aloud. Then tell Ss to read the text again and answer the questions. Let them compare with a partner and then check the answers with the whole class.

Answers
1   While he was in prison and after he was freed.
2   Because it was a small taste of freedom for him.
3   It was on the roof.
4   It took him years.
5   It gave him some control and freedom in his life.
6   Because of Mandela's garden – and because it made him and other prisoners feel good.
7   They get food, but also a little happiness and a taste of freedom.

▶ Ask the Ss if there are any words they don't understand in the text and encourage other Ss to explain before giving an explanation yourself.

4 ▶ Put the Ss in pairs or small groups to discuss the questions. Get feedback from various Ss.

OPTIONAL EXTENSION

Tell the Ss that Mandela's birthday, 18 July, is known as 'Mandela Day' to mark his contribution to world freedom. Put them in small groups to plan a celebration of this day in the place where they live. Ask them to do some research about Mandela first on the Internet and refer them to the Mandela Foundation website (www.nelsonmandela.org). Encourage them to make plans for the whole day, making notes about the different organisational details. Get each group to present their ideas to the rest of the class and the class votes for the best plan.

Grammar | countable and uncountable nouns

OPTIONAL GRAMMAR LEAD-IN

Write *garden* and *rain* on the board and ask the Ss: *Which word is countable?* (garden) *Which word is uncountable?* (rain) Put Ss in pairs to make a list of ten countable nouns they can see in the classroom. Get feedback and write the words on the board. Now ask Ss to make a list of five nouns they think are uncountable. Get feedback and write the correct ones on the board.

5 ▶ Focus on the Active grammar box and read through the rules for countable and uncountable nouns with the whole class. Ask Ss to underline the rules and expressions that are the same in each column (singular nouns, *some*, *a lot of*, *any*) in order to highlight those that can be used with both countable and uncountable nouns. Now focus on the differences by asking:
With what type of nouns can we use a *or* an? (singular countable nouns) *We use* a few *before countable nouns. What is the same before uncountable nouns?* (a little *or* a bit of) *We use* many *before countable nouns. What is the same before uncountable nouns?* (much)

▶ Put Ss in pairs to look back at the text in ex. 2 and decide if the underlined nouns are countable or uncountable. Elicit the answers from the class.

Active grammar

Countable: garden, people, things, years, seed, tree, plant, vegetables, prisoners
Uncountable: sunshine, equipment, money, help, soil, food, control, freedom, time, work, happiness

▶ Focus on *people* and explain that although it is countable and takes the plural verb, we never add an *s* because this is already plural. Ask: *What's the singular form?* (person) Now focus on *time* and write the following sentences on the board: *1 I haven't got much time; 2 I've been to Paris many times.* Ask Ss if *time* is used as a countable or uncountable noun in these sentences (1 – uncountable; 2 – countable). Elicit the different meaning of *time* in each sentence and explain that some words can sometimes be both as they have two different meanings. Point out that Ss can check in a dictionary for [U] or [C] if they're not sure about a noun.

▶ Ask Ss to look at the Reference on page 67. Read through the other examples of countable and uncountable nouns with the whole class, checking they understand them.

6 ▶ Ss choose the correct options. Let them compare with a partner and then elicit the answers from various Ss.

Answers	1	any	3	a bit of	5	a lot of
	2	a few	4	many	6	much

7a ▶ Ss correct the mistakes. Let them compare with a partner and then elicit the answers from various Ss.

Answers
1 I like my city because it's got <u>a lot of</u> trees.
2 There <u>aren't</u> many parks in my city.
3 I've got <u>some</u> beautiful flowers in my garden. They are mostly red and white.
4 There are <u>a few</u> small mountains near where I live.
5 There aren't <u>any</u> big lakes in my country.
6 I sometimes sit in my garden to get a bit <u>of</u> peace.

b ▶ Ss rewrite the sentences from ex. 7a so that they are true for themselves. Ss then compare with a partner. Try to arrange the pairs so that people from different places are working together.

OPTIONAL EXTENSION

Write the following things on the board: *pollution, sports facilities, good clubs, good food, cinemas, violence, traffic, job opportunities*. In small groups, Ss talk about these factors and say how much or how little there is/are in the place where they live. Go around the class monitoring the use of countable and uncountable nouns. Get feedback from the whole class.

Vocabulary | describing a place

8a ▶ In pairs, Ss talk about the meaning of the words in italics. Get various Ss to explain the meanings for the whole class.

▶ Ss now choose the correct options in pairs. Encourage them to use the context given by the other words in the sentence to help them guess which one is the most appropriate. Ask various Ss to read out the correct sentences for the whole class.

Answers			
1 pleasant	3 relaxing	5 impressive
2 beautiful	4 crowded	6 idyllic

b ▶ Ask Ss to answer the question in pairs and elicit the answer.

Answers *crowded* and *noisy* are negative

c ▶ Ss write sentences with the adjectives from ex. 8a for places they know. Put the Ss in small groups and ask them to compare sentences, saying whether they agree or not where possible.

9a ▶ 1.43 Play the recording and Ss match what Gavin and Heather say to one of the two places. Check the answer with the whole class.

Answers
a Southern Thailand – H
b Northumberland, UK – G

b ▶ Ss listen again and note down the adjectives from ex. 8a that each speaker uses. Check the answers with the whole class.

Answers
Gavin: impressive, unspoilt, idyllic
Heather: beautiful, unspoilt, relaxing

Pronunciation | diphthongs

10a ▶ 1.44 Write *diphthong* on the board and explain that this is the pronunciation of two vowels together. Play the recording and Ss repeat the words from the table. Now let Ss practise saying the words in pairs before getting individual Ss to say them aloud for the whole class.

b ▶ 1.45 Play the recording and Ss listen and match the underlined sound to a diphthong in the table. Let Ss compare with a partner and then elicit the answers.

Answers	unspoilt /ɔɪ/	where /eə/
wild /aɪ/	mountain /aʊ/	tour /ʊə/
romantic /əʊ/	lake /eɪ/	year /ɪə/

▶ Draw Ss' attention to the Pronunciation bank on page 147.

Speaking

11a ▶ Give Ss a little time to make notes about their favourite place. Help them with any vocabulary they need. Now put Ss in small groups to tell each other about those places.

b ▶ Ss decide which two places they would most like to visit, and why. Get feedback from the whole class.

OPTIONAL VARIATION

Put Ss in groups of three or four to invent a holiday destination or choose one they already know and make notes about the features of this place, including adjectives of description. Tell them they have to imagine they are travel agents who want to sell this destination to their customers. When they have prepared their description, two members of each group stand up and move around the room, visiting other groups who are going to try to sell them their holiday destination. When they have visited all the other groups, they return to their original group and tell the other members about the different holidays they have been offered. The groups then decide where they would like to go, and why. Get feedback from all the groups.

6.3 Virtual world

SimCity is a computer strategy game first released in 1989. The objective of the game is to build and design a city. This involves creating residential, business and industrial areas as well as developing the different infrastructures such as transport systems and electricity, gas and water supplies. The player may also face natural disasters such as floods or earthquakes. It has won many awards and led to many other related games such as *The Sims* (2000), which is a life-simulation game in which the player creates characters who make friends, buy houses, get a job, have children, etc.

In this lesson, Ss listen to two friends talking about *SimCity* and through this context consider the grammar of *too*, *too much/many*, (*not*) *enough*.

OPTIONAL WARMER

Write *city* on the board and give Ss two minutes in pairs to write down a list of places you can find in a city. After two minutes, stop them and ask the pairs how many words they've got. Get the pair with the longest list to read out their words and write them on the board. Ask other pairs if they have any more to add. Now give a clue for one of the words e.g. *You can study in this place after you have finished school* (university). Put Ss in new pairs and tell them to take it in turns to give each other clues for the other places.

Vocabulary | urban environment

1a ▶ Put Ss in pairs to discuss the difference in meaning between the different places. Get feedback from Ss.

Answers
1 A *sports stadium* is a place where people go to watch sports and a *leisure centre* is a place where people go to do sports.
2 A *library* is a place where you can borrow or consult books and a *bookshop* is a place where you can buy books.
3 A *restaurant* is usually more expensive and provides good quality meals. A *café* is usually cheaper and sells mainly snacks and drinks.
4 A *bar* is smaller, doesn't have a dance floor and closes earlier. A *nightclub* has a dance floor and closes later.
5 A *hospital* is a big building where patients stay and all kinds of medical practice takes place. A *doctor's surgery* serves a local area only and people go there to see a family doctor.
6 People go to the *cinema* to watch films whereas they go to the *theatre* to see plays.
7 At a *museum*, people can see exhibitions of all kinds, e.g. archaeological remains or old books, whereas at an *art gallery*, people can only see different types of painting, photography or sculpture.

Answers (continued)
8 A *school* is for children from four/five years old to eighteen years old. A *college* is a place of higher adult education. They often teach vocational courses.
9 A *bus station* is where all the buses start and finish their routes and a *bus stop* is a place they stop on their routes to pick people up.
10 A *train station* is where people can catch overground trains and a *tube station* is a place where people can catch underground trains in big cities.

1b ▶ Ss match the areas of a town with the buildings you can find there. Elicit the answers from the whole class.

Answers   1   c   2   a   3   b

2 ▶ Ss complete the sentences with words from ex. 1a and ex. 1b. Let them compare with a partner and then get various Ss to read out the completed sentences for the whole class.

Answers
1 cinema
2 leisure centre
3 college
4 nightclub
5 commercial area
6 bookshop
7 bus stop
8 train station
9 doctor's surgery
10 residential area

3 ▶ Ss answer the questions in pairs. Get feedback from the whole class.

OPTIONAL EXTENSION

Tell Ss to look back at the places in ex. 1a and tick the ones that they have where they live. Write the following questions on the board and ask them to answer the questions with a partner in relation to three or four of those places: *How many are there? Are they good places? How could they be better?*

Listening

4 ▶ 🔘 2.2 Ask Ss if they have heard of the computer game *SimCity*, but don't ask them to tell you about it yet. Tell them they are going to listen to two friends talking about the game. Read the questions out loud for the whole class and play the recording. Let Ss consult with a partner and then ask two Ss to answer the questions for the class.

Answers
1 You have to build a city.
2 Because it's about choice and control and it's open-ended. It's not about killing or destroying things. It's well-designed and it holds people's attention.

5 ▶ Have different Ss read out the sentence stems for the whole class and check they understand them. Play the recording again and Ss complete the sentences with one word. Let them compare with a partner and then elicit the answers from various Ss.

Answers	3	libraries	6	crowded
1 happy	4	tax	7	natural
2 commercial	5	working	8	positive

6 ▶ Ss work in pairs to answer the questions. Get feedback from the whole class.

OPTIONAL EXTENSION

Write: *computer games*: *advantages and disadvantages*? on the board. Put the Ss in small groups and tell them to make a list of all the advantages and disadvantages of computer games. Get feedback from the whole class and finally get the class to vote on whether there are more advantages or disadvantages.

Grammar | *too, too much/many, (not) enough*

OPTIONAL GRAMMAR LEAD-IN

Write the following sentences on the board with the words in the wrong order:
enough have There everything isn't space to. (There isn't enough space to have everything.)
money You spend can't much too. (You can't spend too much money.)
about many killing games Too computer are. (Too many computer games are about killing.)
Put Ss in pairs to put the words in order. Elicit the answers and write them on the board.

7a ▶ Ss answer the two questions with a partner. Check the answers with the whole class.

Answers
1 Sentences a and b describe a problem.
2 Sentences a and b have the same meaning.

---

b ▶ Focus the Ss on the Active grammar box. Tell them to match the rules with the examples.

Active grammar

A	Sentence 2	D	Sentences 1 and 7
B	Sentence 3	E	Sentences 4 and 6
C	Sentence 5		

▶ Read through the rule at the bottom of the Active grammar box with the whole class and emphasise the difference by writing the following stems on the board and asking Ss to complete them in an appropriate way in pairs:

This hotel is very popular ... . This hotel is too popular ... .
(e.g. *1 This hotel is very popular and it's making a lot of money. 2 This hotel is too popular and it's so noisy you can't sleep*).

▶ Focus Ss' attention on the Reference on page 67.

8 ▶ Ss use the words from the box to complete the sentences. Let them compare with a partner and then have various Ss read them out for the whole class.

Answers	1 enough	3 much	5 enough
	2 too	4 very	6 many

9 ▶ Ss complete the sentences. Let them compare with a partner and then ask various Ss to read them out for the whole class.

Answers	5	enough nightclubs
1 too noisy	6	too many people
2 big enough	7	too far
3 too much traffic	8	enough space
4 too cold		

OPTIONAL EXTENSION

Write the following things on the board: *free time, good clubs in your town, good food in England, sports facilities, job opportunities in your town, good films, reality shows on TV*. Ss discuss them in groups using *too, enough, too much* and *too many*. Tell them to exchange opinions and make suggestions about how they can be improved. Give Ss the example: *I think there aren't enough sports facilities in my town. They are also too expensive. I think they should be free.* Get feedback from the whole class.

Speaking

10 ▶ Focus the Ss on the *How to...* box and get them to complete it with the headings. Get various Ss to read out the headings and the example sentences for the whole class.

Answers	1 c	2 a	3 b

11a ▶ Ss choose five things they would like to have in their perfect city and make notes about their reasons, using ideas from the *How to...* box. Help the Ss with any vocabulary they need at this point.

b ▶ Put the Ss in pairs to discuss their ideas. Tell them they have to agree on five things.

▶ Reorganise the class so that each student has a new partner. Get them to tell each other about the five things they choose to see if they came up with the same ideas. Finally, get feedback from the whole class.

OPTIONAL VARIATION

Put Ss in small groups of three or four and tell them they have to think of one idea each for the ideal city. Let them make notes individually about the idea and the reasons they have chosen it. Then each person has to present their ideas to the rest of the group. When all the members of the group have presented their ideas, the group decides which one is the best. Finally, the group chooses a spokesperson who then presents the idea to the rest of the class. The class can decide which idea they like the most.

---

6 Communication

In this lesson, Ss read information about four important tourist destinations and they then listen to two people deciding where to go before discussing which destination they would prefer to visit.

1a ▶ Ss match the photos and the cities and then say what they know about each place. Get feedback from the whole class.

Answers
Photo 1: Edinburgh
Photo 2: Barcelona
Photo 3: Cairo
Photo 4: Rio de Janeiro

b ▶ Ss discuss with a partner which topic is the most important and what other factors are important when choosing a holiday destination. Get feedback from the whole class.

2 ▶ Put the Ss in groups of four and get them to divide the texts among them. Each student then reads their text and explains to the other members of the group whether they would like to go on holiday there and what they found out about the place. Get feedback from the class.

3a ▶ 🌐 2.3 Tell the Ss they are going to listen to a conversation between two people deciding where to go on holiday. Play the recording and Ss say where they have decided to go. Elicit the answer from the class (Barcelona).

b ▶ Ask various Ss to read out sentences 1–4 and then play the recording again. Ss mark the sentences true (T) or false (F). Check the answers with the whole class.

Answers
1 T
2 F
3 T
4 T

c ▶ Tell Ss to look at audioscript 2.3 on page 155 in order to complete the sentences. Get various Ss to read out the sentences and point out that in each sentence the speakers are expressing their preferences.

Answers
1 fun
2 prefer
3 idea
4 keen
5 like

4 ▶ Put Ss in groups of four and tell each student to individually decide which city in ex. 1 they would like to visit, and why.

▶ Now ask them to try and reach a group decision. Tell them to use language from ex. 3c when explaining their preferences.

▶ Each group now explains their choice to the rest of the class, and the group sees which place was the most popular.

Review and practice

1 ▶

Answers
1 might
2 might
3 will
4 won't
5 will
6 might not
7 will
8 won't

2 ▶

Answers
1 few
2 of
3 many
4 a
5 bit
6 of
7 few
8 much

3 ▶

Answers
1 much
2 a lot
3 bit
4 some
5 little
6 many
7 much
8 any

4 ▶

Answers
1 The food was too hot to eat.
2 There isn't enough sugar in my tea.
3 It's too far to walk home from here.
4 She isn't old enough to get married.
5 There were too many people in the pool.
6 Don't eat too much chocolate.
7 There aren't enough waiters in this restaurant.
8 She always eats her dinner too quickly.

5 ▶

Answers
1 This suitcase is too heavy for me to carry.
2 The hotel was too noisy for us to sleep.
3 The food is too spicy for me to eat.
4 The homework was too difficult for anybody to do.
5 The top shelf is too high for me to reach.
6 The table was too big for us to get it in the car.

6 ▶

Answers
1 idyllic
2 library
3 mountain
4 commercial
5 pleasant
6 island
7 surgery
8 unspoilt

Writing bank

1 ▶ Ss read the text and answer the questions.

Answers
1 It's a competition entry.
2 Because it makes him feel calm. It's peaceful and wild and it has amazing views.
3 Open answers

2a ▶ Ss read the text again and match the headings (a–c) to the paragraphs (1–3).

Answers
a 3
b 2
c 1

b ▶ Ss decide which topics are included in the text and give details of each.

Answers
1 Things you can see: tall trees, views across the valley, deer
2 Things you can hear: dry leaves under your feet, little animals
3 Things you can smell: X
4 How the place makes you feel: calm

3a ▶ Ss complete the *How to...* box with phrases from the text.

Answers
1 In any season
2 At first
3 One day I was there
4 One of my favourite places
5 The part of the forest
6 The main reason that the forest is one of my favourite places

b ▶ Ss rewrite the paragraph starting each sentence with the words in bold.

Answers
One of my favourite places is my grandmother's house. The part of the house which I like best is the garden. The main reason why I like it there is because there are lots of really big trees. In any season, it is a relaxing place to be, but I especially like it in the summer. The last time I was there, we had a lovely picnic sitting under the trees.

4a ▶ Ss make notes about their favourite place following the paragraph headings in ex. 2a.

b ▶ Ss write their descriptions.

Overview

Lead-in	Revision: Body
7.1	**Can do:** Talk about possible events and situations in the future **Grammar:** First Conditional **Vocabulary:** Appearance **Speaking and Pronunciation:** Intonation in conditional sentences **Reading:** Cover girl
7.2	**Can do:** Describe someone's personality **Grammar:** Gerunds and infinitives **Vocabulary:** Personality **Speaking and Pronunciation:** Schwa /ə/ on unstressed syllables **Listening:** Hands and personality **Reading:** Your skills are in your hands
7.3	**Can do:** Discuss illnesses and give advice **Grammar:** *stop*, *try*, *remember*: gerunds and infinitives **Vocabulary:** Illness **Speaking:** **How to...** give and respond to advice **Listening and Reading:** Different remedies
Communication	Discuss how you feel
Reference	
Review and practice	
Writing bank	Write an apology with an explanation **How to...** use punctuation
Extra resources	Active Teach and Active Book

CEFR Can do objectives

7.1 Talk about possible events and situations in the future
7.2 Describe someone's personality
7.3 Discuss illnesses and give advice
Communication Discuss how you feel
Writing bank Write an apology with an explanation

CEFR Portfolio ideas

a) What is beauty? Write a description of a beautiful person and say why you think he/she is beautiful.
b) Write an email to a friend who lives an unhealthy life. Warn your friend about the likely results of their unhealthy life. Use conditional sentences such as: 'If you eat a lot of sweets things, you will get fat and have bad teeth.'
c) Pair work recording. Record a conversation between a parent and a son/daughter who is at university. Ask about studies, health, and money. Respond to what the son/daughter says and give advice if you want to. Prepare notes for the conversation and record it with your partner.

Lead-in

OPTIONAL WARMER

Write *body* on the board and check that the Ss understand. Tell them to brainstorm parts of the body in pairs. Now write *point to your hand* on the board and tell the Ss to do this. Now explain that you are going to play a game. Have the Ss stand or sit in a circle. One S begins by saying '*point to (+ a part of the body)*' to the next S. If the S follows the instruction correctly, they have a turn and must tell the next S what to do. If they don't follow the instruction correctly, they are eliminated, and the next S continues. The game finishes when Ss can think of no more words to say. While the Ss are doing this, write the words on the board. At the end of the game, give instructions to the whole class to point to the parts of the body that have seemed more problematic.

1a ▶ Ss work in pairs to categorise the words. Tell them to practise saying the words as they do this and go around the class checking pronunciation. Check the answers with the whole class.

Answers
a head: ear, eye, face, forehead, hair, lips, mouth, nose
b torso: back, shoulder, stomach, waist
c arm: elbow, finger, palm, thumb, wrist
d leg: ankle, knee, toe

b ▶ In their pairs Ss discuss which of the words from ex. 1a they can see in the photos.

2a ▶ Ss match the phrases from the box with the definitions. Get various Ss to read out the answers.

Answers
1 physical appearance
2 personality
3 to look like someone
4 to put on weight
5 to go on a diet
6 to get stressed

b ▶ Ss complete the sentences with the correct form of the phrases from ex. 2a. Let them compare with a partner and then get various Ss to read out the answers.

Answers
1 appearance
2 look like
3 get stressed
4 put on weight
5 on a diet
6 personality

c ▶ Ss work in pairs to say if they agree with the statements from ex. 2b. Encourage them to give their reasons. Get feedback from the whole class.

7.1 Changing bodies

Airbrushing is a design technique which is used to hide the signs that a photograph has been altered. It has a long history, for example during Stalin's leadership in the USSR it was often used to 'rewrite' history for political purposes, sometimes removing people entirely from a photo. Recently, this technique (also known as 'photoshopping') is used almost universally for the digital retouching of photographs of models and other celebrities that appear in the media. All imperfections are removed and attributes are enhanced, thus creating an idealistic picture of beauty, which is rarely found in the real world.

In this lesson, Ss read about the impact of airbrushing and through this context look at vocabulary of appearance and the grammar of the First Conditional.

OPTIONAL WARMER

Write *celebrity* on the board and ask the Ss what this means (a famous person who appears frequently in magazines or on TV). Ask the Ss to give you the names of some celebrities and why they are famous. Now ask: *Would you like to be a celebrity?* Allow Ss to discuss the question in small groups and get feedback. Now ask: *Do you think celebrities really look like their photos?* Ss discuss their answers in groups and then get feedback from the whole class.

Reading

1 ▶ Ss discuss the questions in pairs. Get feedback from the whole class.

2 ▶ Ss read the text quickly and answer the two questions with a partner. Tell them not to worry about any words or phrases they don't understand at this stage. Get two Ss to answer the questions for the whole class.

Answers
1 Airbrushing – how photos are changed to make celebrities and models look perfect.
2 She thinks that celebrity magazines put pressure on young people to look perfect.

3 ▶ Have various Ss read the questions out loud for the rest of the class and check they understand them. Now Ss read the text again more carefully and answer the questions. Let them compare with a partner and then elicit the answers from the whole class.

Answers
1 She is tall and slim, with perfect skin and glossy dark hair. She is naturally beautiful.
2 Because of her own experience of airbrushing and because she noticed a contradiction between people saying they like 'natural' beauty when magazines show 'unnatural' beauty.
3 very few
4 The pressure comes from the need for magazines to sell more copies and from the celebrities themselves.
5 She admits she looks better in airbrushed photos.
6 Many young people are desperate to look like the photos and they don't know they aren't real.

▶ Ask the Ss if there are any words or phrases in the text that they don't understand. Encourage other Ss to explain before explaining yourself.

4 ▶ Put Ss in pairs to discuss the statements. Get feedback from the whole class.

Vocabulary | appearance

5a ▶ Focus Ss on the table and read the headings (weight/build; height; attractive or not; colouring) with the whole class and check they understand them. Tell the Ss to put the words from the box in the correct category. Let them compare with a partner when they have finished.

▶ Ask different Ss to read out their answers so that you can check for correct pronunciation. Elicit/teach the meaning of any words Ss are unsure of, but avoid explaining the differences they have to discuss in ex. 5b.

Answers
weight/build: fat, muscular, overweight, skinny
height: medium height, short
attractive or not: (un)attractive, beautiful, good-looking, handsome, ugly
colouring: blonde, dark-haired, dark-skinned, fair-haired, fair-skinned, red-haired

b ▶ Ss discuss the differences in pairs. Get feedback from the whole class.

Answers
1 *Slim* is always positive and is considered to be an ideal build. *Skinny* often means too thin and can therefore be negative.
2 *Fat* is a less polite way of saying overweight. However, *overweight* can also be used to describe someone who is heavier than the average weight for their height and gender, e.g. you can be 2 kg overweight.
3 *Handsome* is traditionally used for men and *beautiful* is used for women.

6a ▶ Focus the Ss on the Lifelong learning box and read through the introduction with the whole class. Have various Ss read out the different strategies for remembering words. Ask Ss to choose one strategy they think will help them the most.

b ▶ Put the Ss in small groups and ask them to compare which strategy they chose, and why.

OPTIONAL EXTENSION

Divide the class into six groups (or fewer if you have a small class) and allocate one of the units of the book already covered, i.e. between 1 and 6, to each group. Get them to go back through the unit and write down between 10 and 15 words that were new for them during this course. Now tell them to use various strategies to group those words. Rearrange the Ss so that the groups are mixed up, and get the Ss to explain and discuss their strategies.

Grammar | First Conditional

OPTIONAL GRAMMAR LEAD-IN

Write the following stem sentences on the board. Ss complete them in pairs:
1 If I'm very tired tonight, I'll … .
2 If I have some free time tomorrow, … .
3 If it rains next weekend, I'll … .
Get feedback from various Ss. Explain that this grammatical structure is called the First Conditional.

---

7 ▶ Tell Ss to read through the Active grammar box and choose the correct alternatives. Ss compare in pairs. Elicit the answers, writing the rules on the board.

Active grammar

A We use the First Conditional to talk about a possible situation in the future.
B The form of the First Conditional is: *If* + Present Simple + will/won't + verb.
C We use a comma after the first clause: only after the 'if' clause.

▶ Refer Ss to the Reference on page 77 and give them time to read through the notes. To check comprehension, ask:

Can we use will *in the 'if' clause?* (no)

Does the 'if' clause always come first? (No, it can come first or second.)

What other types of verbs can we use instead of will? (modals such as *could, may* and *might*)

What other time words can we use instead of 'if'? (when, as soon as)

8 ▶ Ss complete the sentences. Let them compare with a partner and then ask various Ss to read out the completed sentences.

Answers

1 If you eat a lot of junk food, you'll put on weight.
2 You won't have good skin if you wear a lot of make-up.
3 If she continues to spend it all on clothes, she won't have any money left.
4 If you don't start eating healthily now, you'll reduce your lifespan.
5 You'll be late for the hairdresser if you don't leave now.

Pronunciation | intonation in conditional sentences

9a ▶ 🔊 2.4 Write the following questions on the board: *Does the person's voice go up, down, or stay the same?*

▶ Focus the Ss on sentence 1 in ex. 8 and tell them they must decide for each clause in which direction the intonation goes. Play the recording while Ss listen and notice the intonation, as marked by the directional arrows.

b ▶ 🔊 2.5 Play the second part of the recording and get Ss to repeat. Then let them practise in pairs. Get them to focus on good intonation. Draw the Ss' attention to the Pronunciation bank on page 148.

Answers

3 If she continues to spend it all on clothes,
she won't have any money left.

4 If you don't start eating healthily now,
you'll reduce your lifespan.

Speaking

10 ▶ Read through the example with the whole class, showing how a chain of First Conditional sentences can be made, each one leading on from the consequence of the sentence before. Now get Ss to choose a stem and write a total of six sentences. In pairs, Ss read out their chains.

OPTIONAL EXTENSION

Write the following stems on the board:
I'll be very happy if … . I'll be fed up if … . I'll be angry if … .
Get Ss to complete the stems individually. Now tell the Ss that they have to try to find somebody who has written the same as they have. Ss stand up and mingle, reading out their sentences until they find somebody who has the same for at least one of the sentences. Get feedback about how much the class has in common.

7.2 Hands up

People have suggested many ways of analysing personality, from astrology to graphology (the study of handwriting) and palmistry. Palmistry is an ancient practice, dating back thousands of years. There are drawings that have been found of palms and their most important lines in prehistoric caves in Spain and France. It is also thought to have been the subject of one of the earliest known books written by the Hindu Valmiki more than 5000 years ago. It spread from India to other parts of the world and for many important people, such as Aristotle and Alexander the Great, it became a subject of serious study. It later became associated with devil worshipping and was banned by the Catholic Church. These days, people often take it less seriously, although scientific research within this field still continues.

In this lesson, Ss consider the relationship between the shape of a person's fingers and their personality. Through this context they analyse the grammar of gerunds and infinitives with *to*.

OPTIONAL WARMER

Write *personality* on the board and ask Ss to brainstorm related adjectives in pairs. Give them a couple of minutes and then get feedback, writing the words on the board. Now ask: *Which of these adjectives would you use to describe yourself?* Ss discuss their answers in pairs, giving reasons for what they say. Get feedback from a number of Ss.

Vocabulary | personality

1 ▶ Ss label the different fingers in pairs. Get feedback from various Ss.

Answers		
1	thumb	3 middle finger
2	index finger	4 ring finger
		5 little finger

▶ Get the Ss to discuss question 2 with a partner. Get feedback from the whole class.

2 ▶ Read out the adjectives with the class and tell Ss they are going to find definitions for them. Ss match the adjectives and the underlined phrases. Let them compare with a partner and then get feedback from various Ss.

Answers		
1	sensitive	6 chatty
2	open	7 reserved
3	organised	8 ambitious
4	hard-working	9 easy-going
5	unreliable	10 lazy

Pronunciation | schwa /ə/ on unstressed syllables

3a ▶ 🌐 2.6 Write the word *ambitious* on the board and elicit from the Ss where the stress falls (am**bi**tious). Get Ss to write the list of adjectives from the box in ex. 2 in their notebooks. Now play the recording and Ss underline the stress in the words. Ss compare in pairs and practise saying each word. Get feedback from the whole class.

Answers		
chatty	lazy	reserved
easy-going	open	sensitive
hard-working	organised	unreliable

b ▶ Demonstrate the sound of schwa /ə/ for the whole class and have the Ss repeat it. Now ask them to look at the list of adjectives again and pronounce the words with a partner, marking the parts that are pronounced with a schwa /ə/. Play the recording again and Ss listen, check and repeat.

Answers	
ambitious /æm'bɪʃəs/	organised /'ɔːgənaɪzd/
open /'əʊpən/	unreliable /ˌʌnrɪ'laɪəbəl/

4a ▶ 🌐 2.7 Play the recording and ask the Ss to write the questions they hear. Check the questions with the whole class.

Answers
1 Are you ambitious?
2 Are you usually hard-working or lazy?
3 Are you more open or more reserved?
4 Are you an organised kind of person or disorganised?
5 Are you chatty or are you the quiet type?
6 Are you an easy-going person?

b ▶ Ss ask and answer the questions in pairs. Go around the class checking for good pronunciation. Get several pairs to ask and answer questions for the whole class.

Listening

5a ▶ 🌐 2.8 Tell Ss they are going to listen to a conversation between Helen and Daniel about the connection between your hands and your personality. Read out the topics in the box and tell Ss to tick the ones they hear. Play the recording and then let Ss compare with a partner before eliciting the answers from the class.

Answers	
	the shape of fingers
the length of fingers	the length of thumb

b ▶ Refer Ss back to the sentences in ex. 2 and tell them to listen again and mark the ones that Daniel says are true for him. Let them compare with a partner and then elicit the answers from the class.

Answers
sentences 3 and 8

c ▶ Put Ss in pairs to discuss this way of analysing people's personalities. Get feedback from the whole class.

OPTIONAL EXTENSION

Ask Ss to read through audioscript 2.8 on page 155 and underline ways of agreeing and disagreeing. Let them compare with a partner and then elicit structures from the whole class. E.g.

Agrees: *Yes. I think that's true about me. That's absolutely right!*

Disagrees: *I'm not sure about that. Actually, I don't think I'm very open. I don't think so really.*

Tell Ss they will have the opportunity to use these expressions in ex. 10b.

Grammar | gerunds and infinitives

OPTIONAL GRAMMAR LEAD-IN

Write the following questions on the board:

1 What has Daniel decided not to do?
2 What did Helen want to do?
3 What does Daniel avoid telling people about?
4 Who would Daniel never consider showing his feelings to?

Ss discuss the answers in pairs from what they can remember. If necessary, play the recording again. Check the answers with the whole class and write the answers to numbers 1 and 3 on the board.

1 Daniel has decided not to do his essay.
2 Helen wants to look at the shape of Daniel's fingers.
3 He avoids telling people about his feelings.
4 He would never consider showing his feelings to someone he didn't know.

Underline the verbs in each sentence. Elicit the two structures: verb + infinitive and verb + gerund (rub the sentences off the board before the Ss do the next exercise).

6a ▶ Ss read the examples and choose the correct options to complete the rules. Check answers with the whole class.

Active grammar

Some verbs are followed by the gerund (-ing form), e.g. *enjoy, avoid,* _____

Some verbs are followed by the infinitive with to, e.g. *want, decide* _____

---

b ▶ Ss look at audioscript 2.8 on page 155 and put the verbs in the box in the correct list in the Active grammar box. Elicit the answers from the class.

Answers
A   verb + gerund: consider, finish
B   verb + infinitive with *to*: afford, offer, promise, seem

---

▶ Refer Ss to the Reference on page 77 and give them a moment to read through the notes. Ask one of the Ss to read out the list of verbs followed by the gerund and check

that all the Ss understand these verbs. Do the same with the verbs followed by the infinitive with *to*. Explain to the Ss that there are no rules for this, they simply have to remember which verbs are in which list.

7 ▶ Ss choose the correct option. Tell them to do this without referring to page 77, basing their answers on what they remember and what sounds right (very often Ss know these structures subconsciously from having heard or used them before). Check the answers with the whole class.

Answers		4	learning	8	staying
1	to read	5	writing	9	not to be
2	not to be	6	to go	10	to go
3	going	7	to get		

8a ▶ Put the Ss in pairs and get them to complete the sentences for their partner without asking. Tell them to use their imagination or knowledge they have of their partner.

b ▶ Ss read their sentences to their partner who either confirms they are right or says they are wrong and why. Give an example with one student, e.g. '*I think you want to move to England next year.*' '*No, I don't.*' '*What do you want to do?*' '*I want to finish university.*'

OPTIONAL EXTENSION

Ss work in pairs to write questions with two verbs from the lists in the Reference on page 77. They must be personal questions (although emphasise that they shouldn't be too personal) that other Ss could answer, e.g. *Do you expect to get married one day?* They can be in any tense. Ss then take one question each, and mingle with the class, asking and answering questions. Get feedback from each student about the question and the answers.

Reading and speaking

9a ▶ Ss read the text quickly and mark the statements as true (T) or false (F). Tell them not to worry about any words or phrases they don't understand. Elicit the answers.

Answers	1	F	2	T

---

b ▶ Ss read the text again and answer the questions. Let them compare with a partner and then elicit the answers from various Ss.

Answers	1	longer	3	longer
	2	shorter	4	shorter

▶ Ask the Ss if there are any words or phrases in the text that they don't understand. Encourage other Ss to explain them before doing so yourself.

10a ▶ In pairs Ss look at each other's hands and try to explain personality characteristics based on the things they have learned in this lesson.

b ▶ Ss give feedback to their partners about how accurate the interpretation has been. Get feedback from the class.

7.3 Doctor, doctor

Prior to advances in medical science and the widespread availability of over-the-counter medicines from pharmacies, there were many old-fashioned home-made remedies for illnesses. These remedies differed from country to country and were generally passed on from generation to generation. Thousands of such remedies can be found, for example, for the common cold. These range from eating yoghurt mixed with black pepper to eating green chilli paste on chapatti bread.

In this lesson, Ss listen to the advice a woman's colleagues give her when she is ill and through this context consider the grammar of gerunds and infinitives with the verbs *stop*, *try* and *remember*.

OPTIONAL WARMER

Write *illness and symptoms* on the board and check the Ss understand them. In pairs, Ss brainstorm different types of illnesses. Get feedback and write them on the board. Now ask the pairs to discuss what symptoms they associate with each illness. Get feedback from the whole class. If you feel the class are comfortable together, have Ss talk to their partner about the minor illnesses they have had.

Vocabulary | illness

1a ▶ Ss look at the words and phrases in the box and talk to a partner about the meaning. Ss decide which two are illnesses. Check all the meanings with the whole class, asking Ss to read out the words so that you can check pronunciation. Finally, elicit which two are illnesses.

> **Answers**
> A cold and flu are illnesses.

▶ Point out to the Ss that *a cold* is countable and *flu* is uncountable.

b ▶ Point out that we say *I feel sick* (verb + adjective) and *my leg hurts* (noun + verb). Ask Ss to decide what verb we use with the other phrases in pairs. Elicit the answers from the class.

> **Answers**
> We use *have* or *have got*.

▶ Ask Ss *Which of these words and phrases are uncountable?* (backache, earache, stomachache, toothache.) Point out that we don't use the article *a/an* with these things. Write two example sentences on the board: *I've got a headache; I've got toothache.*

c ▶ In pairs Ss look at the six pictures and decide which symptoms from ex. 1a each picture shows.

> **Answers**
> A backache
> B a sore throat
> C a high temperature
> D a rash
> E a cough
> F my leg hurts

2a ▶ Ss correct two mistakes in each answer.

> **Answers**
> 1
> A: You look terrible. What's the matter?
> B: I <u>feel</u> sick and I've got <u>stomachache</u>.
> 2
> A: Are you better today?
> B: No ... I've got flu. I've got a high temperature and a <u>headache</u>.
> 3
> A: How you are? You don't look well.
> B: I've got <u>a</u> cough and sore eyes. I don't think it's serious – <u>I've got</u> a cold. That's all.
> 4
> A: Is your back feeling better?
> B: No. I've got terrible backache and my leg hurts. I've got toothache today, as well.
> 5
> A: How are you feeling?
> B: Terrible! I've got <u>a</u> sore throat and earache. I've got a rash as well.

b ▶ 🔘 2.9 Play the recording and Ss check their answers. Now get Ss to practise the mini-dialogues in pairs.

Listening and reading

3a ▶ Ss read the email quickly and then correct the sentences with a partner. Get various Ss to read out the corrected sentences.

> **Answers**
> 1 Georgia is writing an email to her friends/fellow students at college.
> 2 She is telling them that she is not going to go to college today.
> 3 She asks Jenny to get the homework for her.

b ▶ Ss read the email again and answer the questions with a partner. Ask two Ss to answer the questions for the whole class.

> **Answers**
> 1 She's got a headache, a high temperature, a sore throat and a cough.
> 2 She's going back to bed to try to sleep for a couple of hours.

4 ▶ 🔘 2.10 Tell the Ss they are going to listen to three phone calls between Georgia and her fellow students, Jenny, Ivan and Madison. Explain that they are from different countries and they are going to give her different advice.

Focus the Ss on the table, then play the recording so that they can match the caller with the advice and the country. Elicit the answers from the whole class.

Answers
Jenny: Hot water with honey and lemon. (England)
Ivan: Hot milk with honey and butter. (Russia)
Madison: Hot water with honey and vinegar. (America)

5 ▶ Ask three of the Ss to read out the statements and check that everybody understands them. Play the recording again and Ss mark the statements true (T) or false (F). Elicit the answers from the whole class.

Answers   1 T   2 F   3 F

6 ▶ Put Ss in small groups to discuss the questions. Get feedback from the whole class.

Grammar | *stop, try, remember*: gerunds and infinitives

OPTIONAL GRAMMAR LEAD-IN

Write the following questions on the board:
1 When you are studying or working, how often do you stop for a break?
2 Do you stop speaking your first language when you come into English class?
3 Do you always remember to turn everything off before leaving home?
4 Do you remember going away on holiday when you were a small child?
5 Do you try to learn some new vocabulary every day?
6 When you can't sleep, what do you try doing?
Put Ss in pairs to discuss their answers to the questions. Get feedback from various Ss. Now underline the verbs *stop*, *remember* and *try* in the questions and ask Ss: *What form of verb comes after* stop, remember *and* try? (both the infinitive and the gerund)

7 ▶ 🔘 2.11 Read through the Active grammar box with the whole class, pointing out the difference between the use of these verbs with the infinitive or the gerund. If you have done the optional grammar lead-in, you can refer back to these questions and Ss' answers as examples.

▶ Put Ss in pairs to complete the sentences and then play the recording so that they can check their answers. Ask various Ss to read out the sentences for the whole class.

Answers
1 coughing
2 to get
3 to sleep
4 turning
5 to get
6 having

▶ Ask Ss to look at the Reference on page 77 and read through the other example sentences.

8 ▶ Ss choose the correct options. Let them compare with a partner and then ask various Ss to read out the answers.

Answers
1 to phone   4 feeling   8 to keep
2 putting   5 to cough   9 feeling
3 running   6 to touch
                   7 to take

OPTIONAL EXTENSION

Write the following on the board:
1 *Things you stop doing when you leave school.*
2 *Things you stop to do when you are driving.*
3 *Things you remember doing last year.*
4 *Things you must remember to do before going on holiday.*
5 *Things you try doing to relax.*
6 *Things you have tried to do and couldn't.*
Put Ss in small groups to talk about these things. Go around the class monitoring their work. Get feedback from various Ss.

Speaking

9 ▶ 🔘 2.12 Focus the Ss attention on the *How to...* box. Play the recording and get Ss to complete the gaps. Let them compare with a partner and then get various Ss to read out the examples of how to give advice and how to respond to it.

Answers   1 don't   3 should   5 tried
                2 idea   4 that   6 fancy

10 ▶ Tell the Ss they are going to imagine that they are ill. Give them a few minutes to think about what is wrong and their symptoms. Now put them in pairs. Tell student A to ask one of the questions in ex. 2a and student B responds by talking about his/her illness and the symptoms. Student A then gives advice and student B responds. They then change roles. Ask a couple of the more confident pairs to act out the roleplay for the whole class.

OPTIONAL EXTENSION

Tell the Ss they have to invent a problem. Tell them it can be related to anything and put some suggested categories on the board to guide them: *health, romantic relationships, friends, family, work, studies, money,* etc. Give Ss five minutes to think about their problem and to make some notes. Now ask Ss to stand up and mingle, telling each other about their problems and giving each other advice. After a short time, ask Ss to sit down again and then go around the class asking each student (or some of the Ss if you have a large class) to say what their problem was and what advice they have been given. Ask them what they think the best advice was.

7 Communication

In this lesson, Ss listen to two people doing part of a quiz about stress and then they do the whole quiz in pairs to find out their stress factor. Finally, Ss consider ways of relaxing.

▶ Write *stress* on the board and elicit/teach the meaning (a negative emotional condition caused by external pressures). Ask the Ss: *What's the adjective of* stress? Elicit/teach the two possibilities. *Stressed* (only for people) and *stressful* (things that cause stress).

▶ Focus Ss on the photos and ask: *How do the people feel*? *What stressful things can you see?* Ask them to brainstorm causes of stress in pairs. Get feedback from the whole class.

1 ▶ Ss discuss the questions in pairs. Get feedback from the whole class.

2a ▶ Tell Ss they are going to listen to two people doing part of the quiz about stress. Give them a few minutes to skim the stress quiz so that they have some idea of the questions. Play the recording so that they can identify which questions they talk about. Get feedback from the class.

Answers
They talk about questions 1, 4, 7 and 9.

b ▶ Tell Ss they are going to listen again and they have to say if the two speakers agree or disagree about the level of stress each situation causes. Get feedback from the whole class.

Answers
Question 1: agree
Question 4: agree
Question 7: agree
Question 9: disagree

3 ▶ Put the Ss in pairs to do the quiz. Ask them to take it in turns to read out the question and encourage them to explain their answers in as much detail as possible. Ss also write a number to represent their stress factor in each situation.

4a ▶ Ss add up their points and look at the results on page 130. Ask the Ss which category they fall into.

b ▶ In pairs, Ss discuss whether they agree with the results, giving their reasons why and why not.

5a ▶ Ss work in small groups to discuss the questions.

b ▶ Each group reports back to the class. Write the most popular ways of relaxing on the board.

OPTIONAL EXTENSION

Write the following on the board:
Who is usually in the most stressful situation? Men or women? Politicians or doctors? Drivers or pedestrians? Teachers or students? People who live in the country or who live in the city?
Put Ss in groups to discuss two or three of the questions, giving reasons for their choice. Get feedback from different groups.

Review and practice

1 ▶

Answers
1   We'll be late if we don't leave now.
2   If it rains, we won't play tennis this afternoon.
3   Will you buy me a newspaper if you go shopping later?
4   If I don't see Holly today, I'll phone her.
5   If you put your hand on the cooker, you'll burn yourself.
6   I won't meet you at the cinema if I don't finish my work.
7   If you lend me five pounds, I'll pay you back tomorrow.
8   If you get home before me, will you make the dinner?

2 ▶

Answers
1   If they offer me the job, I'll take it.
2   I'll have a party if I pass my exam.
3   If you don't use sun cream, you'll get burnt.
4   I'll be late for work if I don't get up now.
5   If we don't invite her, she'll be upset.
6   If I see Jon, I won't tell him about the party.
7   You won't have any money left if you buy those jeans.
8   If we don't leave now, we'll be late.

3 ▶

Answers
1   going
2   not to tell
3   to wash
4   doing
5   to go
6   to like
7   using
8   talking

4 ▶

Answers
1   going
2   to go
3   to help
4   arriving
5   to do
6   talking

5 ▶

Answers
1   I can't stop thinking about that horror film I saw last night.
2   ✓
3   Please remember to bring an umbrella tomorrow.
4   She talked all evening and didn't stop to listen to me at all.
5   ✓
6   Could you stop shouting at me, please?

6 ▶

Answers
1   skinny
2   sore throat
3   reliable
4   muscular
5   reserved
6   high temperature
7   ambitious

Writing bank

1 ▶ Ss read the emails and answer the questions.

Answers
1   Michael is apologising for not going to class. Selena is apologising for not going to a party.
2   Michael is apologising to Kate, his teacher. Selena is apologising to Emily, her friend.
3   Michael got very wet and the bus was full. Selena was ill.

2 ▶ Ss read the emails again and number the topics in the correct order.

Answers
a   3
b   4
c   1
d   2

3a ▶ Ss complete the *How to...* box with the parts of punctuation.

Answers
1   full stop (.)
2   exclamation mark (!)
3   question mark (?)
4   comma (,)
5   quotation marks (" ")
6   apostrophe (')

b ▶ Ss punctuate the sentences.

Answers
1   Why don't we go out for dinner next week?
2   I'm sorry I didn't go to Ben's party.
3   Jenny, David and Kevin all said, 'Sorry'.
4   What a fantastic surprise!
5   When I last spoke to Jane, she wasn't feeling well.
6   If you finish your essay, will you come out with us after work?

4a ▶ Ss make notes in preparation for writing the email.

b ▶ Ss write the email.

Overview

Lead-in	**Revision:** Speed
8.1	**Can do:** Discuss the use of technology
	Grammar: Present Simple Passive
	Listening: The pace of life
	Reading: Take your time!
8.2	**Can do:** Talk about special occasions
	Grammar: Prepositions of time
	Vocabulary: Phrasal verbs: relationships
	Speaking and Pronunciation: Phrasal verbs: stress
	Listening: Arranged marriage in India
8.3	**Can do:** Describe past actions
	Grammar: Past Continuous and Past Simple
	Vocabulary: Measurements
	Speaking and Pronunciation: was/were
	Reading: Lightning Bolt!
Communication	Talk for an extended period on a familiar topic
	How to... organise a presentation
Reference	
Review and practice	
Writing bank	Write a short story describing a sequence of events
	How to... use time linkers
Extra resources	Active Teach and Active Book

CEFR Can do objectives

8.1 Discuss the use of technology
8.2 Talk about special occasions
8.3 Describe past actions
Communication Talk for an extended period on a familiar topic
Writing bank Write a short story describing a sequence of events

CEFR Portfolio ideas

a) Write a simple recipe, describing how to make a traditional dish in your country/region, or a dish you enjoy.
b) Choose a photograph of a special moment. Talk about the situation before the photograph, the moment of the photograph and what happened after the photograph. Record your story.
c) Prepare a PowerPoint presentation about your favourite team, musician or piece of technology. Use photographs for the slides. Write your speaking notes on the notes page.

Lead-in

OPTIONAL WARMER

Ask Ss to brainstorm in pairs a list of things that are fast, e.g. *runner/athlete*, *trains*, *cars*, *planes*, *animals*, *food*, etc. Then ask them to choose one or two things from their list and write definitions of the words. Have one student from each pair read out their definitions for the rest of the class to guess the word. Write the words on the board. Then ask Ss to tell you any other words they have on their list and write them on the board too.

1 ▶ Get Ss, in pairs, to look at the photos and say what is the connection between them. Get feedback from the class (Main photo – speed skater; Top photo – cheetah; Middle photo – people running for a train; Bottom photo – a racing car). Elicit the connection and write any words related to speed on the board that Ss suggest (*speed*, *quick*, *fast*, etc.).

2a ▶ Ss complete the sentences in pairs, using the phrases from the box. Check with the whole class.

Answers
1 top speed
2 speed limit
3 speeding
4 speed camera

b ▶ In pairs, Ss discuss which two sentences they think are false. Encourage them to give their reasons. Get feedback, but do not tell them the answers yet.

▶ Ss check their answers on page 131.

3a ▶ Give the Ss a few minutes to work in pairs to discuss the meaning of the underlined words and phrases. Ask for volunteers to explain the expressions one by one or give examples of how they would use them.

Answers
1 in a hurry – going somewhere/doing something quickly
2 on time – according to schedule
3 immediately – straight away/taking your time – to not hurry
4 on the go – without stopping
5 rush hour – the busiest time of day on the roads
6 speed up/slow down – go faster or less fast

b ▶ Ss ask and answer the questions in pairs and then decide who has a 'faster' life. Ask various students to explain how fast their partner's life is.

EXTEND THE LEAD-IN

Draw a chart with two columns on the board with the headings: *Advantages* and *Disadvantages*. Give Ss about ten minutes to think about modern-day society and the advantages and disadvantages of speed in our lives. Then get feedback from each group, allowing other Ss to agree or disagree.

8.1 Fast world

In an increasingly fast world, organisations such as the Slow Movement are springing up to defend our right to take our time in our everyday lives. These organisations claim that the increased speed of modern-day life threatens our health, family and relationships, weakens communities and leads to higher levels of unemployment. The Slow Movement, which started as a protest against the opening of a McDonald's in Rome, is not a single organisation, but is made up of different groups such as Slow Food, Slow Down Now and The World Institute of Slowness.

In this lesson, Ss listen to an interview with a member of the Slow Movement. They then read a leaflet about how fast modern-day life is and tips about how to slow it down. Through this text they analyse the grammar of the Present Simple Passive.

OPTIONAL WARMER

Ask the Ss about their habits with regard to fast food, use of mobile phones and emails. Ask: *How often do you eat fast food? How often do you finish eating in less than five minutes? How many emails do you usually send a day? How many text messages do you usually write a day? When do you switch off your mobile phone?*

Listening

1 ▶ Ss choose the words so that the sentences are true for them. Put them in small groups to compare answers, giving reasons where possible. Get feedback from the whole class.

2a ▶ 🔘 2.14 Tell Ss they are going to listen to a radio interview with Petra van Stroud, who is a member of the Slow Movement. Read through the two statements with the whole class and then play the recording. Ss decide with a partner if the sentences are true (T) or false (F). Elicit the answers from the class.

> **Answers**
> 1 F
> 2 T

b ▶ Give Ss a minute to read through the sentences. Tell them to talk to a partner to predict what words they need to fill the gaps. Encourage them to use the context given by the rest of the sentence. Now play the recording again and have Ss complete the sentences with one or two words. Let them compare with a partner and then check with the whole class.

> **Answers**
> 1 forget
> 2 McDonald's
> 3 social
> 4 communication
> 5 enjoy
> 6 mobile phone

3 ▶ Ss discuss the questions in pairs. Get feedback from the whole class.

Reading

4 ▶ Focus Ss on the Lifelong learning box and read through the tip with the whole class. Read out the two questions about the Slow Movement leaflet and then give Ss one minute to speed read the leaflet to find the answers. Elicit the answers from the whole class.

> **Answers**
> 1 about 31,000
> 2 more than 50 times daily

▶ Point out to Ss that this type of reading is very common in real life and we use this skill when we need to find information quickly and when we're not interested in all the information in a text.

5 ▶ Tell Ss they are going to read the text again, but this time more carefully as they are looking for more detailed information. Ss read the text individually and correct the sentences. Let them compare with a partner before eliciting the answers from the whole class.

> **Answers**
> 1 <u>American</u> people eat about sixty-five million fast-food meals a day.
> 2 The amount of money spent on fast food in the US is going <u>up</u>.
> 3 The text recommends having <u>a proper lunch break</u>.
> 4 British people send more than <u>200</u> million text messages every day,
> 5 In one day, an average office worker spends <u>nearly two hours</u> on email.
> 6 The text says you should have some days when you <u>have an 'email-free' day</u>.

▶ Ask the Ss if there are any words in the text that they haven't understood. Encourage other Ss to explain those words before doing so yourself.

6 ▶ Ss look at the 'slow tips' again and answer the questions with a partner. Ss share their ideas for other tips with the rest of the class. The class can vote on the best extra tip.

Grammar | Present Simple Passive

OPTIONAL GRAMMAR LEAD-IN

Write the following sentences on the board but with the words in the wrong order. Ss close their books and work in pairs to order the words and write the sentences.

1 *million day sixty-five eaten US fast-food every in are meals the.* (Sixty-five million fast-food meals are eaten in the US every day.)

2 *text 200 over million UK the each messages in day sent are.* (Over 200 million text messages are sent each day in the UK.)

3 *with a two Nearly dealing day spent are hours emails.* (Nearly two hours are spent dealing with emails a day.)

Elicit/teach the name of this grammatical structure (Present Simple Passive).

7a ▶ Ss read through the Active grammar box and complete the gaps with the correct form of the verb in brackets. Elicit the answers and write the structures and the examples on the board.

Active grammar

Active form: active subject + verb + object

1   Americans spend more than $110 billion on fast food every year.

2   Sixty-five million fast-food meals are eaten in the US every day.

---

b ▶ Ss find four more examples in the text. (If you have done the optional grammar lead-in, tell them to find two more that you haven't already looked at.) Elicit the answers from various Ss.

Answers

... a huge amount of fast food is consumed every day ... .

... 200 million text messages are sent each day ... .

... nearly two hours are spent dealing with emails ... .

Email isn't switched off at home ... .

▶ Refer Ss to the Reference on page 87 and give them a few minutes to read through the notes. Ask the Ss:

What preposition do we use to say who did the action in passive structures? (by)

What happens to the object of active sentences when we change them to passives? (it becomes the subject)

When do we use is*?* (when the subject is singular)

When do use are*?* (when the subject is plural)

(Note: *am* is not used that often in the passive. If you feel Ss need an illustration of how it is used, write the following sentence on the board: *I am sent flowers for my birthday every year.*)

▶ If the Ss still have some doubts about this structure, work through a few more examples on the board, e.g.

A man in that shop repairs my bike. My bike is repaired (by a man) in that shop.

People in Canada speak two languages. Two languages are spoken (by people) in Canada.

---

8 ▶ Ss complete the sentences individually. Let them compare with a partner before checking the answers with the whole class.

Answers		
1 is reduced	3	are owned
2 are driven	4	is used
	5	are made

---

9 ▶ Ss change the active verb to the passive where necessary. Let them compare with a partner and then check the answers with the whole class.

Answers		
1 are employed	3	are delivered
2 ✓	4	✓
	5	are charged

Speaking

10a ▶ 🌐 2.15 Play the recording and Ss write down the eight questions. Let them compare with a partner and then check the answers with the whole class.

Answers

1   In what language are most international phone calls made?

2   In the US, are more messages carried by email or by post?

3   What percentage of emails are junk email?

4   How much junk mail is delivered by post every year in the US?

5   What percentage of websites are not visited by anybody?

6   How many people visit the website YouTube every day?

7   How many people use the social networking site Facebook every day?

8   In how many different languages do people write messages on Facebook?

---

b ▶ Ss work in small groups and answer the questions from ex. 10a on a piece of paper. Swap the papers around so that a different group is correcting another group's answers. Tell them to check on page 131 and give one point for each correct answer. See which group got the most answers correct. Ask the whole class if they were surprised about anything they found out.

OPTIONAL EXTENSION

Put the class in groups of three and tell them they are going to do a roleplay of a radio interview about the topic. Give one student the role of radio interviewer, one student the role of member of the Slow Movement and the other student the role of somebody who loves a fast way of life. Give them five minutes to think about their roles and make some notes about what they want to say and what they want to ask (particularly in the case of the interviewer). Then get them to act out the roleplay.

8.2 Married in a month

The way in which couples meet each other and eventually marry varies from culture to culture. Arranged marriages, in which family members – often parents or other important members of the community – introduce the couple to each other, have long been a tradition in families around the world, including Europe. It is also a common practice in Indian, Pakistani and Japanese cultures. This type of marriage should not be confused with 'forced marriage' as the couple involved often has a great say in the final choice. In recent years in the US, Britain and other parts of Europe, speed-dating has become popular. This involves single people gathering in a café or bar full of 'tables for two'. The participants are given a short time to talk to a member of the opposite sex on suggested topics to help break the ice. At the end of the set time, there is usually someone who rings a bell or plays music to let everyone know it's time to move on to the next date.

In this lesson, Ss study phrasal verbs that explain relationships and listen to a conversation about arranged marriages and speed-dating. Through this context, they consider prepositions of time.

OPTIONAL WARMER

Write *romantic relationships* on the board. Tell Ss that this is the topic of the lesson. In pairs, Ss brainstorm words related to this topic. Get feedback from the whole class and write the words on the board.

Vocabulary | phrasal verbs: relationships

1 ▶ Write *phrasal verb* on the board and elicit/teach the meaning (verb + one or two particles, e.g. adverb or preposition, which changes the meaning of the verb). Give the Ss an example of a phrasal verb, e.g. *get up*.

▶ Focus Ss on the table. Explain the meaning of *date* (definition d) in this context (a romantic meeting) and tell them to match the phrasal verbs with the definitions. Elicit the answers from various Ss.

Answers					
		3	g	6	b
1	d	4	c	7	e
2	a	5	f		

▶ Point out that *go out with someone* can also mean to do something such as go to the cinema or restaurant with someone who's just a friend. We know from the context whether this phrasal verb has a romantic meeting or not. Write the following on the board: *1 I'm going out with my friends tonight; 2 I went out with Steven for two years*. Ask: *In which sentence does* go out *have a romantic meaning?* (2)

▶ Explain that *get over* and *put up with* can be used with someone or something. Write the following sentences on the board to illustrate their use with something: *It took me three weeks to get over the flu. I can't put up with the noise my neighbours make.*

2 ▶ Ss complete the sentences in pairs. Before they begin, remind them that they may have to change the form of the verb. Ask Ss which of the verbs in the box are irregular and elicit/teach the Past and past participle of those verbs (*go–went–gone; take–took–taken; grow–grew–grown; put–put–put; split–split–split; get–got–got*). Elicit the answers from various Ss.

Answers	
1	split up with
2	asked (me) out
3	puts up with
4	get over
5	took (me) out
6	going out/to go out with
7	grown apart

OPTIONAL EXTENSION

Ask Ss to write sentences about themselves or someone they know with three of the phrasal verbs in ex. 1. Put Ss in small groups to read their sentences to each other. Encourage them to ask follow-up questions about the sentences their classmates say.

Pronunciation | phrasal verbs: stress

3a ▶ ● 2.16 Focus the Ss on the example sentence and play the recording so that they can underline the part of the phrasal verb that has the main stress. Elicit the answer from the class and explain that the stress in phrasal verbs is on the particle. If there are two particles, it is on the first.

Answer	
1	Jade's been single since she split <u>up</u> with her boyfriend last year.

b ▶ ● 2.17 Ss underline the stress in the other phrasal verbs from ex. 2. Play the recording so that they can check and repeat the sentences.

Answers	
2	Pete asked me <u>out</u> yesterday and I said 'yes' because I really like him.
3	Oliver never does the washing-up and Maria just puts <u>up</u> with it.
4	When my sister got divorced, she found it difficult to get <u>over</u> her ex-husband.
5	On our first date, Jack took me <u>out</u> to a really expensive French restaurant.
6	Linda and Guy are a couple. They started going <u>out</u> with each other last month.
7	We used to be good friends, but we've grown <u>apart</u> over the last year.

4 ▶ Put the Ss in small groups to discuss the questions. Get feedback from the whole class.

Listening

5a ▶ Write *speed-dating* and *arranged marriages* on the board. Put Ss in pairs to answer the questions. Get feedback from the whole class.

b ▶ ● 2.18 Tell Ss they are going to listen to two friends, Fiona and Deepa, talking about speed-dating and arranged marriages. Play the recording and ask them to tell a partner if they have heard the answers to the questions they asked in ex. 5a. Get feedback from the whole class.

6 ▶ Get various Ss to read out the statements and check that everybody understands them. Now play the recording again so that Ss can mark them true (T) or false (F). Let them compare with a partner and then check the answers with the whole class.

Answers					
1	F	3	T	6	T
2	F	4	T	7	F
		5	F		

7 ▶ Ss work in pairs to discuss the questions. Get feedback from the whole class.

Grammar | prepositions of time

OPTIONAL GRAMMAR LEAD-IN

Write the following questions on the board: *When do you have English class? When's your birthday? When were you born? When do you go to the beach? When do you have holidays?* Get the Ss to answer the questions in pairs and then ask various Ss to answer them for the whole class. Correct any mistakes they make with prepositions of time. Write *prepositions of time* on the board and explain that this is what they are going to study next.

8a ▶ Ss complete the sentences with a preposition of time.

Answers					
1	in	2	at	3	on

b ▶ Get Ss to look at audioscript 2.18 on page 157 to check their answers and to find six more examples of prepositions of time.

Answers
at Thanksgiving, in November, on my birthday, on 18th November, in the winter, at the beginning of December

9 ▶ Ss complete the Active grammar box. Ask various Ss to read out the answers and write the headings on the board.

Active grammar
A in: for long periods of time
B on: for specific days and parts of specific days
C at: for times and special holiday periods

▶ Test the Ss by saying aloud the following time expressions and having them write them down with an appropriate preposition: *July* (in); *Monday evening* (on); *night* (at); *spring* (in); *12 March* (on); *Christmas day* (on); *2005* (in); *midday* (at).

▶ Point out that *at night* is an exception, as the other parts of the day *morning, afternoon* and *evening* are used with the preposition *in*. Draw Ss' attention to the Reference on page 87.

10 ▶ Ss complete the sentences individually. Let them compare with a partner and then get various Ss read out the answers.

Answers					
1	in	3	At	6	on
2	on	4	on	7	at/in
		5	in	8	in

11 ▶ Ss work in groups to ask and answer questions using the words from the box. Go around the class, monitoring their work.

Speaking

12a ▶ ● 2.19 Focus Ss on the topics in the box and make sure they understand them all. Play the recording. Let Ss answer the questions with a partner before checking them with the whole class.

Answers
1 Valentine's Day
2 mostly positive

b ▶ Read through the questions with the whole class and then play the recording again so that Ss can write down their answers. Let Ss compare with a partner before checking them with the whole class.

Answers
1 Italy
2 Because he helped soldiers to get married secretly.
3 flowers and chocolates
4 to a restaurant
5 He thinks it's good.

13a ▶ Individually, Ss make notes about one of the topics from ex. 12a. Go around the class helping them with any vocabulary they need.

b ▶ Put Ss in groups so that they can talk about the topics they have prepared. Encourage the Ss who are listening to ask follow-up questions.

8.3 Fast men

Usain St Leo Bolt, nicknamed 'Lightning Bolt', is a Jamaican sprinter, who became known as the fastest man on earth at the 2008 Beijing Olympics. Despite considering himself to be a 200-metre specialist at the time, he entered the 100-metre race and broke the world record by completing it in an amazing 9.72 seconds. He also walked away with the world records and gold medals in two other sprinting events, becoming the first athlete to achieve this. Usain had already shown great promise at the age of 15, when he became the youngest sprinter to win a gold medal in the 200 metres at the 2002 World Junior Championships.

In this lesson, Ss read about Usain Bolt and through this context look at the grammar of Past Continuous and Past Simple.

OPTIONAL WARMER

Write *sports* on the board and ask Ss to brainstorm in pairs all the sports they know. Ask Ss to read out the sports and write them on the board. Now play 20 questions. Demonstrate the game yourself by choosing a sport and having the Ss ask you *yes/no* or *sometimes* questions to guess which sport it is, e.g. *Do you play in a team? Do you need a ball? Do people watch it on TV?* etc. Put the Ss in small groups to play the game.

Reading

1a ▶ Write *sprinter* on the board and elicit/teach the meaning of the word (an athlete that runs short races very fast). Now tell Ss that Usain Bolt is a sprinter and get them to guess his top speed.

b ▶ Tell Ss to read the text quickly in order to find the answer (44 kmph). Remind them that they saw a speed reading tip (on page 80) before they do this and see if they can remember what advice was given.

2 ▶ Read the questions out loud with the whole class and then tell Ss to read the text again to find the answers. Tell them not to worry about any words or phrases they don't understand at this stage. Elicit the answers from the class.

Answers
1 He first became well-known at the Beijing Olympics in 2008 because he won three gold medals.
2 He says he was born fast, but he also has the support of his family and his manager, Norman Peart, who keeps him focused.

3 ▶ Read through the example with the whole class and then put them in pairs to explain the significance of the other phrases from the text. Encourage them to use context to help them guess if they're not sure. Get feedback from various Ss.

Answers
1 Lightning Bolt is a play on words. In a storm, a bolt of lightning is very quick – Usain is very quick and his surname in Bolt.
2 A talent for sprinting means he was very good at running very fast over short distances.
3 He didn't train very hard means that he didn't practise very much for his races.
4 He turned professional means he started sprinting as if it were a job.
5 From strength to strength means he got better and better.
6 Something he was born with means that Usain thinks that being fast is a natural talent.
7 Keep him focused means that his manager helped him to concentrate on his objectives.
8 Smashed his own record means he beat his own record, running much faster than he had done before.

▶ Now ask Ss if there are any other phrases or words in the text that they don't understand. Encourage other Ss to explain them before explaining yourself.

4 ▶ Ss retell the story in pairs using the phrases from ex. 3. Go around the class monitoring their work.

OPTIONAL EXTENSION

1 Write the following questions on the board: *Are you good at running? Did you take part in any races when you were a child? What kind of person do you think becomes a top sprinter? What kind of lifestyle do you think they have? Is it easy being a top athlete?*
Put the Ss in small groups to discuss the questions.

Vocabulary | measurements

5a ▶ 🔊 2.20 Focus the Ss on the box and play the recording so that they can circle the number they hear. Elicit the answers from the whole class.

Answers

Answers		
8,880	$6\frac{1}{4}$	$75\frac{1}{2}$
3,235,899	$9\frac{3}{4}$	0.15
		44.9

b ▶ Ss listen again to check and repeat. Ask various Ss to read out the figures for the whole class.

c ▶ Read the question with the whole class and then put the Ss in pairs to identify where we need to say *point* and *and*. Elicit the answers from the class.

Answers
We say *point* before a decimal, e.g. nought point fifteen (0.15) and forty-four point nine (44.9).
We say *and* after the hundreds, e.g. eight thousand, eight hundred and eighty (8,880); three million, two hundred and thirty-five thousand, eight hundred and ninety-nine (3,235,899).

6a ▶ Ss choose the correct words in the questions. Elicit the answers from various Ss.

Answers
1 fast
2 far
3 long
4 tall
5 much

b ▶ Put Ss in groups so that they can ask and answer the questions from ex. 6a. Go around the class monitoring their work.

Grammar | Past Continuous and Past Simple

7 ▶ Focus Ss on the Active grammar box and tell them to complete the gaps with the Past Simple or Past Continuous. Check the answers with the whole class.

Active grammar
A We use the Past Continuous to talk about an action in progress at a particular time in the past.
B We use the Past Simple to talk about complete actions in the past.
C We use the Past Continuous to talk about a longer action interrupted by another action in the Past Simple.

▶ Read through the uses of *when* with the Past Simple and *when/while* with the Past Continuous.

▶ Tell the Ss to look at the Reference on page 87 and give them a few minutes to read through the notes. Ask: *Are Past Continuous actions complete at the time you are talking about*? (no)

8 ▶ Ss complete the text with the Past Simple or the Past Continuous. Let them compare with a partner before eliciting the answers from various Ss.

Answers
1 became
2 was growing up
3 bought
4 was competing
5 was working
6 went
7 was walking
8 met
9 told

Pronunciation | *was/were*

9 ▶ ● 2.21 Explain that we can say *was* and *were* in different ways depending on what kind of sentence they are in. Play the recording and get Ss to listen and repeat.

▶ Explain that the pronunciation of *was/were* is weak in the questions and strong in the short answers.

Speaking

10 ▶ Read through the example with the whole class, then focus the Ss on the story-beginning sentences. Put them in groups and get each group to choose one of the sentences. They now tell a story by taking it in turns to say a sentence that begins with the last letter of the previous sentence. Go around the class monitoring their work.

8 Communication

In this lesson Ss listen to and compare two presentations. They then prepare and give their own presentation in groups.

1 ▶ 🔵 2.22 Tell the Ss they are going to listen to two presentations. Play the recording and have them answer the questions with a partner. Elicit answers from the whole class.

Answers
1   Presentation 1 is about being too busy and presentation 2 is about the benefits of technology in a doctor's professional and private life.
2   Presentation 2 is better because it's more organised and the language is more formal. Main points are backed up with examples. Presentation 1 is repetitive and disorganised and too informal.

2a ▶ 🔵 2.23 Ss look at the introduction of one of the presentations again. Play the first part of the recording and Ss follow it, noting the pauses. Explain that pausing is an important thing to do when making a presentation.

b ▶ Get Ss to turn to page 157 and look at the audioscript. Play the rest of the recording and get them to mark the pauses. Let them compare with a partner and then get one of the confident Ss to read it out for the rest of the class.

3 ▶ Focus the Ss on the *How to...* box and ask them to complete it with the headings. Have various Ss read them out along with the example stem sentences.

Answers
1   c Starting the presentation
2   b Stating the main points
3   a Introducing each point
4   d Finishing the presentation

---

4 ▶ Ss make notes to prepare for their presentation. Encourage them to use the *How to...* box to help them organise their ideas. Go around the class helping them with vocabulary at this point.

5a ▶ Put Ss in small groups to give their presentations. Encourage them to speak slowly and clearly, pausing where appropriate.

b ▶ Reorganise the class so that Ss are in different groups. Give them a few minutes to think about how to improve their presentations before giving them again.

▶ Get feedback from the class to see if they think they have improved their presentations.

Review and practice

1 ▶

Answers
1   are cleaned
2   are invited
3   are sold
4   are cut down
5   is covered
6   are locked
7   is served
8   are opened

2 ▶

Answers
1   don't pronounce
2   are taken
3   is not invited
4   are employed
5   don't use
6   are cancelled
7   is made
8   are played

3 ▶

Answers					
1	at	3	at	6	in	9	in
2	at	4	in	7	on	10	on
		5	on	8	at		

4 ▶

Answers
1   was raining
2   were driving
3   stopped
4   didn't hit
5   fell
6   wasn't
7   was walking
8   was following
9   started
10   looked
11   saw

5 ▶

Answers
1   was she working
2   Was he driving
3   Did he visit
4   were you doing
5   was she waiting
6   Did you go
7   Were you listening

6 ▶

Answers					
1	get	3	up	6	in
2	on	4	hour	7	apart
		5	take	8	top

Writing bank

1 ▶ Ss read the text and answer the questions.

Answers
1   They've been to Austria for a skiing holiday.
2   There was a delay at the airport, there was someone else in their room and they had to wait two hours for another one, it was sunny and the snow was melting, Dinah slipped and broke her leg while bowling.
3   She's bored.

2a ▶ Ss read the email again and choose the correct options.

Answers
1   a
2   a
3   b
4   a
5   b

b ▶ Ss decide which of the three paragraphs could be divided into two parts, and where it would be divided.

Answers
Paragraph 2: Give details of the events of the story. The next paragraph would begin with 'The next morning ... .'

3a ▶ Ss complete the *How to...* box with the underlined phrases from the text.

Answers
1   To begin with
2   While
3   Eventually
4   After we arrived
5   Then

b ▶ Ss choose the correct alternative.

Answers
1   Then
2   After
3   To begin with
4   Finally
5   While
6   At first
7   Eventually
8   After

4a ▶ Ss make notes about one of the topics from the box, organising their ideas under the paragraph headings in ex. 2b.

b ▶ Ss write the email.

Overview

Lead-in	Vocabulary: Work
9.1	Can do: Talk about your abilities
	Grammar: *can, could, be able to*: ability
	Reading: Ben gets dream job
9.2	Can do: Respond to simple job interview questions
	Grammar: Adverbs of manner
	Vocabulary: Work
	Speaking and Pronunciation: Changing word stress
	Listening: Worst job interviews
9.3	Can do: Tell a story from the news
	Grammar: Past Simple Passive
	Vocabulary: Crime
	Reading: Car cleaner sent to prison
Communication	Take part in a simple negotiation.
	How to... negotiate with other people
Reference	
Review and practice	
Writing bank	Write a professional profile
	How to... use positive language in professional writing
Extra resources	Active Teach and Active Book

CEFR Can do objectives

9.1 Talk about your abilities
9.2 Respond to simple job interview questions
9.3 Tell a story from the news
Communication Take part in a simple negotiation
Writing bank Write a professional profile

CEFR Portfolio ideas

a) Write an email to a classmate. Thank him/her for his/her letter and C.V. Invite your classmate to come for an interview at the company office on 28th March at 10 o'clock. Invent any details you need to.

b) Write a newspaper advertisement for a job as a junior sales person in a computer shop. Describe the skills and personality which are required for the job. Offer a small monthly starting salary. Say that after six months, successful sales people can earn 25% more.

c) With a classmate, video an interview for a job as a keeper of lions in the local zoo. Invent any details you need to. The Director of the zoo should prepare questions. The interviewee should invent a suitable background.

Lead-in

OPTIONAL WARMER

Write *work* on the board and tell the Ss that Unit 9 is about work. Have Ss work in pairs to brainstorm a list of jobs. Elicit words from the Ss and write them on the board. Now put the Ss in groups to play 20 questions: One S chooses a job. The others can ask 20 *yes/no/sometimes* questions to guess the job. Brainstorm a few questions before they start playing, e.g. *Do you work inside? Do you use a computer? Do you need to go to university?*

1a ▶ Read out the jobs and check Ss understand them. Now ask Ss to look at the photos in pairs, and match the jobs to the photos. Get feedback from the class.

> **Answers**
> Main photo: construction worker
> Top photo: nurse
> Middle photo: fashion designer
> Bottom photo: stockbroker

1b ▶ Ss say which of the things from the box they associate with each job. Get feedback from the whole class.

> **Suggested Answers**
> construction worker: low salary, working outside
> nurse: long hours, low salary, a lot of training, uniform, shift work
> fashion designer: flexible hours, a lot of training
> stockbroker: long hours, high salary

2 ▶ Ss answer the questions in pairs. Get feedback from the whole class.

3 ▶ Write the following question on the board: *What job would you like to do in the future?* Put Ss in groups of three and ask them to find out what job each of them does (or if they don't work, the answer to the question on the board). Help those Ss who do not know the name of the job in English. Encourage Ss to talk about what the job involves. Get feedback from the whole class.

4a ▶ Read through the phrases in the box with the class and check they understand them. Individually, Ss put the phrases in a logical order. Tell them there is not necessarily one correct answer, and that they must justify the order that they choose.

▶ Ss compare their list with a partner, giving their reasons for choosing the order they did. Get feedback from one of the pairs and see if the rest of the class agree or disagree.

> **Suggested Answers**
> First, you have to prepare a CV, then you apply for a job. Next, you have an interview and then you are offered a job. You take a job and get promoted. Then, you resign and finally, you run your own company.

b ▶ Ss answer the question in pairs. Get feedback from the whole class.

9.1 The best job

Hamilton Island is at the edge of the Great Barrier Reef in Queensland, Australia. Although there are a few permanent inhabitants, it is mainly dedicated to tourism and many facilities, such as hotels, restaurants, shops, a golf club and a yachting club have been developed there. Great care has also been taken, however, to conserve its natural unspoilt countryside and beaches and it has an average year-round temperature of 27 centigrade, making it perfect to visit at any time of year. In 2009, the Queensland tourist board advertised the 'best job in the world' in which the successful candidate would be responsible for looking after the island in return for a high salary and free luxurious accommodation. The advert generated much interest around the world and there were more than 35,000 applications for the job. More importantly for the Queensland tourist board, it acted as a huge publicity campaign, promoting the island on an international scale.

In this lesson, Ss read about Ben Southall, who was chosen from the thousands of candidates for the job on Hamilton Island. Through this context they analyse grammar structures for expressing ability.

OPTIONAL WARMER

Write the following jobs on the board: *musician, doctor, fire-fighter, shop assistant, plumber.* Put Ss in small groups and ask them to discuss what are the good things and the bad things related to each of these jobs. Get feedback from the whole class and see if the different groups agree. Now write: *What would be a perfect job?* on the board and get Ss to discuss this question in groups. Get feedback from the whole class.

Reading

1 ▶ Ss look at the photo and the title of the text and guess what the job is. Get suggestions from the whole class.

2 ▶ Ss read quickly through the text and answer the questions. (Remind them about the speed reading tip they saw on page 80.) Tell them not to worry about any words or phrases they don't understand at this point. Check the answers with the whole class.

Answers
1 Looking after Hamilton Island and promoting tourism there.
2 He felt confident.

3 ▶ Get various Ss to read the statements out loud for the whole class and check that everybody understands them. Now Ss read the text again more carefully and mark the statements true (T) or false (F). Let them check with a partner and then check with the whole class.

Answers
1 F
2 T
3 F
4 T
5 F
6 F
7 T
8 T

▶ Ask the Ss if there are any words or phrases in the text that they don't understand and encourage other Ss to explain them before explaining yourself.

4 ▶ Ss discuss the questions in pairs. Get feedback from the whole class.

▶ Grammar | *can, could, be able to*: ability

OPTIONAL GRAMMAR LEAD-IN

Write the following questions on the board:
Can you swim, run or climb well?
Could you speak any other languages apart from your own when you were younger?
Were you able to finish all the work you had to do last week?
Ss discuss the questions in pairs. Get feedback from the class and then ask Ss which sentences refer to ability in the present and which refer to ability in the past.

5 ▶ Ss complete the Active grammar box and then check with a partner before checking with the text from ex. 2.

▶ Read through each rule with the whole class and have different Ss read out the completed example sentences.

Active grammar
1 can
2 can't
3 could
4 couldn't
5 was able to
6 couldn't

▶ Ask the Ss the following questions to check their understanding:

What verb form do we use after can? (the infinitive without *to*)

What verb form do we use after was/were able? (the infinitive with *to*)

Does can *change in the third person?* (no)

Do we use auxiliary verbs with can *or* was/were able? (no)

Draw Ss' attention to the Reference on page 97.

6 ▶ Individually, Ss decide if both or only one of the options is correct. Let them compare with a partner before checking with the whole class.

> **Answers**
> 1 only *can*
> 2 both
> 3 both
> 4 only *was able to*
> 5 both
> 6 only *can't*
> 7 only *was able to*
> 8 only *wasn't able to*

7 ▶ Ss complete the sentences individually and then compare with a partner. Check the answers with the whole class.

> **Answers**
> 1 was able to
> 2 couldn't/wasn't able to
> 3 could/was able to
> 4 was able to
> 5 can't
> 6 couldn't/wasn't able to
> 7 was able to
> 8 couldn't/wasn't able to

Speaking

8 ▶ Focus the Ss on the Lifelong learning box and read through the tip with the whole class. Tell Ss to write three answers for the question. Let Ss compare what they have written with a partner before getting feedback from the whole class.

9a ▶ Ask Ss to choose two areas of their lives and to make notes about their abilities in the past and now. Go around the class helping Ss with any difficult vocabulary.

b ▶ Put Ss in groups so that they can tell each other about their abilities. Encourage the 'listeners' to ask follow-up questions.

> **OPTIONAL VARIATION**
>
> Brainstorm possible activities which people generally have ability to do or not, e.g. play musical instruments, do sports, ride a bike or drive a car, use a computer, speak a foreign language, etc. Divide the class into pairs and give one activity to each pair. Tell the pairs to write two questions (one present, one past) about that activity, e.g. *Could you use a computer when you were seven? Can you usually solve all your problems on the computer now?* Each student in the pair takes one of the questions and the whole class mingles, asking and answering each other's questions. At the end, each pair reports back to the whole class about what they found out.

9.2 Interview horrors

Nowadays, there are hundreds of books and websites that give advice on how to do well in a job interview. Advice is generally given about the pre-interview stage, e.g. finding out about the company, the interview stage itself, e.g. answering difficult questions, and the post-interview stage, e.g. sending a thank-you letter. These books and sites also offer tips on writing CVs and covering letters. They also tell you what not to do and give advice on what to do if an interview goes badly.

In this lesson, Ss consider vocabulary related to work and listen to three stories about terrible interview situations. Through this context, they look at the grammar of adverbs of manner and roleplay a job interview.

OPTIONAL WARMER

Ask Ss about their experience with job interviews:
Have you ever had a job interview? For what job(s)? Did you get the job? Did you feel very nervous? Have you ever interviewed somebody for a job?

Vocabulary | work

1a ▶ Ss work in pairs to discuss the differences between the two words in each pair. Get feedback from the class.

Answers
1 An *interviewer* is the person who conducts the interview; an *interviewee* is the person who is applying for the job.
2 An *employer* is the boss; an *employee* is the worker.
3 An *application form* is provided and you complete it to apply for a job; a *CV* is a summary that you provide about your qualifications and experience.
4 *Experience* refers to the things you have done related to the job; *qualifications* refer to education and courses you have completed.
5 A *salary* is a fixed amount of money you earn from your job monthly or annually and is usually used when referring to professional jobs; a *wage* is often a variable amount of money paid by the hour or the day for work or services and it is often used when referring to non-professional jobs.
6 A *bonus* is a special payment you are given for good work; *commission* is a percentage payment that corresponds to how much a worker has sold.
7 A *receptionist* works on a desk at the entrance to a business and deals with new arrivals; a *secretary* deals with general administration.
8 A *sales rep* is a person who travels around selling his or her company's products; a *sales assistant* is someone who works in a shop or store.
9 A *managing director* is a person who manages the overall running of a company; a *marketing director* is the person who is in charge of the publicity and advertising of the products.

b ▶ Ss choose the correct alternative and then compare with a partner. Check the answers with the whole class.

Answers
1 employees
2 experience (Point out to the Ss that experience is the correct answer because it is uncountable; qualifications is countable.)
3 receptionist
4 bonus
5 interviewer
6 application form
7 salary

Pronunciation | changing word stress

2a ▶ 🔵 2.24 Explain to the Ss that the stress on words that come from the same word family is sometimes different. Play the recording and get them to underline the stress on each word or phrase. Check the answers with the whole class.

Answers
1 to <u>in</u>terview / an <u>in</u>terviewer / an interview<u>ee</u>
2 to em<u>ploy</u> / an em<u>ploy</u>er / an employ<u>ee</u>
3 to ap<u>ply</u> / an <u>app</u>licant / an appli<u>ca</u>tion form
4 to <u>qual</u>ify / a qualifi<u>ca</u>tion
5 a <u>sec</u>retary / a secre<u>tar</u>ial job

b ▶ Play the recording again and Ss listen, check and repeat.

3 ▶ Ss discuss the questions in small groups. Get feedback from the whole class.

Listening

4a ▶ Focus Ss on the pictures and ask them, in pairs, to discuss what they think is happening in each one. Get feedback from various Ss.

b ▶ 🔵 2.25 Tell Ss they are going to listen to three people talking about their worst job interviews. Play the recording and get them to match the stories to the pictures. Check the answers with the whole class.

Answers	1 C	2 A	3 B

▶ Get Ss to say with a partner whether the ideas they had in ex. 4a were right or not. Ask them to say if they found out any extra information about what was happening. Get feedback from various Ss.

5 ▶ Get various Ss to read out the sentences for the whole class. Now play the recording again and get the Ss to number each one according to the story they hear it in. Check the answers with the whole class.

Answers

a	1	d	3	g	1
b	2	e	3	h	2
c	1	f	3	i	2

6 ▶ Ss discuss the questions in small groups. Get feedback from the whole class.

Grammar | adverbs of manner

> **OPTIONAL GRAMMAR LEAD-IN**
>
> Write the following stem sentences on the board and ask the Ss to complete them individually:
>
> *1 I feel* happy *when … .*
> *2 I feel* tired *when … .*
> *3 I listen to music* loudly *when … .*
> *4 I speak* quietly *when … .*
>
> Now get the Ss to compare what they have written with a partner.
>
> Ask: *What are the underlined words*, *adjectives or adverbs?* Elicit/teach that in sentences 1 and 2 they are adjectives and in sentences 3 and 4, they are adverbs.

7a ▶ Read through part A of the Active grammar box with the whole class. Put the Ss in pairs and tell them to look back at the sentences in ex. 5 and decide if the underlined words are adverbs of manner or adjectives. Check the answers with the whole class.

> **Answers**
> adverbs: slowly, angrily, carefully, quickly, badly, well
> adjectives: embarrassed, desperate, worried

b ▶ Focus Ss on part B of the Active grammar box and ask them to read the rules and write the adverbs. Elicit the answers from the Ss and write them on the board.

> **Active grammar**
> 1   quickly
> 2   angrily
> 3   well

c ▶ Tell Ss to read through the rules in part C of the Active grammar box and then decide which of the four sentences is incorrect. Check the answer with the whole class.

> **Answer**
> Sentence 2 is incorrect.

▶ Ask Ss to turn to page 97 and give them a few minutes to read through the Reference. Now ask the following questions:

What are the adverbs of beautiful *and* nervous? (*beautifully* and *nervously*)

What do we do with an adjective like friendly, *which already ends in '-ly'?* (We say *in a friendly way*.)

What are the adverbs of the adjectives fast, late *and* hard? (*fast*, *late* and *hard*)

8 ▶ Individually, Ss choose the correct options. Let them compare with a partner before checking with the class.

> **Answers**
> 1   carefully   5   angrily
> 2   good/well   6   happy
> 3   Sadly   7   quickly/confidently
> 4   rude   8   nervous/quietly

9 ▶ Individually, Ss find and correct mistakes in four of the sentences. Let them compare with a partner before checking with the whole class.

> **Answers**
> 1   He wrote his CV <u>carefully</u>.
> 2   She spoke to the interviewees <u>angrily</u>.
> 3   ✓
> 4   She pronounced the word <u>carefully</u>.
> 5   ✓
> 6   He asked the question confidently.

Speaking

10 ▶ In pairs, Ss write five pieces of advice, including an adverb of manner, for someone who is going to a job interview. Get feedback from various Ss.

11a ▶ Tell Ss to look at the job adverts on page 131 and choose one of them with their partner. Student A decides which of the questions 1–8 are relevant to the job and then writes two or three more questions. Student B decides which questions they might have to answer and makes notes to prepare for the interview.

b ▶ Ss roleplay the interview. Get one of the more confident pairs to roleplay the interview for the class.

▶ Ss can now choose another advert and change roles so that student A becomes the interviewee and student B the interviewer.

> **OPTIONAL VARIATION**
>
> Ask the class to choose just one of the adverts. Ss act out the interview as above but each 'interviewer' interviews all the 'interviewees' in turn (Ss rotate around the class) and chooses the person who they think is the best for the job. Allow a maximum time (e.g. four minutes for each interview). Tell the interviewees that they can either tell the truth or invent their 'CV'. Finally, have each interviewer tell the rest of the class who they chose, and why.

> **OPTIONAL EXTENSION**
>
> Students give feedback to each other about the interview roleplay, focusing on the positive as much as possible, e.g. '*You spoke clearly. You have good qualifications and speak French well. However …*'. The interviewee can then comment on the interviewer's questions and style. Then various pairs report back to the whole class.

9.3 Career criminals

Many crimes are committed every year all over the world and punishments for these crimes are decided with reference to the legal system of the country in which the crime takes place. While most countries have civil law systems involving a written criminal code (which evolved from ancient Roman law), Britain and the US have a common law system, which is based on customs and general principles. In civil law systems, judges not only pass sentence on the criminal but can also investigate crimes. In common law systems, trial by jury is much more important. When a decision is made by a jury, the judge then passes sentence and this then becomes a precedent for future cases.

In this lesson, Ss work on vocabulary related to crime, read a news story about an unusual crime and, through this context, analyse the grammar of the Past Simple Passive.

OPTIONAL WARMER

Write *crime* on the board and ask Ss to brainstorm any words related to this topic. Get feedback from the whole class and write the words on the board. Ask Ss if they can make any other word (adjectives, nouns, verbs or adverbs) from the words already on the board, e.g. if you have written *prison*, elicit *prisoner*. Now ask Ss, in pairs, to choose one of the words and write a definition for it. The pairs read out their definitions for the rest of the class, who have to guess which word they are defining.

Vocabulary | crime

1a ▶ In pairs, Ss look at the underlined words in ex. 1b and check they understand them. Get feedback from the class, encouraging Ss to explain any of the words that some Ss don't understand before explaining them yourself.

b ▶ Ss answer the questions using the words from the box. Let them compare with a partner and then check the answers with the whole class.

Answers
1 police officer
2 victim
3 jury
4 judge
5 witness

2 ▶ Ss complete the sentences. Remind them that they may have to change the form of the verbs. Let them compare with a partner and then check the answers with the whole class.

Answers
1 thief
2 criminal
3 steals
4 punishment
5 victim
6 judge
7 arrested
8 guilty
9 jury
10 witness

3 ▶ Ss discuss the questions in pairs. Get feedback from the whole class.

OPTIONAL EXTENSION

Ss work in pairs to think of a crime that they have heard about recently in the news. (If they haven't heard of one, they can invent it.) They make notes about what happened and explain the story to the rest of the class. Each pair has to decide what punishment they think is suitable for each crime. Get feedback and encourage Ss to discuss the different possibilities.

Reading

4a ▶ Focus the Ss on the words and phrases from the box and check that they understand them. Tell the Ss that all these words are included in a news article. Put Ss in pairs to predict what the article is about. Get feedback from the whole class.

b ▶ Tell Ss to read the text quickly and then talk to a partner to say how good their predictions were. Tell them not to worry about any words or phrases they don't understand at this point. Get feedback from the whole class.

5 ▶ Ss read the text again more carefully and complete the sentences with one or two words. Let them compare with a partner and then check the answers with the class.

Answers
1 six
2 40,000
3 buy
4 roads
5 important
6 (rich) businessman
7 damage
8 divorce

▶ Ask Ss if there are any words or phrases in the text that they don't understand. Encourage other Ss to explain them before explaining yourself.

6 ▶ Ss discuss the questions in pairs. Get feedback from the whole class.

Grammar | Past Simple Passive

OPTIONAL GRAMMAR LEAD-IN

Write the following incomplete sentences and verbs on the board:

A huge amount of fast food _____ every day.
200 million text messages _____ each day.
Nearly two hours _____ dealing with emails.
Email isn't _____ at home.

Tell Ss that these are sentences taken from the text in Lesson 8.1 about slowing down in a fast world. In pairs, and without looking back at the text, ask them to complete the sentences in an appropriate way. Get feedback and tell the Ss to check their version with the original on pages 80–81. Write the full sentences on the board. Now ask: *How do you think you say this in the past?* Allow Ss to talk about this with a partner and then get feedback. Elicit the correct form.

7a ▶ Focus the Ss on part A of the Active grammar box and get them to complete it with the correct form of the verbs in brackets. Ss check their answers in the text from ex. 4. Elicit the answers and write them on the board.

Active grammar

1 cleaned
2 was sent

b ▶ Focus the Ss on part B of the Active grammar box. Get them to read through the rules and complete example 3 with an appropriate ending. Elicit the answer from the class.

Active grammar

3 a witness

▶ Bring Ss' attention to the grammar reference on page 97.

8 ▶ Refer Ss back to the text in ex. 4 and tell them to underline six more examples of the Past Simple Passive. Get various Ss to read them out for you.

Answers
... he was not paid ... .
All the cars were stolen ... .
Every car was later found ... .
He was called ... .
Blain was arrested ... .
The cars weren't damaged ... .

9 ▶ Ss read the text and choose the correct options. Let them compare with a partner before checking the answers with the whole class.

Answers
1 was given
2 felt
3 was told
4 waited
5 ran
6 took
7 told
8 was arrested
9 was taken

Speaking

10a ▶ Put Ss in pairs. Tell student A to look at the two stories on page 131 and student B to look at the two stories on page 134. Ss complete their stories using the Past Simple or the Past Simple Passive. Go around the class checking their work as they do this.

Answers

Student A		Student B	
1	was arrested	1	was broken into
2	used	2	discovered
3	noticed	3	phoned
4	was sent	4	was arrested
5	was broken into	5	were threatened
6	put	6	demanded
7	decided	7	noticed
8	were caught	8	was arrested

b ▶ Now the pairs work together to retell their stories, using their own words as much as possible.

11 ▶ Ss discuss the questions in small groups. Get feedback from the whole class.

OPTIONAL EXTENSION

Play a game of 'Alibi' with the whole class. Write the following on the board: *Yesterday at 6:00 p.m. a bank in the High Street was broken into by two thieves.*
Choose two of the Ss to be suspects. Tell them they have to leave the class and invent their alibi (explain that this is a reason which is given to the police that proves that they couldn't have committed the crime). They must think of all the details of their alibi. The rest of the class are going to act as police officers. While the suspects are outside inventing their alibi, the rest of the class think of questions to ask them. After a few minutes, call one of the 'suspects' into the classroom to be interrogated by the 'police officers'. When they have finished, the first 'suspect' leaves and the second 'suspect' comes in to be interrogated. If their alibis match exactly, they are innocent, but if they don't match, they are guilty. You can then play this game in small groups.

9 Communication

In this lesson, Ss read some advice on how to negotiate and listen to an unsuccessful and a successful negotiation process. Then they practise negotiating in small groups.

OPTIONAL WARMER

Write *negotiation* on the board and elicit/teach the meaning. Put Ss in small groups to discuss the following questions:
1 *Who do you have to negotiate with in your everyday lives?*
2 *What do you negotiate about?*
3 *Do you usually get what you want?*
Get feedback from the whole class.

---

1 ▶ Focus Ss on the photos and ask them to discuss the questions in pairs. Get feedback from the whole class.

Answers
1
Left photo: (b) family
Top right photo: (a) work colleagues
Bottom right photo: (c) friends

Suggested Answers
2
(a) work colleagues: negotiations about distribution of work, deadlines, days off, etc.
(b) family: negotiations about housework, holidays, TV, finances, etc.
(c) friends: negotiations about free time activities, holidays, presents for other friends, etc.

---

2 ▶ Focus Ss on the five-step negotiation plan. Tell them to read through it and underline anything they don't understand. Go through any problems of comprehension with the whole class.

▶ Ss discuss in pairs whether they agree with all the points or not and if they have anything to add. Get feedback from the whole class.

3a ▶ ◉ 2.26 Tell the Ss that they are going to listen to a boss and an employee negotiating. Ask the Ss, in pairs, to predict what it might be about. Get feedback from various Ss. Read through the questions with the whole class and play the recording. Allow Ss to discuss the answers with a partner before checking with the whole class.

b ▶ ◉ 2.27 Read the question with the whole class. Play the recording. And allow Ss to discuss their answer with a partner before checking with the whole class.

4 ▶ Focus Ss on the *How to...* box and read through the headings for each section. Now play the recording again and ask Ss to number the phrases in the order they hear them. Check the answers with the whole class.

Answers
1 If possible, I'd like to have the day off.
2 I understand what you're saying.
3 I'll work late this week if necessary.
4 I'm very pleased with your work.
5 Thank you very much for your understanding.

---

5 ▶ Divide the class into two groups, A and B. Ss A look at page 131 and Ss B look at page 134. Give Ss time to read through the information with a partner from the same group and discuss how they are going to approach the 'negotiation'.

6a ▶ Two Ss A and two Ss B work together to act out the negotiation process. Encourage them to use language from the *How to...* box. Give them a limited time (e.g. ten minutes) and tell them when to stop.

b ▶ The groups report back to the rest of the class, saying who was most successful at negotiating, and why.

OPTIONAL EXTENSION

Divide the class into two groups, A and B. Tell Ss A that they are going to pretend to be parents who have a teenage son or daughter. Ask them to think of problems they might have with the teenager and what they would like to change. Tell Ss B that they are teenagers and that they must think of problems they have with their parents and what they would like to change. When they have thought of some ideas, reorganise the class so that a student A is with a student B and get the pairs to act out the negotiation. Get feedback from the class to find out how well their negotiations went.

Review and practice

1 ▶

> **Answers**
> 1 can tell
> 2 couldn't take
> 3 can help
> 4 could stand
> 5 can't play
> 6 couldn't sleep
> 7 can't finish

2 ▶

> **Answers**
> 1 Can she read music?
> 2 Could you/Were you able to see the sea?
> 3 How much can he afford (to spend)?
> 4 Could you/Were you able to answer all the questions?
> 5 What can it do?
> 6 How many languages could she/was she able to speak?

3 ▶

> **Answers**
> 1 Tina looked at me <u>sadly</u> and walked away.
> 2 My brother plays the guitar <u>well</u>.
> 3 ✓
> 4 He sat down and opened the letter <u>carefully</u>.
> 5 The children played <u>happily</u> in the park all afternoon.
> 6 ✓
> 7 The security guard <u>politely</u> asked him to leave.

4 ▶

> **Answers**
> 1 More than fifty people were arrested by the police.
> 2 The store was opened at exactly 9 a.m.
> 3 I was paid a lot of money to do the job.
> 4 We weren't met at the airport.
> 5 Everybody was rescued from the ship.
> 6 All the classrooms were cleaned yesterday.

5 ▶

> **Answers**
> 1 interviewee
> 2 qualifications
> 3 bonus
> 4 receptionist
> 5 employee
> 6 work

6 ▶

> **Answers**
> 1 jury
> 2 community
> 3 witness
> 4 arrested
> 5 guilty
> 6 victim

Writing bank

1 ▶ Ss read the text and match the headings (a–d) with the paragraphs (1–4).

> **Answers**
> 1 d Introduction
> 2 b Experience
> 3 a Skills and abilities
> 4 c Interests for future career

2 ▶ Ss read the text quickly and answer the questions.

> **Answers**
> 1 on a professional online website (somewhere people go to 'network' with other professionals)
> 2 because she's looking for a job

3a ▶ Ss complete the *How to…* box with adjectives from the text.

> **Answers**
> 1 committed
> 2 good
> 3 enthusiastic
> 4 keen
> 5 interested

b ▶ Ss underline other phrases in the text that show a clear and positive attitude.

> **Answers**
> I am efficient and have good time-management skills.
> I can deal with pressure … .
> I can speak Spanish and Portuguese fluently.
> I also have some understanding of French and Italian.

c ▶ Ss choose the correct options.

> **Answers**
> 1 good
> 2 interested
> 3 enthusiastic
> 4 committed
> 5 keen

4a ▶ Ss prepare to write a professional profile, using the headings from ex. 1

b ▶ Ss write their profile.

10 Travel

Overview

Lead-in	Revision: Travel
10.1	**Can do:** Describe a holiday **Grammar:** Present Perfect Simple: *just, yet, already* **Speaking and Pronunciation:** Showing interest **Reading:** My backpacking holiday in Brazil
10.2	**Can do:** Make generalisations about customs **Grammar:** Verbs with two objects **Vocabulary:** Greetings and gifts **Speaking:** **How to...** make generalisations **Reading:** Advice for UK business travellers
10.3	**Can do:** Recommend a film **Grammar:** Past Perfect Simple **Vocabulary:** *-ed* and *-ing* adjectives **Speaking and Pronunciation:** Using fillers: *anyway* **Listening:** *The Motorcycle Diaries*
Communication	Talk about a journey **How to...** tell a story in an engaging way
Reference	
Review and practice	
Writing bank	Write about recent travel experiences **How to...** avoid repetition
Extra resources	Active Teach and Active Book

CEFR Can do objectives
10.1 Describe a holiday
10.2 Make generalisations about customs
10.3 Recommend a film
Communication Talk about a journey
Writing bank Write about recent travel experiences

CEFR Portfolio ideas
a) Imagine that you have won a round the world air ticket. You can stop in four different places. When you return, you give a talk to the rest of your class. Prepare your talk. Use a world map to illustrate your journey. Say where you stopped and what you did. Talk about the things you liked and the things you didn't like about your journey. Make a video of your talk.
b) Write an email, giving advice to a friend who lives abroad, but is planning a trip to your country. Use your ideas from Exercise 10 on page 103.
c) What do you hate about travelling by car, bus, train, or plane? Write a magazine article about you ideas. Describe a very bad journey.

Lead-in

OPTIONAL WARMER
Write *travel* on the board. Put Ss in pairs to make a list of eight words that are related to travel. Now put two pairs together and ask them to take it in turns to describe their travel words, without using the actual words. The other pair has to guess the words.

1a ▶ Focus Ss on the words in the box and check they understand them. Explain the difference between a motorbike and a moped (a moped is small and has a low-powered engine, whereas a motorbike is bigger and has a high-powered engine) and coach and bus (a coach is normally for long journeys and a bus for shorter journeys). Ss then say which words they can see in the photos.

b ▶ In pairs, Ss ask and answer questions about what pairs of words from the box have in common. Give them a few prompts on the board and explain any of the words Ss don't understand. Ask various Ss to ask and answer questions for the whole class.

2a ▶ In pairs, Ss write down verb phrases for the different forms of transport. Get feedback from various Ss, then check the answers. Point out that all the verbs in the box take an article except *go by*.

> **Answers**
> catch: a bus, a coach, a ferry, a plane, a train (forms of timetabled public transport)
> get into/out of: a car, a lorry, a taxi, a van
> get on/get off: a bicycle, a bus, a coach, a ferry, a moped, a motorbike, a plane, a train
> go by: bicycle, bus, car, coach, ferry, moped, motorbike, plane, taxi, train
> miss: a bus, a coach, a ferry, a plane, a train
> ride: a bicycle, a moped, a motorbike
> take: a bus, a coach, a ferry, a plane, a taxi, a train

b ▶ In pairs, Ss discuss the difference in meanings. If they only know one of the words, encourage them to talk to their partner about that meaning. Get feedback from Ss.

> **Answers**
> - A *commuter* is a person who lives in one place and travels every day to another place for work; a *traveller* is someone who enjoys going around the world visiting different places.
> - A *journey* refers to the time you spend moving from one place to another using any kind of transport; a *voyage* is a long journey, usually by boat.
> - A *passenger* is someone who is travelling but is not driving or in charge of the vehicle; a *pedestrian* is somebody who is walking in the street.

3 ▶ Ss correct the underlined words individually. Let them check with a partner before you check with the whole class.

> **Answers**
> 1 missed 2 by 3 on 4 off 5 commuters 6 passenger

10.1 Travel companions

Travelling is not always easy and it's not surprising that travel companions often get on each other's nerves. Some companies and many Internet websites now help you find travel companions and give advice on who to choose. They suggest that before your trip, you speak openly about the activities you want to do, the type of accommodation preferred, and your money situation, as well as considering each other's personality traits.

In this lesson, Ss read a travel blog about an annoying travel companion and through this context consider the grammar of the Present Perfect Simple with *just*, *yet* and *already*.

Reading

1 ▶ Ss discuss the questions with a partner. Get feedback, focusing particularly on question 3.

2 ▶ Focus Ss' attention on the photo and ask them what they can see (a woman on holiday, backpacking).

▶ Ss read the travel blog quickly and say which annoying habits are mentioned (he talks a lot, snores and complains). Tell them not to worry about any words they don't understand at this stage.

3 ▶ Ss read the summary of Lucy's blog and find three things that are different from her blog. Let them compare with a partner and then elicit the answers from the whole class.

Answers
1 The summary says that Lucy was worried about travelling with Andy, but in the beginning she thought it was a good idea.
2 The summary says that Andy started talking in his sleep, but he actually started snoring.
3 The summary says that on Wednesday afternoon Andy was shouting and annoying Lucy, but he was singing to himself and this annoyed her.

▶ Ask Ss if there is any vocabulary in the travel blog that they still don't understand and encourage other Ss to explain before doing so yourself.

4a ▶ Ss work in pairs to write a dialogue in which Lucy tells Andy that she doesn't want to travel with him anymore. Go around the class monitoring and picking up any mistakes.

▶ Ss practise their dialogue. Ask for volunteers to roleplay their dialogue for the rest of the class.

b ▶ 🔊 2.28 Tell Ss they are going to listen to the conversation between Lucy and Andy. After they have listened, Ss comment on the dialogue in pairs, saying in what ways it was the same as or different from theirs. Get feedback from the whole class.

Grammar | Present Perfect Simple: *just, yet, already*

5 ▶ Read through the example sentences with the whole class. Then focus Ss on the Active grammar box and tell them to read through the grammar notes and complete the rules with *just*, *yet* or *already*. Check with the whole class and draw their attention to the Reference on page 107.

Active grammar
A   already
B   yet
C   just

▶ Check that the Ss have understood the rules by asking the following questions: *Where do you usually put* just *in the sentence?* (between *has/have* and the Past Participle) *Where do you usually put* already *in the sentence?* (between *has/have* and the past participle or at the end of the sentence) *Where do you usually put* yet *in the sentence?* (at the end) *With what type of sentences do we usually use* yet? (negative and interrogative)

▶ If Ss are having problems with these structures, give them more examples, e.g. *We have just completed the Active grammar box. We have already studied units 1–9. We haven't finished the course book yet.*

6 ▶ Read through the example sentence with the whole class and then ask the Ss to write *just, yet* or *already* in the correct place in the rest of the sentences, using the notes in brackets. Let them compare with a partner and then check the answers with the whole class.

> **Answers**
> 1   Simon's just arrived at the bus station.
> 2   Diana hasn't phoned from the airport yet.
> 3   I've already spent all my holiday money.
> 4   Have you written any postcards yet?
> 5   My parents have just come back from holiday.
> 6   She's already booked the flight.

7 ▶ Put Ss in pairs (A and B) and ask them to look at page 132. Tell them to read the list of things they must do before going on holiday, then ask and answer questions about the things that they have already done or haven't done yet. Get various pairs to ask and answer questions for the whole class.

> **OPTIONAL EXTENSION**
> Tell Ss to think back to a week ago and to write a list of the things they had to do at that point. Now in pairs, ask Ss to show each other their lists. Ss ask and answer questions to find out what their partner has already done and what they haven't done yet.

Speaking and listening

8 ▶ ◉ 2.29 Read through the questions with the whole class and check they understand them. Now play the recording and get Ss to make notes about their answers. Let them compare with a partner and then elicit the answers from the whole class.

> **Answers**
> 1   positive
> 2   Andy and an Australian woman called Emily
> 3   She's put some up on Facebook already and she's going to put some more up today.

Pronunciation | showing interest

9a ▶ ◉ 2.30 Explain to the Ss that we use the tone of our voice to show that we are interested in what someone is saying. Draw the Ss' attention to the Pronunciation bank on page 148.

> **Answers**
> person number 2

▶ Play the recording and tell Ss to notice the intonation and identify which person sounds more interested. Check the answer with the whole class.

b ▶ Play the recording again and ask the Ss to repeat, trying to copy the intonation. Ask a few Ss to read out the sentences for the whole class.

▶ In preparation for the speaking task in ex. 10, refer Ss to audioscript 2.29 on page 158 and ask them to find other ways the listener shows interest in what the other person is saying. Elicit examples from the class (e.g. follow-up questions in general, such as *Did you have a good time? That's amazing! Wow!*)

10a ▶ Ss make notes about a real or imaginary holiday they have had. Go around the class helping with any difficult vocabulary at this point.

b ▶ In pairs, Ss take it in turns to talk and to ask questions about their holidays. Encourage the listener to show interest using the strategies they have seen in ex. 9.

> **OPTIONAL EXTENSION**
> Put Ss in pairs and tell them they are going on holiday and want to find a travel companion to go with them. Ask them to write between six and eight questions they would ask to discover if that person would be a good companion or not. If you feel they need guidance, you can say it's a good idea to ask about accommodation preferences, the amount of money they have to spend, activities they like, etc.
> When they have finished the questions, one member of each pair stands up and moves on to the member of the next pair who is still seated, who interviews him or her for two minutes and takes notes of the answers. Then they move on to the next person, and so on, until the Ss sitting down have interviewed three or four prospective travel companions. At the end, the original pair get back together and look at the notes to decide who they want as their travel partner. Get feedback from the whole class.

10.2 Customs worldwide

Customs vary enormously from culture to culture and successful communication between people from different countries and regions depends in part on an intercultural understanding of those customs and ways of behaving. Failure to comprehend factors such as ways of greeting a stranger, hospitality or certain forms of body language can cause grave problems and embarrassment. This can be of particular importance to people travelling on business, so much so that there has been a remarkable growth in the number of companies who are dedicated to teaching business people about intercultural awareness and competence.

In this lesson, Ss read some advice for UK business travellers and through this context consider the grammar of verbs with two objects.

OPTIONAL WARMER

Write *intercultural differences* on the board and elicit/teach the meaning (the differences between different cultures in ways of behaving and customs). Write the following categories on the board: *timetables*; *food and eating*; *clothes*; *nightlife*; *homes*. Now put Ss in small groups and ask them to think about these categories and brainstorm some intercultural differences that they have noticed between their own culture and other cultures, e.g. when travelling. Get feedback from the whole class.

Vocabulary | greetings and gifts

1 ▶ Focus Ss on the photos and tell them to discuss with a partner what they can see, using the words from the box. Get feedback from the whole class and ask them in which cultures they think this behaviour is common.

Answers
a bow D
a gift E
a handshake A
a kiss B
a wave C

2a ▶ Ss complete the sentences with the correct form of the words from the box. Let them compare with a partner and then ask various Ss to read out the sentences for the whole class.

Answers					
	2	shake hands		4	kiss
1 wave	3	bow			

b ▶ Ss discuss the questions in pairs. Get feedback from the whole class.

Reading

3 ▶ Divide the class into two groups, A and B. Ss A look at the text on page 102 and Ss B look at the text on page 132. Ss read through the text quickly to see which of the things in ex. 2a are mentioned. Tell them not to worry about any vocabulary they don't understand at this stage. Get feedback.

Answers
Student A's text mentions giving gifts and student B's text mentions shaking hands, bowing and kissing.

4a ▶ Ask Ss to read the text again and to make a note about the significance of the things listed in the box. Go around the class helping them with any problems of vocabulary they might have.

b ▶ Pair student As and Bs. Student A asks student B about his/her text.

c ▶ Follow the same procedure with student B asking student A about his/her text.

▶ Tell Ss to close their books and check the answers with the whole class.

Answers
Group A's questions:
1 No, they normally use surnames.
2 in the Middle East.
3 Because they feel uncomfortable if you stand too close.
4 No, your handshake should not be too strong or too weak.
5 Yes, sometimes when greeting Westerners.
6 No, they don't.
Group B's questions:
1 At the end of a visit.
2 Pens or something not available in Japan.
3 No, because four is an unlucky number.
4 No, because the word *clock* is similar to the word for death.
5 Because a lot of the world's best leather products come from South America.
6 No, because red flowers are often associated with romance.

5 ▶ Tell Ss to answer the first question with a partner and get feedback from the class. (This is a traditional English saying which means that when we are in a different country/region, we should adopt the habits and customs of the local people.)

▶ Now ask Ss to discuss the second question in small groups and get feedback. This needs to be handled with some sensitivity, so don't prolong the discussion if some Ss are likely to be offended by the opinions of others.

Grammar | verbs with two objects

6 ▶ Give Ss a few minutes to read through the Active grammar box and then ask them to decide with a partner which of the sentences 1–4 are correct. Get feedback from the whole class.

Answers
Sentences 1, 2 and 4 are correct. Sentence 3 is incorrect.

▶ Ask the following questions to the Ss to check their understanding of the rules:

What is the indirect object usually? (a person); *Where does the indirect object usually come when it is a pronoun?* (first); *What do we add when the direct object is first?* (to)

▶ Focus Ss on the list of verbs at the bottom of the Active grammar box and check they understand them. Tell them to look at the Reference on page 107 and point out the three extra verbs that commonly take two objects (*buy*, *teach* and *write*).

7a ▶ Ss correct the mistakes and then check with a partner. Elicit the answers from the whole class.

Answers
1 You should always *give a tip* to your waiter after a meal.
2 It's traditional to *send your mother* a bunch of flowers on Mother's Day.
3 It's usual for people *to offer old people a seat on the bus.*
4 When guests come to my house for dinner, I like them to bring me a gift.
5 It's best to *tell someone the truth* if you don't like the food they've cooked.
6 It's bad manners *to owe money to people who are not in your family.*

b ▶ In groups, Ss say if they agree with the sentences in 7a and discuss if this behaviour is common in their countries/culture.

8a ▶ Read through the example question with the whole class. In pairs, Ss write five similar questions using the verbs at the end of the Active grammar box.

▶ As Ss write the questions, go around the class monitoring their work. Encourage Ss to self-correct mistakes before correcting yourself.

b ▶ Reorganise the class so that Ss are working with a different partner. Ss ask and answer each other's questions.

▶ Ask some pairs to repeat one of their questions (with answer) for the whole class.

Speaking

9 ▶ Focus Ss on the *How to...* box and ask them to complete the sentences with one word. Ask the Ss to check their answers with the texts from ex. 3 and then get various Ss to read out the completed sentences.

Answers
1 Many
2 tend
3 generally
4 usually
5 probably

10 ▶ In pairs, Ss spend a few minutes thinking about customs in their country in relation to the topics shown in the box and ideas of their own, if they wish. If you have mixed nationalities, group Ss from the same country together. Get them to make some notes about these customs using language from the *How to...* box and help with any vocabulary they need.

▶ Reorganise the class in small groups (of Ss of different nationalities, if possible). Ss then tell the other members of the group their advice. If the Ss are from the same country, see if they agree with each other. Encourage them to use language from the *How to...* box where possible.

10.3 Travel movies

Travel movies are a very popular genre, particularly with movie fans who have a nomadic streak. They allow us to explore the world from our armchairs (or a cinema seat), discovering new places and cultures – or to remember things that we loved about places we've already visited. They can also act as an inspiration for choosing our next travel destination or holiday. Many of these films are successful because they combine beautiful scenery with an interesting plot, a good script and great acting. Some of the most popular travel movies include: *Lawrence of Arabia* (1962); *The Sheltering Sky* (1990); *Thelma and Louise* (1991); *Seven Years in Tibet* (1997); *The Beach* (2000); *A Good Year* (2006).

In this lesson, Ss listen to a radio programme in which a reporter talks about the travel movie *The Motorcycle Diaries* (2004). Through this context, Ss study *-ed* and *-ing* adjectives and the grammar of the Past Perfect Simple.

OPTIONAL WARMER

Write *movies* on the board and ask Ss to write a list of five movies (in English) in pairs. Go around the room checking that their titles are correct and spelt correctly. Now put two pairs together and tell them they are going to play a game of 'charades'. Each pair must take it in turns to mime the titles to the other pair who must guess them.

Listening

1 ▶ Focus Ss' attention on the photo and get them to answer the questions in pairs. Get feedback from the whole class and elicit or tell them the name of the film (*The Motorcycle Diaries*).

2 ▶ ◉ 2.31 Tell Ss they are going to listen to part of a radio programme called *Travellers' Tales* in which the TV reporter, Ben Gardner, is talking about the film *The Motorcycle Diaries*. Read through the topics in the box and make sure everybody understands them. Now play the recording so that Ss can tick the ones Ben mentions. Get feedback from the whole class.

> **Answers**
> He mentions:
> where and when the film is set
> the main actors/characters
> the scenery
> the supporting actors/characters

3 ▶ ◉ 2.31 Ask various Ss to read out the statements for the whole class and then play the recording again so that the Ss can mark them true (T) or false (F). Let them compare with a partner and then check with the whole class.

> **Answers**
> 1 F
> 2 T
> 3 T
> 4 F
> 5 T
> 6 F

4 ▶ Ss discuss the questions in pairs. If you feel it necessary, you can prompt Ss' answers to question 2 by writing titles of travel movies on the board (see the lesson warmer). Get feedback from the whole class.

Vocabulary | *-ed* and *-ing* adjectives

5 ▶ In pairs, Ss answer the questions about the underlined adjectives. Elicit the answers from the class.

> **Answers**
> 1 inspired – describes how the speaker feels (a)
> 2 inspiring – describes what makes the speaker feel this way (b)

▶ Ask the following questions to check further understanding of this difference: *Which adjective is normally used for people?* (inspired) *Which adjective can be used for people and things?* (inspiring)

6 ▶ Ss choose the correct option and then check with audioscript 2.31 on page 158. Get various Ss to read out the sentences for the whole class.

> **Answers**
> 1 amazing
> 2 exciting
> 3 fascinated
> 4 depressing
> 5 surprised
> 6 disappointed

7 ▶ Focus the Ss' attention on the box and check that they understand all the adjectives. Now put the Ss in pairs (A and B). Student A looks at page 132 and student B looks at page 134. Ss take it in turns to ask and answer each other's questions using the adjectives in the box. Encourage them to give more details to explain their choice of adjective. Get feedback from various Ss.

Grammar | Past Perfect Simple

OPTIONAL GRAMMAR LEAD-IN

Write the following question and prompt words on the board:

Had you learned to …

ride a bike / read and write / use a computer / swim / speak a foreign language / cook / drive a car … by the time you were 4 / 10 / 16 / 20?

Demonstrate the complete question by asking one of the Ss: *Had you learned to read by the time you were four?* Elicit the answer, checking that they use *Yes, I had* or *No, I hadn't* and ask follow-up questions, e.g. *Who taught you? When did you learn?* Now, get the Ss to stand up and mingle, asking and answering each other's questions. Encourage them to ask follow-up questions where possible.

8a ▶ Ss look at the example sentences (1–4) in the Active grammar box and decide which of the actions in bold came first. Let them discuss this with a partner and then elicit the answers from the class.

Active grammar

1. had lived
2. had become
3. hadn't thought
4. Had (he) starred

b ▶ Ss look at the rules A and B and choose the correct options. Check the answers with the whole class.

Active grammar

A   before
B   had + past participle

▶ Ask the Ss to turn to the Reference on page 107. Give them a few minutes to read through the information and then ask:

Does the Past Perfect Simple change with the person, e.g. he, we *or* they? (no) *When is the Past Perfect Simple common?* (after verbs of saying and thinking and after when) *What's the short form of* I had eaten? (I'd eaten) *How do we form the negative?* (Elicit both the contracted and full form: *hadn't* and *had not*.) *How do we form the interrogative?* (had + subject + past participle)

9 ▶ Ss choose the correct options. Let them compare with a partner and then check the answers with the whole class.

Answers

1. arrived/had begun
2. saw/had broken down
3. had read/knew
4. hadn't been/was
5. went/had checked-in
6. had arranged/didn't come

10 ▶ Ss complete the sentences with the Past Perfect Simple or Past Simple. Let them compare with a partner and then check the answers with the whole class.

Answers

1. realised/had met
2. Had he finished/saw/had
3. arrived/had left
4. asked/had lost
5. got/had not (hadn't) packed
6. wanted/had forgotten

OPTIONAL EXTENSION

Write the following questions on the board and put Ss in small groups to discuss their answers: *What had you done … by 8 o'clock/11 o'clock this morning? What had your parents done before you were born? How long had you studied English before you started this course?* Get feedback from the class.

Pronunciation | using fillers: *anyway*

11 ▶ 🔵 2.32 Explain that *anyway* is a very common word in English and that we use it as a filler in natural speech. Read the two options with the whole class and tell them they are going to listen to two extracts from the radio programme in ex.2. Play the recording and Ss choose the correct option. Check the answer with the whole class (option b) and draw the Ss' attention to the Pronunciation bank on page 148.

Speaking

12a ▶ Individually, Ss prepare to talk about a film which they enjoyed or which inspired them. They make notes, using the topics from ex. 2 to guide them. Point out that they must include at least two sentences in the Past Perfect Simple. Go around the class, helping them with any vocabulary they may need.

b ▶ Ss talk about their films in small groups. Encourage them to use *anyway* as a filler.

c ▶ Get feedback from the class about which film they would most like to see, and why.

10 Communication

In this lesson, Ss talk about problematic journeys and listen to a man telling a story about an unusual and frightening flight. Then they tell their own travel stories.

1 ▶ Focus Ss' attention on the photos and tell them to answer the questions in pairs. Get feedback from various Ss, writing any new vocabulary on the board.

> **Answers**
> Top left photo: The man's got a puncture in the tyre of his bike.
> Top right photo: The train is overcrowded/packed and the people can't get on
> Bottom right photo: The man is afraid or feeling sick

2a ▶ ● 2.33 Tell the Ss they are going to listen to a man talking about an unusual/difficult journey. Play the recording and the Ss make a note of the two problems he had. Let them compare with a partner and then elicit the answers from the class.

> **Answers**
> His flight was cancelled and the plane couldn't land because there was a lorry on the runway.

2b ▶ ● 2.33 Read through the first part of the *How to...* box with the whole class. Then tell Ss to listen to the recording again and complete the second part. Let them compare with a partner and then check the answers with the whole class.

> **Answers**
> 1 ... suddenly we started climbing again.
> 2 ... this went on for about five minutes.
> 3 ... a lorry had been on the runway.

3a ▶ Read through the prompt questions with the whole class and then get them to make notes about a journey they have had. Go around the class helping with any vocabulary they might need.

b ▶ Focus the Ss back on the *How to...* box and ask them to choose two or three of the sentences to include in their story.

4a ▶ Put Ss in small groups to tell their stories. Encourage follow-up questions.

b ▶ Get feedback from the class about which stories were the most interesting to listen to and why.

> **OPTIONAL VARIATION**
> Ss prepare their travel stories in groups of three. Two of the members of the group must tell a true story and one must tell a false story. Each group then tells their stories to the rest of the class, who must guess which story is false.

Review and practice

1 ▶

Answers
1 already
2 yet
3 just
4 yet
5 just
6 already
7 yet

2 ▶

Answers
1 She hasn't phoned me yet.
2 Natalia has just brought them.
3 Have you moved in yet?
4 I've just painted it.
5 Have you finished it yet?
6 She's already gone home.
7 I haven't asked him yet.

3 ▶

Answers
1 I told him all my secrets.
2 Juan owes me a lot of money.
3 Can I offer you some tea?
4 He promised me a pay rise this month.
5 My grandmother always gives me really good advice.
6 I sent some flowers to the nurse who looked after me.
7 Could you bring us the bill please?

4 ▶

Answers
1 decided/had seen
2 arrived/had missed
3 closed/had left
4 had eaten/felt
5 saw/hadn't studied
6 tried/had forgotten

5 ▶

Answers
I went to the ticket office to buy my train ticket. When I <u>tried</u> to pay for the ticket, I <u>realised</u> I didn't have my wallet. I remembered that when I <u>had got off</u> the bus, someone <u>had pushed</u> past me. I <u>realised</u> that this person <u>had taken</u> my wallet.

6 ▶

Answers
1 shake
2 pedestrians
3 missed
4 passenger
5 waved
6 riding

Writing bank

1 ▶ Ss read the travel blog and answer the questions.

Answers
1 Fatephur Sikri and the Taj Mahal
2 Both

2 ▶ Ss read the text again and complete the sentences.

Answers
1 beautiful
2 miserable
3 excited
4 crowded
5 stunning
6 amazed

3a ▶ Ss answer the questions in the *How to...* box.

Answers
A
2 feeling miserable
3 boy
4 the older boy/tour guide
5 the Taj Mahal
B
1 stunning
2 great
3 amazed

b ▶ Ss rewrite the paragraph.

Suggested answer
We're on holiday in Faro, Portugal. It is a lovely town and the weather is great. Our hotel is called Hotel Bellavista. It is charming and the people are very friendly. They do everything they can to help us. I was surprised – I really didn't expect them to be so kind. There are two beaches near our hotel. We've just come back from the smaller one. I was amazed how clean the sea was. It is completely clear.

4a ▶ Ss prepare to write their travel blog.

b ▶ Ss write their travel blog.

Overview

Lead-in	**Revision:** Influence
11.1	**Can do:** Talk about people who influenced you
	Grammar: *would*: past habits
	Vocabulary: Phrasal verbs
	Reading: Raised by animals
11.2	**Can do:** Discuss adverts and their influence
	Grammar: Articles
	Vocabulary: The media
	Speaking and Pronunciation: Using fillers: *well*, *so* and *erm*
	How to... use persuasive language
	Listening: Advertising on television
11.3	**Can do:** Talk about decisions and plans for the future
	Grammar: *will* and *be going to*: decisions and plans
	Vocabulary: verb + preposition (1)
	Reading: *Yes Man*
Communication	Justify your opinions about people
Reference	
Review and practice	
Writing bank	Write about your opinions of a film
	How to... join ideas and sentences (2) *although* and *however*
Extra resources	Active Teach and Active Book

CEFR Can do objectives

11.1 Talk about people who influenced you
11.2 Discuss adverts and their influence
11.3 Talk about decisions and plans for the future
Communication Justify your opinions about people
Writing bank Write about your opinions of a film

CEFR Portfolio ideas

a) Write a short report on a sports event, music concert, book, fashion show, or TV programme. Say why you liked or didn't like it and explain your reasons.
b) Record a radio advertisement for a sports event, music concert, fashion show, or TV programme. Think about the people who will be interested in the event.
c) Do you usually prefer adverts in magazines, on the Internet, on the radio or on TV? Explain your preference. Give reasons and mention examples.

Lead-in

OPTIONAL WARMER

Write *influence* on the board and ask the Ss to say, with a partner, what they think this word means. Elicit/teach the answer (the power to affect the way someone or something develops, behaves or thinks without using direct force or orders (*Longman Dictionary of Contemporary English*). Now ask the following questions: *Is it a verb or a noun?* (both) *What is the adjective?* (influential)
Now put the Ss in small groups and ask them to discuss the following question: *Who and what influences you in your everyday lives?*
Get feedback from the whole class.

1 ▶ Ask the Ss to look at the words in the box and tick the ones they understand. In pairs, ask them to explain the meaning of the ones they have ticked and then ask various Ss to explain them for the whole class. Explain the words that nobody has ticked.

▶ In their pairs, Ss discuss the questions, using the words from the box to help them.

Suggested Answers
1 In the main photo and the middle left photo, we can see fans. They are often influenced greatly by the sportspeople they support and admire in that they spend a lot of time watching them and talking about them. In the top left photo, we can see an advert for Coca-Cola. Advertising in general deliberately sets out to influence consumer behaviour. The bottom left photo shows an older man, possibly a grandfather, with a young boy. Older generations often influence the upbringing of the young.
2 Often people's ideas and opinions are shaped by the media. The media select the stories we read about and present them in the way they think is appropriate. This affects the knowledge we have of the world and influences the way we think. Also, advertising in the media often affects our choices when we purchase something.

2a ▶ Read through the list with the whole class and check they understand. Now ask Ss to individually tick the phrases they think describe themselves.

b ▶ Ss work in small groups to exchange opinions. Encourage them to give reasons for what they say. Get feedback from the class, asking Ss if they have similar views to the other people in their group.

OPTIONAL VARIATION

Write the following questions on the board: *What was the last thing you bought from a shop? When was the last time you had to make a decision? What influenced your choice in both cases?*
Put Ss in groups to discuss the questions and then get feedback from the whole class.

11.1 Childhood influences

There have been many well-known cases of 'feral' children (children raised in confinement or isolation or by animals in the wild) throughout history. Those children believed to have been raised by wild animals grew up learning the behaviour of their animal 'parents'. They included wolves, apes, bears, gazelles and even an ostrich (Africa, 1945). The authenticity of many of these stories, however, has yet to be proved and there are probably more documented cases of children who have been brought up in isolation rather than by animals. Tales of children raised by animals have also been popular in fiction and in film, notably in *The Jungle Book* and *Tarzan*.

In this lesson, Ss read about Romulus and Remus and the wolf girls, Kamala and Amala. Through this context they learn various phrasal verbs and analyse the grammar of *would* for past habits.

OPTIONAL WARMER

Write *raising a child* on the board and elicit/teach the meaning. Ask: *What are the most important things you have to think about when you are raising a child?* Ss discuss the question in pairs. Get feedback from the whole class.

Reading

1 ▶ Focus Ss on the pictures. Working in pairs, ask Ss to say what they think is the relationship between the people and the animals. Get feedback from the class.

Suggested Answers
The pictures show children who live with or have been raised by animals. (The top photo is from *The Jungle Book* in which the 'man-cub', Mowgli, is raised by animals. The bottom left photo shows a child on all fours and the bottom right photo shows a wolf suckling two children.)

---

2 ▶ Ss read quickly through the text and answer the question. Tell them not to worry about any vocabulary or phrases they don't understand at this point. Check with the whole class (two examples/four children are mentioned).

3 ▶ Read through the questions with the whole class and then tell the Ss to read the text again and answer the questions. Check the answers with the whole class.

Answers
1 the god Mars
2 by the banks of the River Tiber
3 a wolf
4 a shepherd
5 They built a town in the place where they were found.
6 Romulus killed Remus.
7 a wolf
8 Their relationship with the other children was very bad.
9 They could see and hear very well.
10 Amala died after one year in the children's home and Kamala died eight years later.

---

4 ▶ Ss work in pairs or small groups to discuss the questions. Get feedback from the whole class.

Vocabulary | phrasal verbs

OPTIONAL WARMER

Write the following phrasal verbs on the board: *ask someone out*; *go out with someone*; *take someone out*; *grow apart from someone*; *put up with someone/something*; *split up with someone*; *get over someone/something*
Remind Ss that you studied these phrasal verbs in lesson 8.2. Put them in pairs to say what they mean, without looking back in their books or their notes. Now ask different pairs to give definitions. The rest of the class listen and guess the phrasal verb.

---

5 ▶ Ss look at the underlined phrasal verbs in the text from ex. 2 and read the sentence around each one again. Then, Ss match the phrasal verbs (1–6) and the definitions (a–f). Encourage them to use the context to work out the meaning of those phrasal verbs that they don't know. Check the answers with the whole class.

Answers						
	2	f	4	e	6	b
1	d		3	a	5	c

6a ▶ Ss complete the questions with the correct form of the phrasal verb. Let them check with a partner and then check the answers with the whole class.

Answers		
1 did you grow up	4	did you look up to
2 to bring up	5	you picked up
3 you ever looked after	6	you ever come across

---

b ▶ Ss ask and answer the questions in pairs. Encourage them to give detailed answers and to ask follow-up questions. Get various pairs to ask and answer the questions for the whole class.

7 ▶ Focus Ss on the Lifelong learning box. Read through the tip and the example definition and sentences with the whole class, then get Ss to complete the exercise. Go around the class monitoring their work as they do this.

Listening

8a ▶ ⏺ 2.34 Tell the Ss they are going to listen to two people, Emma and George, talking about their childhoods. Play the recording and get them to say who influenced each person the most. Elicit the answers from the class.

Answers
Emma – her grandmother
George – his ice hockey coach

▶ Ask the Ss to talk to a partner about any other information they remember from the recording about the childhood of each person.

b ▶ Ask various Ss to read out the statements and then play the recording again so that Ss can correct the mistakes in each one. Let them compare with a partner and then check the answers with the whole class.

Answers
1   Most of the time, Emma's father worked in Japan and China.
2   Emma usually lived with just her mum.
3   When George first started ice hockey he found it easy.
4   George's sports coach always went to his training sessions.

Grammar | *would*: past habits

OPTIONAL GRAMMAR LEAD-IN

Write the following questions on the board and ask Ss to answer them in pairs:
1 Did both your parents use to work when you were a child?
2 How often did you use to see your grandparents when you were a child?
3 Did you use to play any sports when you were a child?
4 How often did you use to play?
Ask various Ss to answer the questions for the whole class and check they are getting the grammatical structures correct. Remind the Ss that they studied this structure in Lesson 5.3 and that it is used to talk about past habits. Tell them that they are now going to study another similar structure.

9a ▶ Read through the first sentence of the Active grammar box with the whole class. Point out that this use of *would* is different from the use of *would* in the sentence *I would like to go to India.* Get Ss to complete the example sentences and then check their answers with audioscript 2.34 on page 159. Check the answers with the whole class.

Active grammar
1   would look after
2   wouldn't say

▶ Give the Ss a few minutes to read through the rest of the information in the Active grammar box and then ask the following questions to check comprehension:
Can you give me an example of a state verb? (*be, have, believe*, etc.) *What can't we use with state verbs to talk about past habits?* (*would*) *What do we use for an action that happened only once?* (Past Simple)

▶ Write on the board: *What do we use to talk about habits in the present?* Tell Ss to look for the answer in the Reference on page 117. Elicit the answer (*usually*).

b ▶ Ss look at audioscript 2.34 on page 159 and find more examples of *would* + infinitive. Elicit the answers from the class.

Answers
Emma:
I would see him three times a year … .
… I would see her almost every day.
… she would always spend time with me.
George:
… I would see him all the time!
I would play six or seven times a week … .

10a ▶ Ss rewrite the sentences with *would* + infinitive, where possible. Let them check with a partner and then check with the whole class.

Answers
1   My cousin and I would play together for hours.
2   ✗
3   My maths teacher would help me when I didn't understand something.
4   ✗
5   My older brother was my hero, but he wouldn't talk to me much.
6   ✗
7   I would spend hours every day listening to The Beatles in my bedroom.

b ▶ Ss discuss in pairs which of the sentences you could rewrite with *used to* + infinitive and write out the sentences. Get feedback from the class.

Answers
1   My cousin and I used to play together for hours.
2   The footballer Pelé used to be my role model when I was growing up.
3   My maths teacher used to help me when I didn't understand something.
4   ✗
5   My older brother was my hero, but he didn't use to talk to me much.
6   My parents used to be very supportive of me when I was a child.
7   I used to spend hours every day listening to The Beatles in my bedroom.

Speaking

11a ▶ Ss make notes about a person who influenced them when they were growing up. Go around the class helping with vocabulary.

b ▶ In pairs, Ss tell each other about this influential person. Encourage them to use *would* + infinitive and to ask follow-up questions.

OPTIONAL VARIATION

Ss write the name of a person who influenced them as a child and the relationship they had with that person, e.g. *Claire – older sister.* They swap papers with a partner who then spends five minutes thinking of at least five questions they can ask about that person. Ss take it in turns to interview each other.

11.2 The power of advertising

Although advertising has a long history dating back to Ancient Egypt, when merchants hired 'criers' to walk through the streets shouting about the arrival of their ships and their cargo, it wasn't until the emergence of advertising agencies in the late 19th century that it became a fully established institution. Major developments in mass media technology throughout the 20th century made advertising an ever more important industry, both in terms of the money it moved and the influence it had on people's ideas and behaviour. In 2007, an estimated $385 billion was spent on advertising worldwide. Although some claim it is a form of art, others criticise its often manipulative aspect and the way in which it can foster unnecessary consumerism.

In this lesson, Ss study vocabulary related to the media and listen to a radio programme about advertising. Through this context, they study the grammar of articles and practise using persuasive language.

OPTIONAL WARMER

Write *mass media* on the board and ask Ss to discuss in pairs what they think this includes. Get feedback from the class (it's a way of communicating with a large audience and includes such things as newspapers, magazines, TV, radio, the Internet, etc.). Now write the following questions on the board and get Ss to discuss them in groups.
1 How often do you watch TV/listen to the radio/use the Internet/read a newspaper?
2 How do you usually find out what is going on in the world?
3 Do you think these forms of media influence your ideas and your behaviour? In what ways?
Get feedback from the whole class.

Vocabulary | the media

1 ▶ In pairs, Ss divide the words into two groups. Check with the whole class, explaining the meaning of any words the Ss don't understand. (A direct email advert tells carefully chosen potential customers, often people who the company has done business with before, about products and special offers they may be interested in. This is different from a pop-up advert, which simply appears on the screen to anybody who accesses a particular website.)

Answers
a on television: a channel; a commercial break; a documentary; a drama series; a soap opera; a TV advert
b on a computer: a blog; a computer game; a direct email advert; a podcast; a pop-up advert; a search engine

2 ▶ Ss choose the correct options. Let them compare with a partner and then ask different Ss to read out the sentences to check the answers.

Answers
1 advert
2 commercial break/channel
3 pop-up adverts
4 blog
5 computer games
6 search engine
7 documentary
8 podcast

3 ▶ Put Ss in pairs to discuss the questions. Get feedback from the whole class.

Listening

4 ▶ 🌐 2.35 Tell Ss they are going to listen to a radio programme about advertising. Read through the questions with the whole class and then play the recording. Elicit the answers from the class.

Answers
1 annoying, informative and entertaining
2 two

5 ▶ Ask the Ss to talk in pairs about any other information they heard on the radio programme before they do the true/false exercise.

▶ Get various Ss to read out the statements for the whole class and check everybody understands them. Play the recording again so that Ss can mark the statements true (T) or false (F). Let then compare with a partner and then check with the whole class.

Answers					
1 T		3 T		6 T	
2 F		4 F		7 T	
		5 F		8 F	

6 ▶ Ss work in pairs or small groups to discuss the questions. Get feedback from the whole class.

Grammar | articles

OPTIONAL GRAMMAR LEAD-IN

Write the following sentences on the board and ask Ss to complete them with *a/an/the* or *no article (–)*:
1 Is it a good idea to have … TV channel with no adverts? (a)
2 What products are advertised … most on TV? (the)
3 How do adverts persuade people to buy … expensive product instead of a cheap one? (an)
4 Are … adverts a form of art? (–)
Check the answers with the class and then get Ss to discuss their answers in pairs. Now ask the class what the grammatical name is for these types of words (articles).

7 ▶ Ss match sentences 1–4 with the rules in the Active grammar box. Check the answers with the whole class.

> **Active grammar**
>
> A   2
> B   3
> C   1
> D   4

▶ Ask the Ss: *Do we use the article* the *with people's names*? (no) Get them to look at the Reference on page 117 to find the answer.

8 ▶ Ss complete the sentences. Let them compare with a partner and then get various Ss to read out the sentences.

> **Answers**
> 1   the
> 2   the
> 3   (–)
> 4   an
> 5   the
> 6   a
> 7   (–)
> 8   (–)

9 ▶ Ss correct the mistakes in the sentences. Check the answers with the whole class.

> **Answers**
> 1   What's the funniest advert you've ever seen?
> 2   Would you like a job thinking of ideas for adverts?
> 3   What do you do during a commercial break on TV?
> 4   Do you think it's effective to use celebrities in adverts?
> 5   Do any of your clothes have an advert on them?

Pronunciation | using fillers: *well, so* and *erm*

10a ▶ ◉ 2.36 Explain to the Ss that in normal conversation, speakers often use fillers like *well, so* and *erm*. Read through the possible reasons (a–c) for doing this. Play the recording and Ss decide which is the correct option. Check the answer with the whole class.

> **Answer**
> Option c is correct.

b ▶ Ask Ss to look for more examples of *well, so* and *erm* in audioscript 2.35 on pages 159. Draw Ss' attention to the Pronunciation bank on page 148.

Speaking

11 ▶ ◉ 2.37 Read through the questions with the whole class and then play the recording so that Ss can note down their answers. Let them compare with a partner before you check the answers with the class.

> **Answers**
> 1   Advert 1:
>   a hair product (shampoo/conditioner) – ShinePower.
>   Advert 2: 1 a car – G5.
> 2   Open answers
> 3   Open answers

12 ▶ Ss complete the *How to…* box with the headings. Get various Ss to read out the headings and the example sentences for the whole class.

> **Answers**
> 1   a
> 2   d
> 3   c
> 4   b

13 ▶ Tell Ss they are going to prepare an advert. Read through the questions and put Ss in groups to discuss them. Ask one person in each group to take notes. Remind Ss to use fillers in their discussion where possible. Go around the class helping them with any vocabulary they may need as they do this.

> **OPTIONAL EXTENSION**
>
> In their groups, ask Ss to act out their advert for the rest of the class. They should do it as a 'presentation' to the company that makes the product. Give Ss plenty of time to prepare and practise their adverts before they do their 'presentation'. At the end, the class can vote for the best advert.

11.3 Positive thinking

Yes Man (2005) was originally a book by British journalist and comedy producer, Danny Wallace, which tells the true story of what happened to him after a conversation on a bus with a man who suggested he should say 'yes' more often. He decided he would say 'yes' to everything for the next six months and this changed his life radically, taking him on adventures all around the world. In 2008, it was made into a film starring Jim Carrey, who plays a Los Angeles bank employee who changes his boring, uneventful life after attending a 'Yes!' seminar. Although the reviews of the film were mixed, it was a box office success worldwide.

In this lesson, Ss read an email in which the writer talks about a film he has seen and through this context they analyse the grammar of *will* and *be going to*. Then they look at various verbs and their dependent prepositions.

OPTIONAL WARMER

Write the following question on the board: *Would you say 'yes' or 'no' in the following situations?*
1 Your boss asks you to work abroad for the company for a year.
2 A friend suggests travelling around the world for a year.
3 A friend suggests going bungee-jumping (jumping from a high place like a bridge with special equipment).
4 You're invited to go on a reality TV programme like Big Brother.
Put the Ss in small groups to discuss the questions. Encourage them to give reasons for their answers. Get feedback from the whole class.

Reading

1 ▶ Focus Ss on the photo and tell them that it is the poster for a film. Ask them to answer the questions in pairs. Get feedback from various Ss, asking those who have seen the film or read the book to talk about the plot and to give their opinion on the book/film.

2 ▶ Ask Ss to read quickly through Adam's email and answer the question. Tell them not to worry about any words or phrases they don't understand at this point. Get feedback from the whole class.

Answer
He describes the film as both funny and serious.

3 ▶ Ask Ss to read the text again and complete the sentences with between one and three words. Let them compare with a partner before checking the answers with the whole class.

Answers
1	his exams	5	decided to say
2	hilarious	6	self-help class
3	stranger	7	quite weak
4	lonely and boring	8	more positive

▶ Ask Ss if there are any words or phrases in the text that they don't understand and encourage other Ss to explain them before doing so yourself.

4 ▶ Get Ss to discuss the question in pairs and then get feedback from the whole class.

OPTIONAL VARIATION

Write the following contexts on the board: *your family/ flatmates at home; your teachers/classmates at school/university; your boss/colleagues at work; your friends in your social life or in general; neighbours or acquaintances in general.*
Put Ss in small groups and ask them to choose two or three of the contexts. Now tell them to talk about what these people normally ask/invite them to do and ask them to talk about how often they say 'no', and what to. Ask them to talk about how their lives would change if they always said 'yes'. Would their lives be better or worse?

Grammar | *will* and *be going to*: decisions and plans

OPTIONAL GRAMMAR LEAD-IN

Write the following questions on the board, followed by the answers with the words in the wrong order:
1 What did Danny decide when he spoke to the man on the bus?
yes everything will to I say. (I will say yes to everything.*)*
2 What did Adam say to himself when he saw the film?
be I anymore won't negative. (I won't be negative anymore.*)*
3 What did Adam decide after seeing the film?
to be I positive going am more. (I am going to be more positive.*) home not so going I to much stay am at. (I am not going to stay* at home so much.*)*
Put Ss in pairs to order the words without looking back at the text on page 114. Elicit the answers and write them on the board. Ask Ss to underline the verb forms in each sentence and identify the tense. Ask what rules they already know about this tense. If they can't remember, allow them to look back through the book. (*will/won't* + infinitive – future simple for prediction – Lesson 6.1; *be going to* + infinitive for future plans – Lesson 3.1).

5 ▶ Refer Ss back to the underlined sentences in the text from ex. 2 or, if you've done the optional lead-in, the sentences that are written on the board, and ask them to complete the rules in the Active grammar box. Elicit the answers from the whole class.

Active grammar

A   1 We use *will* to talk about decisions about the future, when we decide at the moment of speaking.

B   2 We use *be going to* to talk about future plans and intentions, when we've decided before we speak.

▶ Tell Ss to turn to the Reference on page 117 and give them a few minutes to read through the notes. Now ask the class the following questions:

What phrases can we add to sentences with will/won't *to say that something is not certain? (I (don't) think, maybe* or *I'm not sure) What phrase do we often add to sentences with* be going to*? (I've decided) What do we usually use in questions when we are asking about plans and intentions? (*be going to*) When do we use the Present Continuous and not* be going to *to talk about future plans?* (when it's an arrangement, i.e. important details, time, place, etc. have been decided.)

▶ If you think Ss are not comfortable with these structures yet, write three more examples on the board to illustrate the three tenses:

1 Student: It's cold. Teacher: I'll shut the window.
2 I'm going to study French next year. I don't know where yet.
3 I'm meeting Susan after class in the café across the road.

6 ▶ Ss complete the dialogue. Let them compare with a partner and then ask two of the Ss to read it out for the whole class.

Answers	
1	are you going to do
2	am ('m) going to go
3	will ('ll) go
4	are you going to get
5	am ('m) going to work
6	will ('ll) get

7 ▶ Put the Ss in small groups to ask and answer questions about their plans. Ss will mainly have to use *be going to* but if you feel they are confident enough, you can encourage them to use the Present Continuous if it is an arrangement. Go around the class monitoring their work and get feedback from various Ss.

OPTIONAL VARIATION

Tell the Ss to write a number between 1 and 3 in a secret place. Now put the Ss in groups to ask and answer the questions about their plans. Each student must answer truthfully except when asked the question that corresponds to the number they have written, in which case they must lie. Encourage the other Ss in the group to ask follow-up questions to guess which answer is false.

Vocabulary | verb + preposition (1)

8 ▶ Ss complete the sentences with the prepositions. Ask them to check with a partner and then check with the text from ex. 2. Get various Ss to read out the sentences for the whole class.

Answers					
		3	about	6	in
1	for	4	about	7	to
2	on	5	to	8	in

9a ▶ Tell Ss to cover ex. 8 and then choose the correct options, trying to remember the correct prepositions. When they've finished, get them to uncover ex. 8 and check. Get various Ss to read out the sentences for the whole class.

Answers					
		3	for	6	about
1	to	4	on	7	in
2	in	5	about	8	to

b ▶ Put Ss in pairs to ask and answer the questions. Encourage them to give detailed answers and to ask follow-up questions. Get feedback from the whole class.

Speaking

10 ▶ 🔊 2.38 Tell the Ss they are going to listen to two people playing a game. Read through the questions with the whole class so that the Ss can find out how to play the game and number the questions in the right order. Let them compare with a partner and then check the answers with the whole class.

Answers		
1	You are asked questions and you are not allowed to say 'Yes' or 'No'.	
2	a	3
	b	1
	c	2
	d	4

11a ▶ Ss look at audioscript 2.38 on page 160 and underline the answers they use to avoid saying 'Yes' or 'No'. Then they add six more questions to the ones in ex. 10. Go around the class checking their work as they do this.

b ▶ Ss play the game in pairs.

OPTIONAL EXTENSION

Remind Ss that *Yes Man* was originally a book that was then turned into a film. Write the following questions on the board and put Ss in small groups to answer them:
1 Do you know any books that were later turned into films?
2 Was the film better than the book or the book better than the film? Why?
3 Think of a book you have read recently and imagine you are going to make it into a film. Which actors would you choose to play the main characters, and why?

11 Communication

In this lesson, Ss read an extract from a magazine in which they are asked to choose an influential and important person for their front cover. Then they work in groups to choose the person.

OPTIONAL WARMER

Write the following question on the board: *What do you think about … ?* and add a short list of famous, influential people (e.g. David Beckham, Shakira, Bill Gates, Barack Obama, etc. Make sure you don't include any of the people used in this lesson and try to include some local celebrities if you can). Put Ss in small groups and ask them to answer the question, justifying their opinions. Get feedback from the whole class and then explain that in this lesson they are going to learn how to justify their opinions about people.

1 ► Get Ss to read the text quickly and then answer the question with a partner. Check the answer with the whole class.

Answer
The magazine wants them to choose an important and influential person to appear on the cover of the following month's issue.

2a ► Put Ss in small groups and ask them to individually choose a famous, influential person who they think should be on the cover of the magazine. Tell them they can choose one of the people shown in the photos on page 116 and use the information that is given about that person on page 133, or they can choose somebody else that they know about (if you have access to the Internet, you can ask them to do a bit of research). Ask them to check with each other to make sure they have all chosen different people. If they haven't, some of the Ss must change their person.

b ► Ss make notes about the person they have chosen, following questions 1–4. Encourage them to add some additional information.

3 ► Ss tell the other members of their group about the person they have chosen. Encourage them to try to persuade the others that their person is the best choice. After the discussion, each group should decide who is the best person.

► Get feedback from the class about the people they have chosen and write the names on the board. Where Ss have used their own ideas, ask the rest of the class to ask them questions to find out more about these people. Finally, have a class vote to decide who is the best person to appear on the cover.

OPTIONAL EXTENSION

Repeat the activity but with people that the Ss know personally. Ask them to think of one person each who they believe has been influential in their lives, has achieved a great deal or is special in some way. Ask them to make notes about this person and then put them in groups to talk about their people. They must choose someone for the front cover of the magazine.

Review and practice

1 ▶

Answers
1 both
2 both
3 moved
4 both
5 didn't use to be
6 started
7 both
8 both

2 ▶

Answers
1 a/a/the
2 a
3 the
4 (–)
5 the
6 the
7 (–)/(–)
8 the

3 ▶

Answers
1 will ('ll) go
2 am ('m) going to stay
3 am ('m) not going to do
4 will ('ll) invite
5 am ('m) going to have
6 will ('ll) have

4 ▶

Answers
1 in
2 across
3 in
4 to
5 up
6 about
7 up
8 on

5 ▶

Answers
1 channel
2 blog
3 commercial break
4 pop-up advert
5 documentary
6 search engine

Writing bank

1 ▶ Ss read the text and answer the questions.

Answers
1 They write these kinds of texts because they want to share their opinions with other people. They read them because they want to know other people's opinions after they have seen the film or as recommendations before seeing it.
2 They have different opinions.

2 ▶ Ss read the text again and answer the questions.

Answers
the acting/main stars: Anna47, SimonP, Sunny
the differences between the book and the film: Anna47, SimonP, Sunny
the plot/story: Anna47, Sunny
their overall opinion of the film: Anna47, SimonP, Sunny

3a ▶ Ss read the sentences and then choose the correct underlined words in the *How to...* box.

Answers
1 the same sentence
2 before
4 two different sentences
5 second

3b ▶ Ss complete the sentences.

Answers
1 Although
2 However
3 however
4 although
5 However
6 Although

4a ▶ Ss write some notes about a film.
4b ▶ Ss write their comments about the film.

Overview

Lead-in	Revision: Money
12.1	**Can do:** Discuss imaginary or unlikely situations **Grammar:** Second Conditional **Vocabulary:** Money **Reading:** How much do you want to pay?
12.2	**Can do:** Report what someone said to you **Grammar:** Reported speech **Vocabulary:** Money in education **Speaking:** **How to...** report back on discussions **Listening:** Money in education
12.3	**Can do:** Describe similarities and differences **Grammar:** *both, either, neither* **Vocabulary:** Verb + preposition (2) **Speaking and Pronunciation:** Emphasising details **Reading:** Making baseball history
Communication	Ask survey questions and report the results
Reference	
Review and practice	
Writing bank	Write a formal email/letter **How to...** structure a formal email/ letter
Extra resources	Active Teach and Active Book

CEFR Can do objectives

12.1 Discuss imaginary or unlikely situations
12.2 Report what someone said to you
12.3 Describe similarities and differences
Communication Ask survey questions and report the results
Writing bank Write a formal email/letter

CEFR Portfolio ideas

a) Make a video for a foreign friend who will be visiting your country. Show the notes and coins which are used in your country. Show each note and coin. Explain how much each one is worth by saying what you can buy with it.
b) FOR SALE: English coursebooks in good condition. Contact Elaine.Stubbs@mail.co.uk
You read the advertisement above. Write to Elaine Stubbs and ask her which coursebooks she has, which level they are for and how much they cost. Also ask if you can pay with a credit card.
c) A friend who teaches English to adults phones you. He/She wants to know about the English course you have just done. Prepare the phone conversation with your partner. Record the conversation.

Lead-in

OPTIONAL WARMER

Write *money* on the board and tell Ss to work in pairs to brainstorm words related to the topic. Give them a few minutes and then get feedback from the whole class. Write the words on the board. Now tell the Ss, in pairs, to choose two or three of the words and write a definition of each word. Then ask Ss to read out their definitions without saying the word and the rest of the class guess the word.

1a ▶ Tell Ss to look at the photos in pairs and say what they can see, using words from the box. Get feedback from the whole class and write the new words on the board.

Answers	
Main photo: coins	Middle photo: a cash till; cash
Top photo: a bill	Bottom photo: a discount

b ▶ Ss discuss the difference in meaning between the pairs of words. Allow them to use dictionaries if you have them. Get feedback from various Ss, and explain any words that they don't understand.

Answers
- A *bargain* is something which is cheaper than you expected. A *discount* is when money is taken off the usual price.
- A *coin* is made of metal and a *bank note* is made of paper.
- A *cashpoint* is a machine in or outside a bank or shop and you can take money out of it. A *cash till* is used in a shop or a restaurant, and it's where the money you have paid is put.
- A *credit card* is a small plastic card which allows people to buy goods without using cash and pay for them later. *Cash* is coins and notes.
- A *currency* is the money of a country, e.g. pounds, dollars, and an *exchange rate* is the price at which we buy and sell money.
- A *receipt* is what we get after we buy something and a *bill* is a piece of paper that tells us how much we have to pay.
- A *wallet* is for notes or bank cards and a *purse* is for coins.

2 ▶ Ss ask and answer the questions in pairs. Get feedback from several Ss.

3a ▶ Ss individually choose the correct words. Let them compare with a partner and encourage them to discuss why they think the one they have chosen is correct. Check the answers with the whole class.

Answers					
1	spending	3	afford	6	won
2	save	4	owe	7	earn
		5	withdraw		

▶ Write the other words that haven't been used (*borrow* and *lend*) on the board and elicit the meanings.

b ▶ Ss ask and answer the questions in pairs. Encourage them to give detailed answers and ask follow-up questions.

12.1 Honesty is the best policy

An 'honesty box' is a box at locations like airports, stations or farms where people are asked to deposit their money in a box (unsupervised) in exchange for some goods, e.g. a newspaper or a service such as parking facilities. The system was used by the British chain of newsagents WH Smith at Heathrow airport and it was a great success. It is also very common in the US. The band Radiohead made musical history when they introduced their own idea of an 'honesty box' by releasing an album digitally and allowing fans to download it at a price they felt appropriate. More recently, this term has become well-known in a different way as an application on Facebook. This application allows people to send anonymous messages in which they can tell the truth to a friend without that person knowing who they are.

In this lesson, Ss read a text about what influences how honest people are and study some money vocabulary. Through this context, they consider the grammar of the Second Conditional.

OPTIONAL WARMER

Write *honesty* on the board and ask Ss what part of speech it is (a noun). Elicit/teach the adjective and the prefix to form the opposite of both (*honest*; *dishonest*; *dishonesty*). Ask Ss to discuss *honesty* in pairs by asking: *In what kind of situations are people sometimes dishonest? What is a white lie?* (a lie told to avoid hurting somebody's feelings) *In what situations would you tell a white lie?* Get feedback from the whole class.

Reading

1 ▶ Ss discuss the questions with a partner. Get feedback from the whole class.

2 ▶ Tell Ss to read through the text quickly and answer the question. Tell them not to worry about any words they don't understand at this stage. Check the answer with the whole class.

Answers
One factor is whether you think you are being watched and the other is loyalty.

3 ▶ Ask Ss to read the text again and complete the sentences with one word. Let them compare with a partner and then ask various Ss to read out the completed sentences.

Answers
1 fares
2 queue
3 decide
4 eyes
5 change
6 small

▶ Ask Ss if there are any words or phrases in the text that they don't understand. Encourage other Ss to explain before explaining them yourself.

4 ▶ Ss discuss the questions in pairs. Get feedback from the whole class.

Vocabulary | money

5a ▶ Ss match the beginnings (1–8) with the endings (a–h) of the questions. Let them compare with a partner and then check with the whole class.

Answers
1 f
2 d
3 b
4 h
5 g
6 c
7 e
8 a

b ▶ Ss ask and answer the questions in pairs. Encourage them to give reasons and ask follow-up questions where possible. Get feedback from the whole class.

Grammar | Second Conditional

OPTIONAL GRAMMAR LEAD-IN

Write the following stem sentences on the board:
If a cashpoint gave me too much money, I would … .
If I won a lot of money, I would … .
Ss complete the sentences individually and then compare with a partner. Get feedback from a few Ss and then elicit/teach the name of this grammatical structure (Second Conditional).
Remind Ss that they studied the First Conditional in lesson 7.1 and ask them if they remember the structure. If they don't, let them look back at the Active grammar box in that lesson. Ask Ss to think of an example First Conditional sentence in pairs. Get various Ss to read out their examples and choose one to write on the board (e.g. *If it is expensive, I won't buy it.*). Elicit the use of this structure (to talk about a possible situation in the future).

6 ▶ Focus Ss on the Active grammar box and read through the example sentences with the whole class. Now tell Ss to read through the rules and choose the correct alternatives. Check the answers with the whole class.

Active grammar
1 future
2 present
3 Past Simple
4 only after the 'if' clause

▶ Write the following sentences on the board:

1 If I won the lottery, I'd travel around the world.

2 If you were English, you wouldn't be in this class now.

Ask the Ss which sentence refers to an imaginary situation in the present (2) and which refers to an unlikely future (1).

▶ Tell Ss to turn to page 127 and give them a few minutes to read through the grammar notes. Now check their understanding by asking the following questions.

Does the 'if' clause come first or second? (either)

What do we use instead of would *when we are less certain?* (*might*)

▶ Write the following sentence openers on the board: *I would go … . I would not go … .* and ask Ss how they can be contracted (*I'd go; I wouldn't go*). Point out that the first contraction cannot be used in short answers in affirmative sentences, e.g. *'Would you like a coffee?'* *'Yes, I would.'*

▶ Write the following sentence on the board: *If I were rich, I'd travel around the world.* Explain to the Ss that *were* is normally used instead of *was* in Second Conditional sentences with *I* and *he/she/it* (although in spoken English both can be used). This is what is sometimes referred to as the subjunctive mood.

7 ▶ Ss complete the sentences. Let them compare with a partner and then check the answers with the whole class.

Answers
1 gave/would ('d) give
2 had/would ('d) pay
3 would not (wouldn't) pay/asked
4 earned/would ('d) give
5 would ('d) eat/was not (wasn't)
6 Would you leave/was

8 ▶ Read through the example sentences with the whole class and then get Ss to complete the second sentences so that they mean the same as the first. Let them compare with a partner and then check the answers with the whole class.

Answers
1 If my bank didn't give good rates of interest, I would ('d) change it.
2 If the waiter didn't work so hard, I would not (wouldn't) leave him a big tip.
3 We'd go to Australia if it didn't cost so much.
4 He'd pay in cash if he had enough change.
5 If I didn't want to earn more money, I would not (wouldn't) work longer hours.

OPTIONAL EXTENSION

Write *If this person were a country, which country would they be?* on the board. Explain that you are going to play a game. Choose a student but don't tell the class who you have chosen. Now Ss have to ask you questions, like the one above, in order to guess that student. In each question, *country* is substituted for words such as *food, colour, type of music, famous actor/actress, film, book, clothes, animal.* When somebody guesses, it is their turn to choose a person and the game begins again.

Speaking

9 ▶ Ss work in pairs or in small groups to discuss the questions. Get feedback from the whole class.

OPTIONAL EXTENSION

In pairs, Ss write two more situations related to honesty. These don't necessarily have to be about money, they could also be about relationships, work, school, etc. Ss then stand up and mingle, asking each other what they would do in these situations. After a short time, Ss sit down and compare answers with their original partner. Finally, they report back to the rest of the class.

12.2 The price of success

In order to increase student motivation, many schools offer prizes and awards for high achievement. This idea has been taken one step further by a school in Bristol, in the west of England, where students are being given quite large sums of money for meeting their targets. This system is also becoming increasingly popular in the US, especially in the poorer areas of New York, Washington and Dallas. These programmes are often funded by charities and sometimes include paying the teacher as well as the pupil for high achievement rates. While some teachers, students and indeed businessmen and women and economists seem to like the idea, others are critical of the 'commercial' values it conveys and believe that students should be motivated because they want to do well, not because they will get paid.

In this lesson, Ss listen to a radio news report about money in education and look at related money vocabulary. Through this context they analyse the grammar of reported speech.

OPTIONAL WARMER

Write *motivation* on the board and elicit/teach the meaning (something that makes us want to do something/an incentive). Now ask the Ss to discuss the following questions in pairs or small groups: *What motivates students to do well? How well did you do at school/university? How motivated were you at school/university?* Get feedback from the whole class.

Listening

1 ▶ Focus Ss on the newspaper headlines and get them to discuss the possible stories in pairs. Get feedback from the whole class.

2a ▶ Focus on the Lifelong learning box and tell Ss that it is very useful to make predictions about what you are going to hear before doing a listening task. Tell them to read through the tips and make predictions with a partner. Get feedback from the whole class.

b ▶ 2.39 Play the recording and Ss identify which of the news stories from ex. 1 are mentioned. Check with the whole class.

Answers
Average graduate owes £15,000
Prizes for grades
Do your homework for $100

3 ▶ Read through the questions with the whole class and then play the recording again. Ss make notes of their answers and then compare with a partner. Ask various Ss to answer the questions for the whole class.

Answers
1 They get a loan from the bank.
2 They owe around £25,000.
3 £11,000
4 £500
5 Because it rewards every student for doing well, not just the best ones.
6 She doesn't like it. She thinks students should study because they want to do well.
7 a laptop computer
8 MP3 players

4 ▶ Ss discuss the question in pairs. Get feedback from the whole class.

Vocabulary | money in education

5 ▶ Ask Ss to find the phrases from the box in audioscript 2.39 on page 160. Tell them to discuss the meaning of the phrases in pairs. Encourage them to use the context to guess the meaning when they don't already know it. Ask various Ss to explain the meaning of each one for the whole class. Point out that the *b* in *debt* is silent and model the pronunciation.

6a ▶ Ss complete the sentences with one word of the verb phrases from ex. 5. Let them compare with a partner before checking the answers with the whole class.

Answers
1 grant/fees
2 loan
3 debt
4 reward
5 prize

b ▶ Ss ask and answer the questions in pairs. Ask various Ss to answer the questions for the whole class.

Grammar | reported speech

OPTIONAL GRAMMAR LEAD-IN

Write the following on the board. Ss rearrange the words to make sentences, working in pairs.
1 *told The teacher was exam not us difficult the.* (The teacher told us the exam was not difficult.)
2 *had My exam failed she sister her said.* (My sister said she had failed her exam.)
Ask Ss: *What's the name of this grammatical structure?* (reported speech)
What do you think each person actually said? Ss to discuss this in pairs then get feedback. (1 'The exam is not difficult.' 2 'I have failed my exam.')

7a ▶ Focus Ss on part A of the Active grammar box and get them to complete the sentences (1–7). Ask various Ss to read out the answers.

Active grammar

1 were working
2 would continue
3 was
4 had made
5 had earned
6 was going to buy
7 could afford

b ▶ Ss complete parts B and C of the Active grammar box. Let them compare with a partner and then elicit the answers from the class. Point out that in spoken English *that* is usually omitted.

Active grammar

1 said
2 told
3 she/her

▶ Tell the Ss to turn to the Reference on page 127 and give them a few moments to read through the information. Now ask: *When don't we change the tenses in reported speech?* (when what somebody said is still true)

8 ▶ Ss change the sentences to reported speech. Let them compare with a partner and then check the answers with the whole class.

Answers

1 He said (that) he was going to save money for university.
2 She told me (that) her school gave prizes to the top students.
3 He said (that) he didn't want to be in debt for years.
4 She told me (that) she would pay back the loan as quickly as possible.
5 He said (that) they had offered him a scholarship to study medicine.
6 She told me (that) her school was taking part in a reward scheme.
7 He said (that) he couldn't afford to pay the fees for his university course.

OPTIONAL EXTENSION

Write the following stem sentences on the board: *I love going … . Yesterday I … . Next week I'll … . At the moment I'm reading … . I can … .* Put Ss in pairs and get them to choose one of the stems and complete it orally with true information about themselves. One of the pair then stands up and moves to a different pair. They report what their last partner said and complete another stem sentence. They then move pairs again and repeat the same procedure. Do this five times. Then get feedback from various Ss about what they have found out.

Speaking

9 ▶ Ask Ss to look at audioscript 2.39 on page 160 and to complete the *How to…* box. Get various Ss to read out all the example sentences, including the ones they have completed, for the whole class.

Answers

1 Most of us … .
2 Some of us … .
3 We all agreed … .

10a ▶ Put the Ss in small groups and get them to elect a 'secretary' who will take notes of the group's opinions. Ss then discuss the questions.

b ▶ Each group reports back to the class using reported speech structures where relevant.

OPTIONAL VARIATION

Write the following statements on the board: *University should be free. School uniform should be compulsory. Children should be able to leave school at fourteen. School holidays should be longer.* Put the Ss in groups and ask them to choose one of the statements. Ss then discuss it and one person takes notes. Each group reports back to the rest of the class, who say if they agree or disagree with what has been said. Alternatively, rearrange groups and ask Ss to report back in these small groups.

12.3 The $1 million baseball

It is thought that baseball, a sport which is played between two teams each of nine players, is based on the British game of rounders (a simple bat and ball game played mostly in schools) and was taken to the US by British and Irish immigrants. The first American league was created in New York in 1857 and baseball quickly became what we might call America's national sport. Although it has enjoyed many years of unchallenged popularity, it does seem that in recent years, American football has started to attract more fans.

In this lesson, Ss read about a million dollar baseball and study verbs with dependent prepositions. Through this context, they analyse the grammar of *both*, *neither* and *either*.

OPTIONAL WARMER

Play 'Twenty questions' with sports. Tell Ss that you are thinking of a sport and that they have to guess that sport by asking *yes/no* questions, e.g. *Do you play inside? Do you play in a team?* When Ss have guessed, they then play the game in small groups.

Reading

1 ▶ Ss discuss the questions in pairs. Get feedback from the whole class.

Answers
1 baseball
2 The aim of the game is to get more runs than the opposing team. The pitcher throws the ball and the batter hits it. A run is scored when a batter hits the ball and then runs to a base. A home run is when the batter runs around the four bases before the opposing team reach a base with the ball.
3 Ss' own answers

2 ▶ Read the questions with the whole class and Ss read quickly through the text to find the answers. Tell Ss not to worry about any vocabulary they don't understand at this stage. Elicit the answers from the class.

Answers
1 The argument was about who owned the record-breaking baseball.
2 No, it didn't have a happy ending because all their money went on lawyers' fees.

3 ▶ Read through the questions with the whole class and tell Ss to read the text again and answer the questions. Let them compare with a partner and then check with the whole class.

Answers
1 He broke the record for the number of home runs in a season.
2 Because it was the ball that broke the record.
3 Popov
4 Other fans knocked it out of his hands.
5 A certificate to say the ball was his.
6 He took Hayashi to court.
7 four months
8 That the ball belonged to neither of them.

4 ▶ Ss discuss the question in pairs. Get feedback from the whole class.

Vocabulary | verb + preposition (2)

OPTIONAL VOCABULARY LEAD-IN

Write the following verbs on the board: *revise, spend, worry, complain, respond, succeed, appeal, believe.* Remind Ss that they studied these verbs in lesson 11.3 and that each one has a dependent preposition. Ask Ss, in pairs, to try to remember their dependent prepositions. (*revise for, spend on, worry about, complain about, respond to, succeed in, appeal to, believe in*).

5 ▶ Focus Ss on the three sentences and ask them to look back at the text in ex. 2 to complete the sentences with the correct preposition. Check the answers with the whole class.

Answers	1 for	2 with	3 to

▶ Explain to Ss that these verbs are often followed by these prepositions, but that some verbs may be followed by different prepositions in different contexts. Write the following sentence on the board as an example and teach/elicit the difference between: *play for a team* (*for* is used before the group you belong to) and *play with your friends* (*with* is used before your partners in the game).

6 ▶ Ss complete the sentences. If you have dictionaries, allow the Ss to consult them where necessary. Let them compare with a partner and then check the answers with the whole class.

Answers					
1 for	3 for	6 for
2 to	4 from	7 to
	5 with	8 on

7 ▶ Ss ask and answer the questions with a partner. Get feedback from several Ss.

OPTIONAL EXTENSION

In pairs, Ss write similar questions to those in ex. 7, using two or three of the verbs (+ preposition) from ex. 5 and ex. 6 that have not been used in ex. 7, i.e. *play for, agree with, belong to, apologise for, apply for, wait for, listen to.* Tell them to write 'realistic' questions that their classmates will actually be able to answer. Go around the class, checking their work. Ss now stand up and mingle, asking and answering each other's questions.

Grammar | *both, either, neither*

> **OPTIONAL GRAMMAR LEAD-IN**
>
> Write the following questions on the board. In pairs, Ss answer them, looking back at the text if necessary.
> 1 *What did both Popov and Hayashi believe?* (That the ball belonged to both of them.)
> 2 *Who said it belonged to neither of them?* (the judge)
> 3 *Do you think either of them was right?* (Ss' own answers)
> Get feedback about the answers and then underline *both, neither* and *either* and tell Ss this is the grammar point you are going to study.

8 ► Focus Ss on the Active grammar box and tell them to read the rules (A–C) and complete the sentences (1–6). Let them compare with a partner and then get various Ss to read out the completed sentences.

> **Active grammar**
> 1 both
> 2 Both/and
> 3 either
> 4 Either/or
> 5 neither
> 6 neither/nor

► Read through the rule that explains how *both/either/neither* can be used with *of* + pronoun/*the*/*these*, etc. and get Ss to complete sentences 7–9. Ask various Ss to read out the completed sentences for the whole class.

> **Active grammar**
> 7 neither of them
> 8 Both of them
> 9 either of them

► Write further examples on the board if Ss are unsure of this point. Make them relevant to Ss in the class, e.g. Both *Pablo and Maria are Spanish.* Both *of them are Spanish.* Neither *Pablo nor Maria is English.* Neither *of them is English. Do you live with* either *Pablo or Maria? Do you live with* either *of them? I don't live with* either *Pablo or Maria. I don't live with* either *of them.*

► Point out the fact that *both* and *neither* are usually used in affirmative sentences whereas *either* is usually used in negatives or interrogatives. Write the following sentence on the board: *Both Pablo and Maria didn't come to the last class.* Tell Ss that we don't say this in English and ask them to rewrite it with a partner. Elicit the answer from the class (*Neither Pablo nor Maria came to the last class*). Draw the Ss' attention to the Reference on page 127.

9a ► Ss correct the mistakes in five of the sentences. Let them compare with a partner and then check with the whole class.

> **Answers**
> 1 I like both buying expensive things <u>and</u> finding bargains.
> 2 I don't like <u>either</u> borrowing or lending money.
> 3 <u>Neither</u> of my two best friends likes going shopping at all.
> 4 I <u>neither</u> pay for things by cheque <u>nor</u> by credit card – always in cash.
> 5 ✓
> 6 My best friend and I <u>both</u> like doing the lottery.

b ► Ss change the sentences in ex. 9a so that they are true for them. Put them in pairs and ask them to tell each other their sentences, giving reasons or explanations where necessary.

Pronunciation | emphasising details

10a ► ⬤ 2.40 Tell Ss to listen to the dialogue and note down the four things that the two women have got in common. Check the answers with the whole class.

> **Answers**
> They both like clothes shopping and finding bargains. They both pay in cash because neither of them has got a credit card.

b ► Explain to the Ss that when we want to emphasise certain details about what we are saying, we put extra stress on particular words. Draw their attention to the Pronunciation bank on page 148. Play the recording again and get the Ss to note down which three words are stressed the most. Elicit the answers from the class.

> **Answers**
> clothes (stressed twice), cheap, always

Speaking

11a ► Focus Ss on the words in the box. Then ask them to discuss these things in pairs to find four things they have in common.

b ► Ss report back to the rest of the class about what they found out. Alternatively, rearrange the pairs and ask the Ss to tell their new partner about what they have in common with their original partner.

> **OPTIONAL EXTENSION**
>
> Ask the Ss to make a list of five things that are very expensive. Get feedback from the class and write the words on the board. Now write the question: *Are these things worth so much money?* Explain the meaning (is the price of these things a good or fair price?) and put the Ss in pairs to discuss the question in relation to the different things. Get feedback from various pairs to see if they agreed or disagreed.

12 Communication

In this lesson, Ss listen to the results of a market survey on attitudes to money. They then write and conduct their own survey and report back on the results.

<blockquote>
OPTIONAL WARMER

Write <i>market research</i> on the board and elicit/teach the meaning. Now put Ss in pairs to discuss why people do market research and to make a list of things that the research is usually about.

Get feedback from the whole class and ask the Ss if any of them have ever been asked to take part in market research and what kind of questions they were asked.
</blockquote>

1 ▶ Ask the Ss to ask and answer the survey questions in pairs. Get feedback from various Ss.

2 ▶ 🔘 2.41 Tell the Ss they are going to listen to someone from Money Matters reporting the results of their survey. Read through the numbers/statistics with the whole class and then play the recording so that they can note down what they refer to. Let them compare with a partner and then check with the whole class.

<blockquote>
Answers
1 were savers
2 were spenders
3 weren't sure or a bit of both
4 would lend £50 to a friend
5 would be worried about doing so in case it spoilt their friendship
6 said they used a credit card regularly
7 paid off their bill completely at the end of each month
</blockquote>

3a ▶ Focus the Ss on the topics from the box and get them to choose one with a partner. Alternatively, allocate a topic to pairs of Ss to ensure that you have a variety.

▶ Ask the pairs to write survey questions about the topic using the prompts (1–6). Go around the class, checking their work as they do this.

b ▶ Ask Ss to mingle asking their questions and making a note of their answers. Alternatively, form small groups, with one member of each pair in different groups so that they can ask their questions.

4 ▶ The original pairs get back together and collate their results. Get them to write one or two sentences to report the results for each question using the language from ex. 2 and audioscript 2.41 on page 160.

5 ▶ Each pair gives an oral presentation of their results for the rest of the class. Get feedback to see if the Ss found any of these results surprising.

Review and practice

1 ▶

Answers
1 I'd do things differently if I <u>had</u> my life again.
2 I'd buy a dog if I <u>didn't</u> live in a city.
3 What <u>would</u> you do if you saw an accident in the street?
4 If Karla studied more, she would <u>pass</u> her exams.
5 If I <u>had</u> Pete's address, I'd send him a birthday card.
6 People would understand me more easily if my English <u>was/were</u> better.
7 What would you take <u>if</u> you went on a cycling holiday in France?
8 If you <u>had</u> more time, would you read more?

2 ▶

Answers
1 had/would ('d) buy
2 would be/spoke
3 got/wouldn't be
4 would ('d) feel/phoned
5 didn't work/wouldn't be
6 would ('d) do/had
7 found/would ('d) take
8 failed/would ('d) retake

3 ▶

Answers					
1	tell	3	say	6	told
2	told	4	said	7	tell
		5	say		

4 ▶

Answers
1 I thought you said you weren't going home soon.
2 I thought you said you wouldn't see Steve and Jim tomorrow.
3 I thought you said you had a lot of time at the moment.
4 I thought you said they hadn't borrowed your car for the weekend.
5 I thought you said you hadn't talked to Tara.

5 ▶

Answers
1 Both men were wearing long black coats.
2 Neither hotel <u>has</u> a swimming pool.
3 ✓
4 ✓
5 I'm afraid the maths teacher has had problems with <u>both</u> of your sons.
6 I don't think I like either of her brothers.
7 ✓

6 ▶

Answers					
1	pension	3	reward	5	depends
2	argue	4	borrow	6	tax

Writing bank

1 ▶ Ss read the email and answer the questions.

Answers
1 He's writing to a language school to find out about Spanish Language intensive courses in the summer.
2 He wants to know about accommodation, dates/times of courses and other students.

2 ▶ Ss read the email again and answer the questions.

Answers
1 no
2 Yours faithfully,
3 one
4 no
5 indirect questions

3a ▶ Ss complete the *How to...* box with the headings.

Answers
1 a
2 d
3 c
4 b

b ▶ Ss complete the sentences with three words.

Answers
1 be grateful if
2 like to know
3 tell me if
4 be possible to
5 am interested in
6 would prefer not

4a ▶ Ss prepare to write a formal email/letter.

b ▶ Ss write the email/letter.

Track 1.3

M = Man, W = Woman.

W: Hey, Jerry, I'm making some coffee … would you like some?

M: Mmmm … ?

W: Coffee? … Would you like some coffee?

M: Mmm? Oh, yes.

W: What are you reading that's so interesting … ?

M: It's an article about Valentino Rossi. You know – the motorbike racer. It's fascinating!

W: He's from Italy, isn't he?

M: That's right – and he's very successful – one of the best motorbike racers ever.

W: Is he the world champion, then?

M: He's actually won nine world championships. It says here that he's won nearly half of all his races in his career …

W: Really? That's amazing!

Track 1.4

M = Man, W = Woman.

M: Yes … The article is about his typical day – it's quite surprising actually!

W: Really? Why's that?

M: Well, his race days are very busy and stressful … and he works very hard. You know, he gets up early – at about six or seven o'clock and prepares for the race in the morning. Then he races in the afternoon.

W: Yes, I'm sure it's really busy … What's surprising, then?

M: Well, most sportspeople work really hard every day, and spend all their time training … but Rossi's 'normal' days – when he doesn't go to a race – are very relaxing. He has quite a lazy lifestyle actually! He says that his normal life is like being on holiday!

W: What does he do?

M: Well, he gets up late … He says he isn't a morning person.

W: What time does he get up?

M: He gets up at eleven o'clock …

W: Eleven o'clock!

M: Yes, and he's always quiet in the mornings. He doesn't talk to his family for the first hour!

W: Oh, same as me! I don't chat to anyone in the morning. Sorry, anyway, what about Rossi's training? Does he go to the gym or something?

M: Yes, he needs to stay fit for his racing, so he goes to the gym between twelve and two in the afternoon.

W: Really? Only two hours in the gym.

M: Mmm … it's not much, is it? I think it's quite an unusual routine for a top sportsperson.

W: Yeah, I sometimes go to the gym for two or three hours.

M: Do you?! Really? How often do you go to the gym?

W: Well, I go about once a week, I suppose!

M: No, you don't! You go about twice a year!!

W: Oh, ok … Anyway, back to Rossi … What does he do for the rest of the day?

M: Umm … it says that in the afternoon, he often listens to music and plays computer games. And he sometimes watches a film.

W: What about the evening? Does he go out late?

M: Yes, he does!! He hardly ever goes to bed early. His evenings are fun and he usually has a plan to go out with friends. He likes going out to parties and clubs. He's a real party animal apparently … He usually goes to bed about three or four in the morning!!

W: That's late!!

M: Yes, he says he's got a lot of energy after 2:00 a.m.

W: What about before a race day? What time does he go to bed then?

M: Before race days, too … he goes to bed at two or three in the morning … and then he usually wins the race!!

W: Wow! Rossi's life is very exciting! My life is really boring! I'd like to have his lifestyle!

M: Me too.

Track 1.6

M = Man, W = Woman.

M: So, let's see … what time do you get up … you know, on a work day?

W: Well, um … I suppose I usually get up at about six o'clock during the week.

M: Six o'clock!!

W: Yes … it's usually about six o'clock.

M: Are you serious?! Why do you get up so early?

W: Um … I often go running in the mornings before work … for about half an hour in the park.

M: Do you?!

W: Well, yes … I mean, I like starting the day with some exercise.

M: Really? I don't!

W: I find it wakes me up … What about you? How often do you do exercise or sport during the week?

M: Oh, probably about four or five times a week.

W: Really? Me too. What kind of exercise do you do?

M: Well … I don't really like going to the gym. It's really boring.

W: Yes, that's the same as me.

M: So, I usually go for a swim after work – you know, Monday to Thursday … I don't usually go on Fridays.

W: What do you do on Fridays then? Do you go out?

M: Yes, of course. It's the end of the week … I always go out with friends.

W: Yes, definitely … It's the start of the weekend.

Track 1.7

Stig

I'm learning Japanese at the moment which is quite a hard language. I want to speak it erh because my wife's parents don't speak English they speak only Japanese. Erh I'm quite good at speaking now and my listening's not bad. The most difficult thing about learning Japanese is learning to read and write. There are so many letters in the Japanese alphabet, so I really want to improve my reading and writing.

Tessie

Erm right well erm I am learning Spanish at the moment erm erm I'm I have decided to learn Spanish because I I I would I'm dreaming of going and living in erm Latin America erh and erm I'm quite good at understanding erm what people say in Spanish because I already speak good French, so there are a lot of similarities erm and I'm I'm also pretty good at reading but I'm finding it rather difficult to express myself and erm I would really like to improve my speaking skills. I'd really like to to erh be a little bit more fluent, not perfect but just enough to get by when we go to Argentina. Erm communication is is the most important thing.

Track 1.9

I = Interviewer

Hello and welcome to *Friday Film Festival* – the programme where we look at films – old and new. Today, we're talking about James Bond films and the incredibly successful music associated with them. The English writer, Ian Fleming created the character of James Bond in 1952. Bond is a spy – also known as double oh seven – who works for the British Secret Service and saves the world from various enemies or 'baddies'. The first Bond film was in 1962 and there are now twenty-two films of the Bond books. Different actors star in the role of Bond, including Daniel Craig, Pierce Brosnan and, of course, the first one, Sean Connery – my personal favourite. The films are probably one of the most successful series of films ever, earning over twelve billion dollars. It's not only the films, however, which are popular but also the theme songs connected with the films … including one of the most recent, *Another way to die* by Jack White and Alicia Keys for the film *Quantum of Solace*. Today, we have Tony Andrews, film critic from *WeLoveFilm* magazine and a fan of everything James Bond, to tell us more about the music for double oh seven. Welcome, Tony …

Track 1.10

I = Interviewer T = Tony

I: Welcome, Tony.

T: Hello. Great to be here.

I: So, we know that the James Bond films are incredibly successful … but as I said, the theme songs are hugely popular, too. I mentioned *Another way to die* … Can you tell us a bit about that one?

T: Yeah, that's right … *Another way to die* is from the film *Quantum of Solace* … It came out in 2008 and was really popular.

I: It's a duet, isn't it?

T: Yes, it's a duet by Alicia Keys and Jack White – the lead singer of The White Stripes. Actually, it's the first duet used for a Bond theme song – all the others are solos, with just one singer. I think it appealed to young people … although some people didn't like it at first. The words of the song are great. Personally, I loved it.

I: Yes, the lyrics are really good and have a strong message. And I think Alicia Keys is very cool. I love that song. Let's hear a bit of it … Mmm … great song! So, when was the first famous Bond theme song?

T: Well, the first Bond film, *Dr No*, and the second one actually, *From Russia with Love*, had great soundtracks. They had music, obviously. But they didn't have a theme song connected with them. *Goldfinger* was the first big song.

I: Mmmm. That's right … *Goldfinger*.

T: When *Goldfinger* came out, <u>in 1964</u>, the real connection between film and theme song started. <u>After that</u>, I suppose the public expected a great theme song in every film.

I: Yes, that was a great film. And Shirley Bassey made *Goldfinger* into a classic song, too.

T: Yes, she's an amazing singer. That song started her career and she became an international star immediately. It wasn't Bassey's only Bond song either.

I: Oh, yes – that's true. How many did she sing?

T: She sang three Bond songs altogether – the only singer to do more than one.

I: Really?

T: Yes, she sang another classic song, *Diamonds are forever* in 1971. And then, <u>eight years later</u>, *Moonraker* although that one wasn't very successful. But it's not just Shirley Bassey. What's good about Bond is that there are different singers and different styles for each film. Many of the songs really are classics ...

I: Tell us about some of the other successful ones.

T: Well, yes, many Bond songs got to the top of the charts in different countries, but *A View to a Kill* by Duran Duran is the only Bond song actually to be Number One on the Billboard Hot 100 chart.

I: The only Number One? *A View to a kill* – really? That's interesting.

T: Mmm ... there are other real classics which did really well. In the 1970s, there were two great Bond songs ... first *Live and let die* by Paul McCartney and Wings, in 1973. Then, *Nobody does it better* by Carly Simon, in 1977.

I: And *Another way to die* of course that we talked about earlier ... Jack White and Alicia Keys had huge success with that one.

T: Yes, that was one of my personal favourites.

I: Not all Bond songs were hits though, were they? There have been some flops, too.

T: Yes, there was a very mixed reaction to Madonna's *Die another day*, when it came out in 2002. It wasn't a complete flop ... but strangely, it got awards for being the best song, but also the worst!

I: I liked that one actually. It had a really catchy chorus.

T: Did you? Yes, I thought so, too.

Track 1.13

M = Man W = Woman

M: I've got an article here about the *Mozart Effect* ... It says music can affect your mood. You know, different music makes you feel happy or relaxed or something. I don't know about that ... Can music change how you feel? Ermm ... What do you think?

W: Erm I don't know, I think maybe when you're in a bad mood or upset about something, and you put happy music on, it makes you feel better. Yeah, I think music can change your mood ... but maybe also, it depends what kind of person you are I suppose ... and what kind of music you like.

M: Mmm ...

W: Sometimes I like listening to music that reminds me of old times. You know, I put on a song the other day and it really reminded me of my summer holidays a few years ago. I remember listening to it when I went to Italy with my family. It's got great memories I suppose and it made me feel really good, you know, listening to it again.

M: Yeah, I know what you mean ... How often do you listen to music, then?

W: I listen to music every single day ... all day, sometimes! From the moment I wake up, the radio is on ... or the MP3 player ... I never go anywhere without my MP3 player – even when I'm out on my bike.

M: So, do you listen to music when you're travelling? You know, when you're going to work or something?

W: Yes ... that's a really good time for listening to music. I have the radio on in the car, and it makes the journey go quicker. You know, you can sing along ... and have fun when you're sitting in a traffic jam!

M: What's your favourite type of music?

W: Erm I love all kinds of music ... anything that's good. I love old stuff, I love new stuff. My favourite type is probably rock, but lots of other stuff too. Erm I think that it's quite difficult to say your favourite, especially because I listen to so much music.

M: What about live music? When did you last see live music?

W: Oh, it was ages ago. The last concert I saw was years ago. Erm ... I don't know why, I suppose it's really expensive usually and sometimes the place is so big, you can't really see the person properly. I'm not really bothered about live music so much ...

Track 1.15

I = Interviewer ML = Mark Leyton:

I: On *My top three* today, we're talking to actor Mark Leyton. What are his top three records? Imagine he is alone on a desert island for ten weeks. Which music would he want? Which three pieces of music would he take with him to this desert island? Let's talk to him and find out. Hello Mark – welcome to *My top three*.

ML: Hello.

I: So, imagine – you're going to be alone on a desert island. You can only take three pieces of music. Which three do you want? First ... tell us about number three.

Track 1.16

I = Interviewer ML = Mark Leyton:

ML: Well, it's very difficult to choose – but I think number three for me is *Feelin' so good* by Jennifer Lopez. I love it!

I: Yes. So do I!

ML: It reminds me of when I was at school. We finished our exams and then this song was on the radio all summer. It makes me feel so happy. I always want to dance when I hear it!

I: Well, let's hear it ... ... Great! So number three is Jennifer Lopez, what about number two?

ML: Number two for me is something completely different ... it's a piece of classical music. It's got great memories for me. I heard it first when I was about ten years old and I didn't know anything about classical music at that time. It's the fourth movement of Mahler's *Symphony number 5*. When I first heard it, it made me cry because it was so beautiful!! And I still love it.

I: OK ... so here it is ... the fourth movement of *Symphony number 5* by Mahler ... ... That really is lovely, isn't it?

ML: Yes ...

I: So, number one ... what's your all-time number one favourite piece of music?

ML: Well, I think my favourite song ever is *Imagine* by John Lennon. I think he's got a fantastic voice. It reminds me of a great holiday I had. I remember listening to it when I was on the beach in Spain. It's so relaxing – I could listen to it every day!

I: Mmm ... here it is ... ... A great choice! Thank you for coming in today to tell us about your top three, Mark.

Track 1.17

1 It reminds me of when I was at school.
2 It makes me feel so happy.
3 It's got great memories for me!
4 When I first heard it, it made me cry!
5 It reminds me of a great holiday I had.
6 I remember listening to it when I was on the beach.

Track 1.18

A: I prefer meat. I never choose fish when I go out to a restaurant.

B: Not really. I think a lot of them are a waste of time. They don't really work.

C: Yes, I have. It was when I was a teenager. I didn't think it was right to eat animals.

D: Yes, I can't eat nuts or seafood. They make me really ill.

E: I like to have a lot of choice in a restaurant. Then you always know there's something you like.

F: I really love apple pie – it's very traditional where I come from.

G: Yes, there are lots. I really like Jamie Oliver. He makes cooking seem simple and fun.

H: Yes, I do. I use them to help me get new ideas.

Track 1.20

1 What are you going to do this year?
2 I want to work in a restaurant as a chef.
3 I'm going to get a job as a waiter in October.
4 I'd like to speak English better because I want to work abroad.
5 I'm going to get a place at college to learn about hotel management.

Track 1.21

T = Tarin M = Marcos

T: Hi Marcos, what are you doing next Thursday? And your brother too ... is he around?

M: Erm ... next Thursday? Ermm ... my brother is staying with friends next week ... but I'm not doing anything ... Why?

T: Well, I'm having a meal at my house to celebrate Thanksgiving and I'd really like you to come.

M: Oh, thanks, I'd love to! That's very kind of you! I've never been to a Thanksgiving meal before. It's an important festival here, isn't it?

T: Yes ... and I'm going to cook roast turkey! Thanksgiving is all about the food ... well ... really just getting together with family and friends and having a lovely meal. Sometimes, after the meal, people go out for a walk or something, but mostly, they just sit around and watch TV together.

M: Mmm ... And what about presents and things? Is it a time when you give presents to people, like at Christmas or ... ?

T: Ermm ... no, not really ... it's a really big and important celebration but it isn't commercial. People don't usually buy lots of presents or anything. There are some big public celebrations like the Macy's parade in New York ... but, for most people, it's just a time for giving thanks, and getting together with family and friends and eating turkey!

M: Mmm ... I love roast turkey!

T: Yes, me too. Traditionally, we have roast turkey as the main part of the meal ... and then there are lots of other dishes. I mean, basically, there are four other essential parts to the meal ... sometimes more than four ...

M: Really ...?

T: Mm ... There are lots of variations, too. It depends on where you come from in the States. I'm from the north east and one of the things we have is sweet potatoes with maple syrup ... it's very sweet, and some people don't like it, but I love it!

M: Mm ... I think it sounds delicious ... sweet potatoes and maple syrup ... mmm.

T: Yeah ... some people have sweet potatoes baked in the oven ... in a sort of pie ... but we usually have them boiled ... and then mashed up and ... then with maple syrup on top. Not everyone has maple syrup – in some parts of the States they have sweet potatoes with fresh fruit – things like apples, oranges and pears.

Audioscripts

M: Really? Mmm … Interesting!

T: The second thing we always have is cranberry sauce. Have you ever had that?

M: Cranberry sauce? No, I don't think so.

T: It goes really well with turkey – it's made of small red berries – it's also very sweet actually … Not everything we have is sweet though. There are some savoury dishes!

M: What else then?

T: Well, stuffing is really important. I love it … it's one of my favourite parts of the meal.

M: Stuffing … ? What's that?

T: It's made of bread and meat … sausages usually – all mixed up together … and it's often very spicy.

M: Mmm … . So, … there are basically four other dishes. What was it? … Sweet potatoes, … cranberry sauce … and stuffing … What's the fourth one?

T: Well, apple pie of course!

M: Aah yes … I've heard about traditional American apple pie.

T: Actually, some people don't have apple pie. In some places, they have pumpkin pie … or pie made of pecan nuts, which is very popular … But in our house, we have apple pie – baked in the oven. It's fantastic!

M: Mmm … I'm getting hungry just thinking about it all. So, is there anything I can bring?

T: Oh, no! Don't worry about that. Just come and enjoy yourself. We're eating at about two o'clock in the afternoon – so why don't you come at about midday for some drinks first?

M: Perfect! See you then. I'm really looking forward to it.

Track 1.23

T = Tarin M = Marcos

T: Hi Marcos, what are you doing next Thursday? And your brother, too … is he around?

M: Erm … next Thursday? Ermm … my brother is staying with friends next week … but I'm not doing anything … Why?

T: Well, I'm having a meal at my house to celebrate Thanksgiving and I'd really like you to come.

M: Oh, thanks, I'd love to! That's very kind of you!

…

M: So, is there anything I can bring?

T: Oh, no! Don't worry about that. Just come and enjoy yourself. We're eating at about two o'clock in the afternoon – so why don't you come at about midday for some drinks first?

M: Perfect! See you then. I'm really looking forward to it.

Track 1.26

W = Woman M = Man

M: So, come on then, Anita, tell me all about it! Have you found a place for your new restaurant?

W: Yes! I'm really excited about it actually. I'm renting a fantastic space … it's on the ground floor of a big building … in the centre of town … near the school.

M: Oh great … That's a really good place for a restaurant. What are you going to call it?

W: Well, I think I'm going to call it 'Anita's' … after me!

M: Why not? Yes … , 'Anita's' … That's good … And, what type of food are you going to serve?

W: Well, traditional English food, mostly … but with some food from Europe … some Italian and modern French food, too – European food, I suppose.

M: That sounds good …

W: The thing is, I want the food to be simple, but delicious …

M: Yes …

W: … and I think it's really important that the prices are reasonable. You know, I don't want it to be really expensive … I want ordinary people to come and to get affordable, good food … I've decided that we're going to keep the menu simple, but change it every two weeks.

M: That's a good idea.

W: So, we're going to have three starters, three main courses and three desserts.

M: Mmm, yes … what kind of things, then?

W: In our opening weeks, we're going to have, as starters: fresh mussels in a garlic sauce, Italian salad and … tomato soup.

M: Lovely!

W: For the main course: cheese and lemon pasta, grilled fish of the day with green beans and roast chicken with potatoes.

M: Mmm …

W: And finally, for dessert: chocolate mousse, homemade ice cream and apple pie with cream.

M: Fantastic! You really have got it all planned out! It sounds delicious! And what about the service? Is it going to be waiter service at the table or self-service?

W: Ermm … waiter service … I think it's really important to have friendly waiters who are really efficient. There's nothing worse than bad service in a restaurant … the customers just won't come back!

M: And what are your plans for the décor? I mean, you must have an idea about the kind of atmosphere you want.

W: Yes, like the food, I want the place to be quite simple, but modern at the same time. And we're going to have music to create a young, lively atmosphere. I'd also like to have paintings on the walls … art by local artists.

M: Yes, that's a nice feature.

W: It's an extra thing really – to attract more customers … Anyway, that's the plan. We'll have to see how it goes …

M: Well, good luck with it all. I can't wait to come and try it out.

Track 1.27

1 It was a few months ago … I was really nervous … really scared. It was for a good promotion and I wanted it so much! I decided to use a kind of meditation – and I repeated positive things to myself to try and stay focused and to control my fear. I think it worked … because the interview went well and I got the job!

2 My brother had a serious illness last year … he had problems with his heart. He's much better now, thankfully, but because of his illness, I decided to do something positive, something to help … I ran one marathon every day for a week to raise money. It was a huge challenge … really difficult … but I did it … and I raised nearly £2,000 for charity.

3 Next year, I'm going to South America with a friend of mine … We want to see the world a bit before we go to university. I'm going to have Spanish lessons and try to learn as much as I can before we go. The thing is that my friend speaks very good Spanish, but I don't speak any … and I don't want to rely on her all the time.

4 When you go on a long trek somewhere – like the Arctic – where it's very cold, or across a desert – where it's very hot – it's obviously hard to survive. You know, … you need a lot of physical strength. You also need a lot of mental strength. You need to be prepared to face difficult things without giving up.

5 I've wanted to be a doctor since I was really young … for as long as I can remember, really. I know that you have to study for years and years, and do very long hours, all through the night sometimes. But I am definitely prepared to do the hard work … I'm determined to achieve my goal and be a doctor.

Track 1.28

1 Carla is much more motivated than Louisa. Louisa isn't as motivated as Carla.

2 Louisa is a bit fitter than Carla. Carla isn't as fit as Louisa.

3 Louisa is a bit more determined than Carla. Carla isn't as determined as Louisa.

4 Carla is much braver than Louisa. Louisa isn't as brave as Carla.

Track 1.30

Good evening and thank you for coming to find out about the Hillside Survival School. My name's David Johnson. I started the school and I'm the school's chief instructor. I learned my survival skills while I was in the army and before starting the Hillside Survival School, I worked in other well-known survival schools. So, first, why do people come on our courses? What are our aims? Well, firstly, we aim to help people to discover nature and the outdoor life … and to remind people that there is more to life than city living. Secondly, and perhaps more importantly, we want people to work well as a team and to have fun together … and a lot of people come to do just that!

Who comes on our courses? Who are our courses for? Well, the answer is anybody and everybody. We get a lot of groups of colleagues – people who work together, like you. The weekend courses are a fantastic way of team-building, and having fun together, as I said. The courses are also popular with groups of friends who want to do something a bit more challenging than lying on a beach! So, let me tell you about what happens on some of our courses … The most popular course we run is our basic survival course which lasts a weekend and takes place throughout the year. This course teaches you the basic skills that you need to survive in the wilderness and costs a hundred and seventy-five pounds per person. Choose this one and you will have the best weekend you've ever had! If you want an even bigger challenge, our extreme survival course takes place between November and February, when the conditions are more difficult. These courses also last for a weekend and cost a hundred and ninety-five pounds per person. The extreme survival course teaches you to survive in a wet and cold environment. In fact, we aim to give you the wettest, coldest weekend ever! The course offers you the chance to push yourself, both physically and mentally. No tents, no gas cookers; just you and the wilderness. You learn to find food and cook it over an open fire. You learn to build a shelter and then you actually sleep in it. It could be the hardest thing you've ever done by far … You won't have the most comfortable weekend of your life, but you will probably be surprised how well you can cope with difficult conditions.

Well … thank you very much for inviting me here to your company to tell you about Hillside Survival School. If you're interested in doing any of our courses with a group of colleagues, speak to your manager. You can also pick up a booklet before you go … it includes information about all the courses, prices, dates and application forms. Push yourself. It really could be the best thing you've ever done! … And, yes,

I think we've got time for a few questions … before you all get back to work. Erm … yes … the man at the back …

Track 1.31

1

A = Assistant P = Train passenger

A: Can I help you?

P: I'd like **a return to Edinburgh**, please.

A: Yes … when would you like to travel?

P: **On Friday afternoon … and coming back on Sunday evening.**

A: OK … uh … there's a train at **five forty-five p.m. on Friday.**

P: Yes, that's fine. Oh, and can you tell me how long the train takes?

A: Erm, yes … it takes **about five hours.**

P: Thank you.

2

P1 = Passenger 1 P2 = Passenger 2

P1: Err … do you know if this is the train to **Cardiff** please?

P2: Yes, it is.

P1: Oh … good. Is this seat free? … I mean, is it OK with you if I sit here?

P2: Yes, of course. No problem.

…

P1: Excuse me, **is this your newspaper? Do you mind if I read it … ?**

P2: No, that's fine. Go ahead.

3

S = Shop assistant C = Customer

S: Hello. How are you?

C: I'm good thanks. How are you?

S: Good thanks … Do you need any help?

C: Oh, yes, please. **Can you tell me if you have this jacket in medium?**

S: Yes, certainly … I'll just have a look for you. … Here you are.

C: Thanks. Oh, and could you tell me how much it is, please?

S: Yes, of course. It's fifty-five dollars.

C: Is it OK if I pay by credit card?

S: Yes, that's fine.

Track 1.34

1

A: Can you tell me if you have this jacket in medium?

B: Yes, certainly … I'll just have a look for you.

2

A: Could you tell me how much it is please?

B: Yes, of course. … It's fifty-five dollars.

3

A: Is it OK if I pay by credit card?

B: Yes, that's fine.

4

A: Do you mind if I read it … ?

B: No, that's fine. Go ahead.

Track 1.35

W = Woman M = Man

M: I'm really excited about this weekend … I think it's going to be difficult, but I'm sure we're all going to have a great time.

W: Yes … I'm really looking forward to it as well. I've always wanted to go on one of these survival courses. It might be a bit strange going with a group of people who you don't know very well. But I suppose it's good to get to know our colleagues better!

M: Yes, I think that's the idea … I'm sure it'll be fun.

W: Anyway, we can take five things, can't we? Shall we think about it now … and try and decide which things to take?

M: Yeah … good idea.

W: Erm … Which of them do you think is the most important?

M: Well, it's quite cold … erm … I don't want to be cold at night! I think we should take the blankets to keep us warm.

W: OK … so, do you think they're more important than the penknife?

M: No, no … not more important. We can have the penknife as well … We are allowed five things after all.

W: That's true. So what else?

M: Well, in my opinion, we should take the matches, so we can make a fire from all the wood you can chop up with the penknife!

W: Good idea … and … how about the tent?

M: Hmmm … I'm not sure. That sounds like cheating a bit. Couldn't we make a shelter from the trees and leaves and things?

W: Well maybe you could!

M: OK … we'll have the tent … and why don't we have the chocolate as number five as a bit of luxury?

W: Yes, great idea … I think we're going to need it!

Track 1.37

M = Man W = Woman

1

W: One of the daughters of a friend of mine has got married and she's eighteen. Now I think that's too young to get married. What do you think?

M: I agree, I think eighteen is far too young to get married because you haven't got any experience of life. I … I think if you get married at eighteen, you have so many responsibilities. At … ah that age, you need to be able to travel and try different jobs and um …

W: Yes, I … I think you're right and um … also, I think at that age you, you really haven't become the person that you you're going to be. You haven't developed, um, so I think you change between eighteen and, say, twenty-five. You change so much and young people who get married at eighteen, by the time they reach twenty five, they might not be interested at all in their, their husband or wife.

M: I agree, I … I think um it's, it's too, ah it's too early to get married. If you make a mistake and um you marry the wrong person then, marriage is for life but … ah the … you should be able to wait just another few years and maybe get married at twenty-five or thirty … um there's still plenty of time.

W: It's better, yes that's definitely better …

2

M: I agree, I think it would be very good if young people these days did military service, because it teaches them responsibility and it also um … teaches them how … ah to cooperate in a group. I think it's a very good idea.

W: Um … I'm not so sure about that. Um, OK, it teaches them cooperation. It teaches them to work in groups, but on the other hand it teaches them how to be aggressive. It teaches them to go out and kill people.

M: Um, yeah well, I … I don't agree. I've spoken to young people in countries where they still have military service and … ah maybe they have military service for a year or eighteen months, and apart from being very pleasant, polite, young people, many of them also say that they enjoyed their military service.

W: Mmm …in

M: And um, met some very good friends and …

W: Yeah, in my opinion, it doesn't have to be military service. Erm, in some countries you have the, the possibility of … um a kind of civil service where they work in hospitals or on farms and generally do good things for their country, but it's not to do with the military and I think you have to give young people the choice because some young people don't want to be in the military service – they don't want to be involved in that kind of thing and I can understand

that. So why can't they do something else which helps their country?

3

W: I don't know, teenagers these days, they only ever think about their girlfriends, their boyfriends, about money, about what they want to do in the evening – they're just terrible! They really are, don't you think so?

M: I … I don't agree. Um, I mean, I think that teenagers have all sorts of problems and things that they have to deal with these days. I'm … I'm always amazed by the amount of schoolwork they have to do for example, far more homework than I did when I was at school.

W: Well maybe …

M: Don't you think so?

W: Maybe some … no, I don't. Um, I think some teenagers are very irresponsible. They, they should be more responsible about their lives … they … I think a lot of teenagers don't study … don't study very much at all … um. They come out of school with no qualifications. They don't get jobs … um. They cause problems in the streets. I don't know, I think that um the parents are to blame really. The, the main reason is their parents um aren't strict enough with them.

M: Well, I … I agree that there are lots of teenagers who do cause problems, but I think most teenagers now are much more responsible than they used to be and ah, there's a lot of pressure on them to do well at school, so that they can go to university and ah and get a good career.

Track 1.38

M = Martin T = Tina

M: It's great to be back … We've got so much catching up to do!

T: Yeah, there's so much to tell you! I know, I'll show you some photos from my birthday party.

M: Oh, that's a good idea … I can see who your friends are.

T: Yes, I had a bit of a party with some of my best … you know, my closest friends. We had a lovely time. Let's see … where are they? OK … here we are … this is a good one. So, well, first, this is Alison.

M: Mmm … yes, I think I remember her …

T: Yes, I've known Alison for years. I mean, we're old school friends – from primary school – so, I suppose I've known her nearly all my life really. We first met when we were in the same class at school from the age of four and a half.

M: Four and a half? Really?

T: Yeah, even when we were at school together, we never fell out with each other about anything. She's a very easy-going person and still a really great friend. I'm very glad we've kept in touch. I suppose we see each other about once a month and we still get on really well.

M: Mmm, that's really nice. And who's that? He looks like a bit of a character!

T: Yes! He's great … That's my friend Jake. Basically, I go to the gym with him! Actually, he was a colleague first. I got to know him at work and we've worked together for about five years now. Then, about a year ago, we started going to the gym together. It's really good because we help each other to keep motivated.

M: I need a friend like that!

T: Well, that's right. It's hard to keep going to the gym and exercising on your own, isn't it? Because I've got someone to go with, it's much easier. He's always encouraging me, and motivating me. I

Audioscripts

think he feels the same, too. So, yes, we see each other at work, and we go to the gym together … and I would definitely say he's a really good friend.

M: Yes …

T: Oh, … and Melanie. That's her … She's a lovely friend – always there for me. I met her at a party, actually – about ten years ago … but then we lost touch for a while.

M: Oh, really?

T: Well, yes, but a couple of years ago, we met again and we've been really close since then. I call her my 'three o'clock in the morning' friend because she really is the kind of person who you can phone up at three o'clock in the morning if you need to, and she really wouldn't mind.

M: That's great …

T: In fact, I have phoned her at that time on a couple of occasions. You know, when I've been really down about something and really needed someone to talk to. I see her at least once a week … She's my best friend … she really is … She's a very special person – she doesn't give you advice, you know. She just listens. It's a great quality in a friend, I think.

M: Yes, definitely … Oh, who's that? I think I recognise him …

Track 1.39

M = Man W = Woman

M: OK … so three things about my childhood. Well, firstly, I used to … well, every summer, I used to go to the same place for my holidays. We used to go camping near a lovely beach in Wales.

W: OK … Did you use to drive there?

M: Yes … it took about three hours from where we lived.

W: Mmm … next one?

M: Next one … we used to have a dog …

W: Right … when did you get it? I mean, how old were you?

M: Well, I wanted a dog so much … I was really upset and I used to ask my mum all the time … And then my parents gave me a dog on my eleventh birthday! I couldn't believe it. I was so pleased.

W: OK … and … erm … the last one?

M: And number three, … well, about school. I used to love playing out on the street with my friends.

W: What did you use to play mostly?

M: Ermm … We used to play football in the middle of the road … you know, there weren't many cars, so it was OK.

W: OK … so … so which one is false? Let's see … Erm … about the dog … What was your dog's name?

M: Ermm … she was called Meg.

W: Meg? What colour was she?

M: Oh, sort of black and white.

W: Did you use to take her out for walks?

M: Yes, but mostly my dad took her out.

W: Oh, but she was your dog…

M: Err … yes, but …

W: It's not true, is it? You didn't have a dog … that one's false …

M: Ermm … no I didn't actually! You're right. It's false. I really wanted a dog – but we never got one! OK … your turn…

W: OK, first one …

Track 1.40

Today on *This is your life*, we are talking about a woman who is probably one of the most famous and influential women in the world. Going back to her early life, she was born on January the seventeenth, 1964, and grew up in Chicago, USA. She did well at school and then went on to get a law degree from Harvard University in 1988.

After graduating, she worked at a law company in Chicago. This is where she met her future husband, who was working for the same company. They got married on October the eighteenth, 1992. She has had an impressive career; with senior positions in several large companies and universities. Looking at family matters, in July 1998, she had her first child; a daughter called Malia. And a second daughter, Natasha – known as Sasha – followed in June 2001. After her husband was elected to the U.S. Senate, she and her husband decided to keep their children in Chicago. She wanted to continue with her career, as well as keeping a stable family life for the children.

Currently, she is the First Lady of the United States, and manages to juggle being a mother, a career woman and the wife of the President. She usually goes to bed by nine thirty and gets up each morning at four thirty, to go running. It is this discipline that helps her keep calm and organised in her busy, stressful life.

Track 1.41

I = Interviewer W = Woman

I: Welcome to *Tourism Today* – the programme that looks at aspects of tourism throughout the world. Today, we're talking about a tourist destination in Europe. With its fantastic summer weather and beautiful islands, Greece is extremely popular with holiday makers. An expert on the Greek islands, Alanna Papadakis, is here to talk about some changes – both positive and negative – that are happening there. … Hello, Alanna.

W: Hello, Mike.

I: Greece is a major tourist destination. And many of the islands – like Crete, Mykonos and Santorini – are familiar to us from the tourist guides … most of us know these names.

W: Yes, that's right. Many Greek islands are well-prepared for the hordes of tourists who come every summer. These islands expect to see thousands of visitors every year. Other islands remain quiet and undiscovered by tourists though … and many of them will stay that way.

I: One island, however, may soon change dramatically. Tell us about that …

W: Well … Skopelos is an island in the Aegean Sea to the east of Athens. It's very small – there are only 4,696 residents there … and yes, they might need to prepare for a huge increase in tourists.

I: 4,696 residents – that is small! So, what's going on there?

W: There are reports that some tourists want to get married there. Others want to have parties in their own private bay. Others just want to dance on the beach. It's called the *Mamma Mia!* effect – and it seems everyone wants to go to Skopelos now. It all started when the film *Mamma Mia!* was released. You know … the film version of the musical … the hit Abba musical, starring Meryl Streep, Colin Firth and Pierce Brosnan.

I: It's proving to be hugely popular, isn't it?

W: Yes, not only the film … but also the island! Until they started filming *Mamma Mia!*, Skopelos was famous for plums, pears and pine forests. It was a surprise to everyone that the island itself became one of the biggest stars of the film!

I: Why did they choose this particular island?

W: Well, producers looked at about twenty-five Greek islands before they decided on Skopelos. In the end, they chose this

one because it has many different places which fitted with the story.

I: Can you tell us exactly where some of those places are?

W: Yes … some of the film takes place around Kastani Bay and the beaches there. Other parts were filmed at the top of the cliffs, above Glisteri Beach. That's where the main character – played by Meryl Streep – has a house.

I: And what about the famous wedding scene at the end of the film?

W: Yes, the wedding scene is filmed on the mountain on the peninsula near Glisteri. It's beautiful … unforgettable really.

I: So, this beautiful location provided the backdrop for an extremely successful film. But will the film bring success for the island of Skopelos? Or will the changes have a negative effect?

W: Well, things will change there. Sometimes films like this have a huge effect on the location … Skopelos won't stay the same …. it won't be the same unknown place that it used to be. There's a positive side and a negative side, I suppose… On the negative side, things may be less peaceful. The local people may not keep the peaceful atmosphere of the island completely. But on the positive side, they are pleased to get more business, at least during the summer months.

I: Yes, the film might be very good for business …

W: Mmm … and I'm sure the *Mamma Mia!* effect will increase tourism on other islands.

I: Yes, it might increase tourism for the whole of Greece, but … at the moment, nobody really knows if these changes will be positive or not … in the long run, I mean …

Track 1.42

1
A: Will tourism change the island of Skopelos?
B: Yes, I think it'll change it a lot.
2
A: Where will you live when you're older?
B: I think I'll live by the coast.
3
A: Where are they going on holiday next year?
B: I think they'll go to Greece.
4
A: Do you think you'll pass the exam?
B: Yes, I think I will.

Track 1.43

Gavin
OK, um, growing up, I used to go on holiday to a place in Northumberland called Seahouses, um, and the most **impressive** thing about Seahouses is the miles and miles of **unspoilt**, **idyllic** beaches. You can walk for miles and miles and only see a man and his dog and it's fantastic. The biggest feeling you get when you're there is being entirely relaxed. Um, it's such a, a good um contrast with the city, um, and generations of my family have been going there. Erm, I think it was my great great grandfather ah discovered this small seaside town ah many years ago and ever since my ahm family's been going there and ah yeah it's fantastic.

Heather
One of the most beautiful places I've ever been to is in Southern Thailand and it's a peninsula called Railay. It's a **beautiful**, **unspoilt** lush scenery. It takes five minutes to walk from one side of the peninsula to the other. Erm, one of the beaches that I used to visit I had to walk through caves to get to

it, ahm, and it was a hidden beach … um um … and when I went swimming um you can see to the bottom in about ten feet of water. There's tropical fish everywhere, the sun is shining and in the distance all you can see is dots of other islands in the distance. It's very **relaxing**, ahm very calm very serene. It's a very tranquil place to spend, spend the afternoon.

Track 2.2

M = Man W = Woman

W: Hi, Jack. … What are you doing?

M: Oh, it's SimCity … have you ever played it?

W: SimCity? No, I haven't … and I can't believe you're still playing that! Aren't you bored of it? It's been around for over twenty years, hasn't it?

M: Well, yes … but it's a fantastic game … really – one of the most popular computer games ever made. And, they bring out new versions all the time. It's a great game …

W: What's does it involve, then? What do you have to do?

M: Well, your basic task is to build a city. You make choices about what things you want in your city, how to keep the people in your city happy and how much to spend.

W: What kind of things are you talking about?

M: Well, you plan the whole city. You decide what different areas there are, for example, a residential area – where people live – or a commercial area, with shops and things. You can also decide where to put things like parks, cinemas, swimming pools and other facilities.

W: Is it only leisure facilities?

M: No, your city shouldn't have too many leisure facilities. There isn't enough space to have whatever you want – and you need to have the basic things, too. So, you decide how much to spend on basic things like roads, bus stations, hospitals and libraries.

W: What about money? Can you spend as much as you want on these things?

M: No … that's a big part of the game – you can't spend too much money. Most of your money comes from tax, but the people don't want to pay too much tax.

W: No, of course not!

M: But, they want enough facilities. You know, if you don't spend enough money on things like schools and hospitals, the workers might stop working … they might go on strike. And if the workers stop working, your city begins to break down. And with each new version, they've added new things; like having areas of the city which become too crowded for people to live in, and so they begin to leave. They're too noisy – you know, they're not quiet enough for some people to live in anymore.

W: So, it's basically about designing your city?

M: Not only … I mean, there are various bad things that happen, like earthquakes and other natural disasters, and you can see how your city survives, or not …

W: So, why do you think it is so popular? I mean, twenty years … that's a long time …

M: Ermm … I think it's about choice and control … and the fact that it's an open-ended game. I mean, I think SimCity is popular because it's not about killing or destroying things. Too many computer games are about killing, I think.

W: Yes, I agree.

M: But, in SimCity, you make decisions and choices which help you in a positive way and you create your own city. The game is really well designed. They've designed it well enough to appeal to a lot of people

… and … it really holds people's attention for a long time. I think people like being in control of their own city. It is a virtual city, but the technology is very good, it feels very real …

Track 2.3

H = Harry L = Linda

H: Well, what do you think? We're going in March, so we need to get the tickets soon. Where would you like to go?

L: Umm … I think Barcelona sounds really good, or maybe Edinburgh … I'm not sure. There are lots of great things to see and do in both places. What do you think?

H: Umm … I think Edinburgh is too cold for me … I mean, cold weather isn't my idea of fun! I like warmer weather … four degrees is too cold! Barcelona is a bit warmer. Is it warm enough?

L: Yes, I think so … it's warm enough for me … I don't like it too hot.

H: Oh really? I'd prefer somewhere very warm … like Rio. I like the idea of going to the beach.

L: Yes, but Rio is too far away. I'm not keen on sitting on a plane for twelve hours or something … And it's too expensive to get there …

H: I suppose you're right … But, look … Edinburgh is expensive, too… the accommodation, I mean.

L: Well, what about Barcelona? I'd like to go somewhere on the coast.

H: OK … it sounds really fun there. And it isn't too far away, is it?

L: OK, then … Shall I book the tickets this afternoon?

Track 2.7

1 Are you ambitious?
2 Are you usually hard-working or lazy?
3 Are you more open or more reserved?
4 Are you an organised kind of person or disorganised?
5 Are you chatty or are you the quiet type?
6 Are you an easy-going person?

Track 2.8

H = Helen D = Daniel

H: Hi Daniel. Have you finished doing your essay? I want to show you something … just five minutes … it won't take long.

D: Yes, sure. I've decided not to do my essay now, actually … It's really difficult and Michael has offered to help me later … What do you want to do?

H: Well, erm … I want to look at the shape of your fingers.

D: What? … Why?

H: I'm going to tell you about your personality.

D: Oh … hmm … I'm not sure about that. What are you going to say about me?! You have to promise to be nice!

H: Well, we'll see what your fingers say!

D: Oh, OK … why not? I enjoy doing this kind of thing actually. So, where do we start?

H: OK, well, erm … there are three main things to look at.

D: Mmm …

H: First, there's the length of your fingers. People with long, slim fingers are quite sensitive. People with shorter, thicker fingers, like yours, are more open. They talk about their feelings more. So, you're quite an open person …

D: No, I'm not sure about that … Actually, I don't think I'm very open. I think I avoid telling people about my feelings most of the time … In fact, I don't think I talk about my feelings much at all.

H: Yes, you do …

D: I don't think so, really … only to really close family and friends. I mean, I'd never even consider showing my feelings to someone I didn't know.

H: No, well, obviously not … But you seem to be quite open with people you know – that's what I mean.

D: Well … I'm really not sure … But let's move on … What else then?

H: Well, secondly, there's the shape of your fingers. Are you fingers straight?

D: Erm … yes … I think they are quite straight.

H: Ermm … that means you're organised. Is that true?

D: Yes. I think that's true about me. I mean, especially with writing essays and things … I'm very organised. You can't afford to be disorganised really. There's so much work at university … it all piles up if you're not organised about it.

H: Yes …

D: So, you said I'm open, organised … OK … what else?

H: Well, finally, the thumb is very important … Let's see how long your thumb is …

D: Hmm … I think it's quite long.

H: Well, a long thumb means you're ambitious. You know, you really want to be successful in what you do. You've got quite a long thumb, so I guess you're quite ambitious.

D: That's absolutely right! I think I am ambitious … yes. Hmmm … not bad … you said I'm ambitious, yes, organised, yes … and open, well, I'm still not sure about that one … but not bad, I suppose.

H: Mmm … I think that's quite accurate, actually.

D: OK, now it's your turn! Let me look at your hands …

Track 2.9

1
A: You look terrible. What's the matter?
B: I feel sick and I've got stomachache.

2
A: Are you better today?
B: No … I've got flu. I've got a high temperature and a headache.

3
A: How you are? You don't look well.
B: I've got a cough and sore eyes. I don't think it's serious – I've got a cold. That's all.

4
A: Is your back feeling better?
B: No. I've got terrible backache and my leg hurts. I've got toothache today, as well.

5
A: How are you feeling?
B: Terrible! I've got a sore throat and earache. I've got a rash as well.

Track 2.10

1
G = Georgia J = Jenny

G: Hello?

J: Oh, Georgia …This is Jenny … I'm so sorry … Did I wake you up?

G: Ermm … no, well … not really …

J: Oh dear … you sound terrible. How are you?

G: Not very well, really. I've got an awful sore throat and I can't stop coughing …

J: Poor you! Have you taken anything for it?

G: Ermm … well, no …

J: I remember having a sore throat a lot when I was a child … and my mother always gave me hot water with honey and lemon. Why don't you try drinking some of that? It really helps.

G: Thanks. That's a good idea.

J: Have you got any honey or lemon at home?

Audioscripts

G: Erm ... well ... I don't think I've got any honey, no.

J: Well, listen – on the way to college, I'll stop to get some honey at the supermarket and bring it round.

G: Oh, no ... don't worry about ...

J: ... It's not a problem – don't worry ... And try not to cough too much ... You should go back to bed now ...

G: Yes, I think I'll do that ...

J: I'll come round in about half an hour.

G: OK ... Thanks, Jenny. Oh ... will you remember to get the homework for me?

J: That's fine ... See you later.

G: Bye.

2

G = Georgia I = Ivan

G: Hello?

I: Hello? Georgia, is that you?

G: Yes ...

I: Oh dear ... I hope I didn't wake you up. It's Ivan here. I got your email and I wanted to check you were OK ... Do you need anything?

G: It's really kind of you to phone, Ivan ... Erm, I think I just need to sleep really ... and Jenny is going to bring me some honey and lemon for my sore throat.

I: Honey and lemon? Oh really, that's an English remedy, isn't it?

G: Yes ... I suppose it is.

I: Well, have you tried having honey and butter in hot milk? In Russia, my grandmother always gave us that. I remember having it a lot when I was a child.

G: Erm, ...I haven't tried that. Did you say it's a Russian remedy?

I: Yes ... it's really good. I used to love it and it makes your throat feel much better. Would you like me to come and see you? I could bring some round for you to try.

G: Oh, no ... really. It's fine ... I mean, Jenny will be here soon.

I: It's no bother really. I'll just come in on my way to college. Try to get some sleep now ...

G: Ermm ... OK – see you in about half an hour ...

3

G = Georgia M = Madison

G: Hello?

M: Georgia? Hi, it's Madison here.

G: Oh, hi ...

M: You don't sound very well. How are you?

G: I'm not feeling very well ...

M: Were you asleep? Sorry – I probably woke you up, didn't I?

G: Well ... it's really nice of everyone to phone me. I mean, Jenny and Ivan just phoned ... and ... well, it's lovely really ...

M: But you can't sleep ...

G: Well, yes ... I suppose ...

M: Oh dear ... you have got a bad cough. You should have honey and vinegar in hot water.

G: Honey and vinegar?! Oh, I don't fancy that!

M: It's good ... You use apple vinegar. It's an old American remedy. My mom used to give to us children when we were ill. It smells bad, but it's really delicious and ... it makes your throat feel better.

G: Really? Jenny said the English remedy is hot water with honey and lemon. Ivan said the Russian remedy is hot milk with honey and butter, and ...

M: Oh! I'm so sorry. You've got all the advice you need, haven't you? Well, OK ... I know what you really need – you need some rest ... and some peace and quiet. You need people to stop phoning you! Why don't you try turning your phone off?

G: Yes, that's a good idea. Oh! That's Jenny, I think ... with the honey and lemon ... or it could be Ivan. Sorry Madison, I'd better go and answer the door.

M: OK ... look after yourself – and try to get some rest ...

G: Bye .

Track 2.12

1

A: Why don't you try hot water with honey and lemon?

B: Thanks. That's a good idea.

2

A: You should go back to bed.

B: Yes, I think I'll do that.

3

A: Have you tried honey and butter in hot milk?

B: No, I haven't tried that.

4

A: You should have honey and vinegar in hot water.

B: Oh, I don't fancy that!

Track 2.13

P = Polly A = Amber

P: Um, waiting too long for a bus is definitely a major stress alert for me. Um, it happens quite often and it's really really annoying.

A: Especially if you're late for work.

P: Yep, definitely if it makes you late for work or anything else, and there's nothing you can do about it – it's out of your control.

A: Um, I get quite stressed out when I'm um on the phone to customer services and, um, I don't actually manage to speak to a human.

P: Oh yeah, that's really really annoying as well.

A: Especially when they ah they play the annoying music, makes me get a little bit tense ...

P: I'd say I get more than tense, I get really really stressed out about that.

A: Would that be a major stress alert for you?

P: I think so yeah, especially if I was having to pay for ah the phone call while I was waiting in line.

A: Yeah ...

P: Definitely. But maybe, ah ... yeah, it's definitely more stressful than, um, than losing a game of tennis or something.

A: I was just thinking that ...

P: I wouldn't really be that worried about that.

A: ... be no problem for me.

P: Naw, it's just a bit of fun, and I'm not really comp, very competitive ... so it wouldn't be a bit of a ...

A: Yeah, especially if you're playing with a friend.

P: Yeah, it'd be just for fun ... umm ... are there any other ones?

A: Um, not being able to sleep, um, doesn't make me very happy um

P: Yeah, but you could always put in earplugs or you could ...

A: You can, but ah, it's not ah a major stress alert but ah if you're tired and you can't sleep and there's a lot of noise going on outside, dogs barking, etc. then yeah that's a, that's pretty stressful.

P: I ... I don't agree that much. I'm er, a quite a heavy sleeper, so I don't think it would be that much of a problem

Track 2.14

I = Interviewer W = Woman

I: Welcome to *Changing World*. Almost everything in the modern world is speeding up. The pace of life is getting faster and faster and most people, it seems, think that 'fast is good'. My guest today, however, is someone who thinks that 'fast is bad' and 'slow is good'. Petra van Stroud is a member of the Slow Movement and

she's here to tell us why. Petra, welcome to the programme.

W: Hello, thank you.

I: So, in a fast world, you have chosen to join the Slow Movement. Why's that? I mean, don't you think that there are benefits from being able to do things faster – like faster communication using computers and mobile phones and things?

W: Ermm ... well, it can be good ... there are some benefits from a lot of new technology. In my opinion, however, the problem is that people get addicted to doing things fast and then they forget about important things in our lives – like, communicating in real time with a 'real' person. People start living in a virtual world ...

I: They just communicate through a computer or something ...

W: That's right. We need to remember to see each other in the real world ... And that's really what the Slow Movement is all about – having some of the good things about the old, slower life.

I: OK. The Slow Movement – tell us about that. How did it all start?

W: Well, it actually started as the Slow Food organisation in 1986.

I: Slow Food?

W: Yes, in 1986, in Italy – in Rome – a group of people protested about a fast food restaurant – McDonald's – opening there.

I: They didn't want a McDonald's in Rome.

W: That's right. They were against fast food and they wanted people to continue to eat home-cooked 'slow' food. It wasn't just about the food, though. Of course food is better if you cook it yourself – but it was also about the social side of food. You know, when people eat fast food, they are often in a hurry and they often don't talk to each other.

I: So, the Slow Food organisation wanted people to slow down – and take their time to eat and socialise together.

W: Exactly. Then, as more people got interested in the idea, the Slow Food organisation grew into the Slow Movement, including communication, for example, and many other aspects of people's lives. You know ... the aim remains the same: to encourage people to slow down and enjoy spending time with each other – whatever they're doing.

I: I mean, I agree with that philosophy – it is important to spend time with people. I'm just not sure that we can slow down the pace of life now, or even that most people really want to. Fast technology is everywhere and for many of us, the benefits are huge. We live busy fast lives and enjoy them.

W: Many people enjoy their busy lives, yes. But many people don't. I suppose the Slow Movement wants to remind people that in your fast life, sometimes, it's good to slow down. And maybe turn your computer off, or leave your mobile phone at home – at least sometimes. People might be surprised how much they enjoy slowing down sometimes.

Track 2.15

1 In what language are most international phone calls made?

2 In the US, are more messages carried by email or by post?

3 What percentage of emails are junk email?

4 How much junk mail is delivered by post every year in the US?

5 What percentage of websites are not visited by anybody?

6 How many people visit the website YouTube every day?

7 How many people use the social networking site Facebook every day?

8 In how many different languages do people write messages on Facebook?

Track 2.18

D = Deepa F = Fiona

D: Hi Fiona. What's the matter?

F: I don't know. I'd like to meet someone nice ... you know, a nice boyfriend. I feel that I've totally got over Daniel now ... You know, we just grew apart really ... and then we finally split up with each other at Thanksgiving. Ermm ... well, it was in November. Oh, actually – I remember now, we split up on my birthday – on the eighteenth of November!

D: Oh dear ...

F: I'm fine now, but ... I haven't found anyone nice to go out with since then, and I don't know where to meet anyone. There's nobody at work, that's for sure! ... How did you meet your husband?

D: Oh, I was lucky, I suppose ... My parents helped me.

F: Your parents? Really?

D: Yes, it's the Indian tradition; you know, arranged marriage. It's different now, though. Nobody forces you to get married to someone you don't like. Your parents help you find someone, but you can say 'no' if you don't like him. You certainly don't have to put up with someone you don't like for the rest of your life!

F: So, what did you do?

D: Well, like a lot of young Asians from Britain, I went to India for a couple of months in the winter. The winter is 'wedding season' – lots of people get married at that time. Indian weddings last about a week, and they are a really good place to meet other young single people.

F: Really?

D: Yes, so my parents came with me and they arranged for me to go to lots of social events. I spent most of the time going to weddings and parties, and visiting lots of friends and family. I met loads of single men there and some of them took me out on dates.

F: So, you meet people properly and talk to them in a social situation?

D: Yes, it's all very normal really. The thing that's different is that it's all speeded up. I mean, most parents would like everything done in about one or maybe two months.

F: One or two months?

D: Yes, I arrived in India in December ... at the beginning of December ... and I got married at the end of January – on the twenty-eighth of January actually. When I came back to Britain, I was a married woman!

F: Really?! That is quick!

D: Yes. The whole process is really fast – meeting people, going out with different boyfriends and then getting married. Job done!

F: It's a bit like speed-dating!

D: Speed-dating? Have you ever done that?

F: Yes, I did it once. It was OK, but you only have three minutes to talk to each person and it feels very unreal. It really is like a job interview and you don't get enough time.

D: Mmm ... The arranged marriage thing is different because although it's quick, you have time to get to know someone in a real social situation.

F: Yes, with speed dating you meet twenty people in one hour! And I was there for two hours!

D: Sounds quite fun though – did you meet anyone you liked?

F: Well, there was one who was quite nice ...

Track 2.19

So, erm ... Valentine's Day started hundreds of years ago. There was an emperor in Italy ... and, well, ... the emperor didn't want his soldiers to get married ... because he wanted the soldiers only to fight. But, a priest called Valentine helped soldiers to get married secretly. The emperor was angry about that and ... he killed Valentine ... on the fourteenth of February. So, now people celebrate love and romance ... on that day ... in memory of Valentine.

So, Valentine's Day is on the fourteenth of February and people celebrate all over the world. Traditionally, people send cards to each other. And they give presents – flowers and chocolates, usually. And of course, it is traditional for a boyfriend to take his girlfriend out for a romantic dinner in a restaurant. It's also a popular date for getting married.

Some people think that Valentine's Day is too commercial. They think that people buy too many cards and presents ... but I don't agree. I mean, people buy things of course, but I think it's really good to celebrate love and romance.

Track 2.20

eight thousand, eight hundred and eighty centimetres

three million, two hundred and thirty-five thousand, eight hundred and ninety-nine metres

six and a quarter kilograms

nine and three-quarter hours

seventy-five and a half minutes

nought point one five seconds

forty-four point nine kilometres per hour

Track 2.22

1

I really think that my life is too busy, I'm always on the go ... and I don't sit down and rest very much... so, that's what my presentation is about today. I do everything in my life very quickly. Every day, I've got too much to do and I spend my time in a hurry. I'm always rushing around and I'm always late for everything because I don't have time to fit everything in. It makes me really stressed because I feel I can't do anything properly. My mobile phone rings all the time and it interrupts me when I'm working. It would be a good idea to turn it off, but I like people contacting me. I think that it might be something really important – but it isn't usually! The other reason why I'm always rushing around is that my work is very far away from where I live. That means I have to travel for about an hour each way ... at least. I mean, usually I spend about two hours or maybe more travelling ... and I'm usually late. I use the time when I'm sitting on the train and I send emails and go on Facebook and things on my laptop. But it's very tiring because I don't get home until quite late. So, yes, all in all, my life is very fast and busy.

2

The topic of my presentation is 'The benefits of technology in my life'. The main points I will talk about are: firstly, how technology benefits my work life and secondly, how technology benefits my personal life.

Let's begin with my work life. I am a doctor and there are huge benefits to my professional life from technology. In the past, I wrote all my patient's notes on paper and sometimes things got lost. It is much easier for me to look at my patients' notes now because they are all on computer. I can also look for symptoms, illnesses and medicines online if I need to. Also, my patients can book their appointments

with a computer system which makes it quicker and more efficient.

Now we're going to look at my personal life. My mobile phone is very important to me; I don't go anywhere without it. I have a very busy life so it is good to have a mobile. I use it on the train to keep in touch with friends or to make arrangements. My laptop is also very important; I can use it anywhere to shop online or book cinema tickets and other things.

I'd like to finish by saying that some people think that there are disadvantages to modern technology, but I think that if you use it thoughtfully, there can be huge benefits.

Track 2.25

1

My worst interview experience was about three years ago. I had a group interview for a sales rep job with a big media company. There were about ten or twelve interviewees ... and about three interviewers, I think. At first, I was quite confident ... I mean, I had good experience and the right qualifications and I felt I was right for the job. But, erm ... I don't know why... but when they asked me the first question ... I began to feel very nervous. My throat went dry and I couldn't speak. Then, I started coughing and ... erm, it was really awful because I just couldn't speak. One of the interviewers gave me a jug of water. I was really nervous and I couldn't really think clearly by that time ... Anyway, he gave me the jug, and ... slowly, I took it from him ... you know, the jug was really heavy and my hands were shaking. I really didn't want to spill it. So, erm ... I poured it very carefully ... but all fifteen or so people in the room stopped and looked at me ... and my hands were shaking so much that the water went everywhere ... all over me ... and all over the floor. It was terrible ... I was really embarrassed! At that point, I grabbed my bag and left the room. I still go cold all over when I think about it.

2

Well, I think my worst experience was about two months ago. I had an interview for a good job as a marketing director. I really wanted the job. I remember that it was raining that day ... so I decided to drive. But the traffic was really bad and when I arrived, I didn't have much time. I didn't want to be late for the interview. So, ... I drove into the company car park and quickly parked my car in the nearest place. Well, it turned out that it was the Managing Director's parking place. That was bad ... but it got worse because ... erm ... just as I was getting out of my car, the Managing Director himself arrived in his car – a great big BMW or something. Well, as you can imagine, he wasn't very happy at all. In fact, he shouted at me angrily ... and told me to park somewhere else. By that time, I was really worried about being late ... so, I ignored him and ran off to the interview. I know I behaved really rudely ... but I was desperate to get to the interview. Well, it got worse ... because he was one of the interviewers and he was really angry about it all and he refused to give me an interview in the end.

3

My first interview after leaving college was for a job as a receptionist for a large company. I prepared myself for the interview really well. You know – I found out about the company and prepared my answers and everything – but, when it came to the actual interview, the whole thing was a bit strange really. Erm ... I arrived on time and I confidently walked into the interview room. But then I got a real shock ... because as soon as I stepped into the room, the interviewer threw a tennis ball at me! I quickly moved to one side and it didn't hit me. Well, unfortunately, I didn't get the job ... I was quite upset about that. They told me afterwards that the tennis ball was to test people's reactions. They wanted to see what people did with it. The person who caught the ball and threw it back got the job! The people who moved to one side or caught it and put it back on the desk, didn't! I wasn't very happy about the whole thing really ... I felt really cheated, to be honest. The whole interview went really badly for me – I just don't think they took it seriously at all and I didn't get a chance to talk about myself or show them what I could do.

Track 2.26
E = Employee B = Boss

E: Oh, hi, can I talk to you a minute, please?
B: I'm a bit busy right now, actually.
E: Well, it's really important because I want to take Friday off. Is that OK?
B: As I said, I'm rather busy. If you come back later, I'll be able to talk to you properly.
E: I need to know now, though. I mean, my brother has got tickets for something. And I need to let him know now.
B: Well, I really don't think you're listening to me. I'm busy now and if it's really urgent, I will talk to you after my meeting this afternoon.
E: But ... I need an answer now ...
B: No, actually, I've changed my mind. I don't like your attitude. The answer is 'no'. You can't take Friday off.

Track 2.27
E = Employee B = Boss

B: Good morning, James. Come in. Now, you wanted to talk to me about taking the day off on Friday?
E: Yes, that's right. The thing is ... if possible, I'd like to have the day off because my brother is over here from Australia for two weeks ... and he's got tickets for a show. It's really special and I'd really like to go.
B: I understand what you're saying, yes. I know that you don't see your brother much and this sounds like a chance you don't want to miss. Ermm ... what about the report? Will you able to finish it by the end of Thursday?
E: Yes ... no problem. Obviously, I'll make sure that the report is finished before I go and I'll work late this week if necessary.
B: Yes, I know that you work long hours and I'm very pleased with your work. Ermm ... I think it sounds fine. Go ahead and have a good day.
E: Thank you very much for your understanding.
B: Not at all. And I hope you have a good time.
E: Thank you.

Track 2.28
L = Lucy A = Andy

L: Andy, umm ... we need to talk ...
A: Yes?
L: Well, I was thinking ... I think we need to travel separately now ...
A: Oh! Really? I'm enjoying being with you so much ... I think that would be a real shame ...
L: Well ... yes ... I like travelling with you, too ... but ... I want to practise my Portuguese and when I'm with you, we just speak English all the time.
A: Oh ... I promise I'll speak Portuguese to you ...
L: No ... I don't think that would work, do you?
A: No ... you're probably right.

Track 2.29
L = Lucy M = Man

M: Hi, Lucy ... you're back! I wasn't sure when your flight was.
L: Yes ... well, I've just got back actually. I arrived last night, so I'm really tired... you know, I haven't got used to the time difference yet.
M: Did you have a good time?
L: Yes! It was great. I mean, there were some difficult moments ... but mostly it was really good. When I was in Rio, I met an old school friend of mine – Andy. I didn't know he was there, but we bumped into each other in an internet café.
M: That's amazing!
L: Mmm ... well, we travelled together for a bit, but actually he was really annoying, so in the end, I told him I wanted to travel on my own. It was a bit difficult, but after that I had a fantastic time.
M: Where did you go?
L: Well, after Rio, I went up the coast to Salvador – it was really lovely. Then I went further north to Fortaleza and to lots of amazing beaches near there. It's completely idyllic actually – miles and miles of beautiful beaches.
M: Wow! Were you on your own all the time?
L: No, actually – there were lots of other people travelling, so most of time I wasn't on my own at all. In fact, I met a really nice woman called Emily – she was Australian. We got on really well and travelled together for the rest of my time in Brazil.
M: That's great!
L: Yes, it was very good.
M: Have you got any photos yet?
L: Well, yes, I've put some up on Facebook already ... and I'm going to put some more up today.

Track 2.31
P = Presenter G = Guest

P: Hello and welcome to this week's edition of *Travellers' Tales*. Later in the programme, we're talking to a group of young people who have just finished a sponsored cycle ride across Europe. But, before that, we're going to start with today's look at 'My travel inspiration' with our special guest, TV reporter, Ben Gardner. Hello, Ben.
G: Hello.
P: So, your travel inspiration ... is it a book, or a film or a piece of music, Ben? Tell us about something inspiring ... which has made you want to travel.
G: Yes, well, 'My travel inspiration' is a film – *The Motorcycle Diaries*. It's set in South America and it's about the early life of Che Guevara when he was a young man.
P: Mmm ... *The Motorcycle Diaries* ... Yes, so, who plays Che Guevara?
G: Well, Guevara is played by Gael García Bernal – he's very good. I really think he is the perfect choice for this role actually.
P: Had he starred in any other films, before he made this one?
G: Yes, yeah, a few ... but this was a turning point in his career I think ...
P: And the film is set in the 1950s, isn't it?
G: Yes, 1952, in fact. Before Che Guevara arrived in Cuba and got into politics, he had lived in Argentina with his family. He and a friend, Alberto, decided they wanted to travel and see South America.
P: Mmm ...
G: Anyway, at the beginning of the film, we see them preparing for their trip in Buenos Aires. They buy an old motorbike ... and the rest of the film then follows

them on their amazing 8-month-long trip through Argentina, Chile, Peru, Columbia and Venezuela ... Basically, it's about two young men seeing a bit more of the world and learning about life. They have some really exciting adventures. There are some dangerous moments, too ... you know, on the motorbike!
P: So, what was most inspiring for you about this film?
G: Well, three things I think. Firstly, I was inspired by the two main characters – they are very believable. García Bernal is brilliant as Guevara, and Rodrigo de la Serna, as his friend Alberto, is also excellent. Anyway, as the film goes on, I was fascinated to see how their personalities grow and change. All their adventures were really inspiring ... and it's great how they learned so much from all the people they met along the way. At the beginning of the trip, they were young men – just interested in having fun – and they had become much more grown up ... and mature, by the time they reached the end.
P: Mmm ...
G: There's a particular scene when they were in a sort of hospital in a poor part of the countryside in Peru ... It was a depressing place and very sad, but Guevara got very close to the people in the hospital. It was inspiring to see that.
P: And the second thing ...?
G: The South American people that these young men met on their travels ... Almost all the people they met were kind and helpful – they went out of their way to help Guevara and Alberto, even though they didn't have much themselves. The supporting cast is excellent at showing that aspect. And the South American people also like a good party ... so they have a lot of fun!
P: Yes, I'm sure! And thirdly?
G: Well, ... the scenery. In fact, I think I'd say that the scenery of South America is possibly the main star of the film!
P: Really?
G: Well, yes. Before I saw this film, I hadn't thought about visiting South America ... but it inspired me to go there almost immediately. I was surprised by the incredible beauty of this continent. I was really amazed by the huge diversity there. I followed the route of the film – more or less. I mean, first, I started in the southern parts of Argentina and Chile where it's really cold. And then, I went up to the hotter desert parts of Chile. Then, I travelled further north into Peru – Machu Picchu in Peru was really incredible. Then, finally, I got to the beautiful jungle areas of Colombia and Venezuela.
P: Well, you've certainly inspired me – and I hope our listeners – to want to go to South America. It sounds fantastic ...
G: Yes, ... well, I'm sure you won't be disappointed.
P: OK ... so Ben, I hope you'll stay with us for the rest of the programme and take some calls from listeners later.

Track 2.33
M = Man

M: Well ... something really frightening happened to me the other day. I had a really unusual – and frightening journey – going from London to Paris. I'd got a really good last-minute deal and I was going for the weekend with my wife. Anyway, it started off badly when our flight was suddenly cancelled and so obviously we were quite annoyed about that. It was really annoying because we were only going for a short time. But then they said there was another flight we could go on … which was only twenty minutes after our cancelled flight. So, we all got on the flight and nothing happened really until we got to Paris. And then, just as we were coming in to land, … it's hard to believe, but suddenly we started climbing again. The wheels were almost touching the ground I think … and the engines came on very, very … very, very loud and we started climbing violently. There was no announcement from the captain. And then the engines went quiet again and then we climbed again violently and then we went sideways and then we went another way and then we climbed again and … believe it or not, this went on for about five minutes – maybe longer. Actually, it felt like about half an hour, but it was probably about five minutes. After a while, the plane started flying normally again and then the captain made an announcement and apologised. It's incredible, I know, but a lorry had been on the runway. He said that a lorry had been in the middle of the runway … and he had had to take off again in order to avoid it. Well, what a journey! Thankfully, we had a really good weekend in Paris, and the flight back was fine!

Track 2.34

1

E = Emma M = Man

M: So, Emma, who was the person who most influenced you when you were growing up? I mean, like a role model … or something?

E: Well erm my parents both worked a lot when I was young, erm especially my dad, and well, he worked abroad a lot of the time so … I would see him three times a year or something. He used to have a job which took him to different countries all the time – mostly Japan and China – so I only saw him in the school holidays really. I lived with my mum, but I was always really close to my grandmother, too. I got on really well with my mum, but I think the person who most influenced me was my grandmother.

M: Mmm … Did you see her a lot?

E: Yes. My mum and my grandmother brought me up really. I mean, she didn't live with us, but she would look after me a lot when my mum was working. I think I would see her almost every day. Erm I really looked up to my grandmother. She's she was a wonderful person. I mean, she was incredibly kind and generous. And she would always spend time with me. You know, she always seemed interested in what I had to say.

2

G = George W = Woman

W: George, who do you think was the most influential person in your life when you were a child?

G: Erm well, I was really into ice skating – particularly ice hockey – when I was young. I loved playing ice hockey … I used to be really good! I picked it up really quickly and … and did it all the time, you know. I started playing when I was about five and … well, went on until … eighteen, or something – when I left school. And my coach was an amazing man called Frank. He was a really good trainer. He, he taught me so much about the sport and was very good at motivating me and keeping me focused. He was a really inspiring person. He was a really good mentor … and role model … in many ways.

W: How often did you see him?

G: Well, I would see him all the time! … You know, … I used to wear my skates more than my shoes probably! I mean I really played a lot. I would play six or seven times a week and he was always there. It wasn't just the training though. I think I really looked up to him. When you asked him something, he wouldn't say much, you know, but what he did say always seemed to be the right thing to say. I remember thinking … I want to be like him!

Track 2.35

P = Presenter W = Woman

P: Today, we're talking about advertising. The aim of any company is to sell; and to continue to sell, more than other companies. And to keep ahead of the competition, companies need to advertise their product better and better in order to influence potential customers. Top advertising executive, Sarah Delaney, is with us today to talk about new developments in advertising and the amazing technological developments which make them possible. Good morning, Sarah.

W: Hello.

P: So … , before we talk about these new developments, Sarah, can you tell us … what kinds of adverts have the most influence on people?

W: Well … , that's an interesting question. Erm, I think that all advertising has some kind of influence on people. I mean, we may think, perhaps, that we make free choices about which products to buy … but actually, the adverts that you've seen will certainly influence what you think about different products … even though you may not think about that consciously.

P: Yes, adverts put ideas in your head, even if you don't want them there! So … , what do you think makes an advert effective? What are the most effective types of adverts?

W: Erm, … the most effective types of adverts … well, I think it depends really. Some people respond to humour; some people like an advert to have a lot of information; other people are very influenced by their favourite celebrity in an advert. I think, in the end, adverts are effective because they are very clearly aimed at certain groups of people … and a lot of research goes into which group of people your advert is aimed at.

P: And it's not just who the adverts are aimed at – there is also a lot of research into how and where to advertise, isn't there?

W: Yes, and with new technological developments, things are changing all the time.

P: So…, what's new in the advertising world, then?

W: Well …, there's one new innovation which means that television viewers may soon see adverts during their favourite documentary or drama series.

P: Oh, really?

W: Yes. Some developers for television companies are planning pop-up advertisements. That means logos or messages can be flashed up on the screen during a programme so the company doesn't have to wait until the commercial break to advertise. Basically, erm … the new technology is used to find a blank space on the screen to put the logo on – like some blue sky or a blank wall – you know, not covering someone's face in your favourite soap opera.

P: Even on a blank space, it sounds annoying!

W: Well, yes – some people would say very annoying! Some people are worried that these pop-up adverts will destroy their enjoyment of a programme. The developers are convinced, however, that consumers will like them.

P: I'm not sure they're right about that! …

W: Well… there are other developers who agree with you. In Japan, they are developing an approach which is very different… almost the opposite really.

P: Mmm…?

W: Yes … Nintendo has created a new internet video site for games consoles, and it uses a new system for advertising. The company did some research about the way customers are influenced by adverts and they decided they didn't want to force viewers to watch adverts. With the new system, no adverts are shown on the screen at all. Consumers choose to watch adverts only if they want to.

P: Ah! That sounds better!

W: Mmm … and if they do choose one, they get a very informative kind of advert … with more detailed and interesting information about the product. And as well as the advert itself, consumers can do other useful things, like receive vouchers to get discounts or even order some free samples of the product. The company hopes that adverts will change from something we avoid watching, to something we want to watch. They may even become one of the most popular things on TV, you never know; … these entertaining adverts may actually become a form of entertainment in themselves, in fact.

P: Yes – that would really turn things around, wouldn't it? Adverts either spoil your favourite show or they become your favourite show!

W: That's right! But you know, in whichever way companies choose to get their message across, one thing is for sure: advertising, in some form, is here to stay …

Track 2.37

1

W1 = Woman W2 = Woman 2 A = Announcer

W1: Hey Lisa … Are you coming out with us tonight?

W2: No, I can't. My hair looks terrible!

A: Are you worried about your hair? Is your hair boring and lifeless? Does it stop you going out? You need ShinePower from Studio-X. With ShinePower, even the most boring hair suddenly comes to life. ShinePower will make your hair shine like never before. After one wash with ShinePower from Studio-X, your hair will look amazing!

W1: Hey Lisa … Are you coming out with us tonight?

W2: Of course I am.

W1: Hey, your hair looks amazing!

A: ShinePower from Studio-X. Your hair will look amazing!

2

The new G5 by Kurama is the car you've wanted all your life … Designed by an expert car designer … Engineered by an expert car engineer … Made by an expert car maker … Now, … driven by an expert driver. You. The new G5 by Kurama: a car by experts – for experts.

Audioscripts

Track 2.38

W = Woman M = Man

W: OK … we're going to play the 'Yes-No' game. Do you know how to play?

M: No, I've never played that. How do you play?

W: Well, basically, I ask you questions and you must not answer with either 'Yes' or 'No'.

M: What can I say, then?

W: You can say anything else … like … 'I'm not sure', or 'Maybe', or 'I'll think about it' or 'Definitely'. You know, anything else, but not 'Yes' or 'No'.

M: OK. That sounds easy!

W: OK. Let's start. Ready?

M: Y … umm … I am!

W: OK. Have you seen any good films recently?

M: I have.

W: Have you ever seen a film that changed your life?

M: Maybe.

W: Did you say 'Maybe'?

M: Err … I'm not sure.

W: What about 'Yes Man'? Have you seen that?

M: I have.

W: You have? Really?

M: Yes! Ohhhh! You tricked me …

W: That's the idea!

M: OK … now I'll ask you. Ready?

W: Definitely.

M: Right. Are you going to go on holiday this summer?

W: I've told you that.

M: Are you going to the seaside?

W: Sure.

M: Are you looking forward to it?

W: I certainly am.

M: Oh. What can I ask you? Do you believe in fate?

W: Fate?

M: Yes, do you believe in fate? You know, that our lives are planned already somehow, and you can't change them?

W: Not at all. I believe that you can change a lot about your life.

M: So you don't believe in fate?

W: No, I don't!

M: Got you! You said 'No'.

Track 2.39

P = Presenter M = Michael Dennis
C = Caroline Clarke PA = Parent H = Holly

P: A quick summary, now, of the main *Money in Education* stories this week … Firstly, as any parent knows, the cost of education can be huge, especially as children get older and want to go to university. You will be faced with huge fees – and the problem of how to pay for them. Earlier this week, I spoke to financial adviser, Michael Dennis, and he told me about this month's figures and the almost unbelievable cost of going to university these days.

M: University has always been expensive and there are schemes in which you can get a grant to help pay the fees, or for the top students, you can sometimes get a scholarship. But these aren't always available, and in most cases, when you're at university, you may need to get a loan from the bank to pay for everything. Of course, you're not earning money when you're studying, so you can't even begin to pay the loan back until you leave university and, hopefully, get a job. It's not much fun starting your working life in debt … and owing the bank a lot of money. Official figures out this month show that the average student debt is around fifteen thousand pounds. For medical students, the figure rises to around twenty-five thousand pounds.

P: Twenty-five thousand pounds … that's a lot of money. And that could take at least twelve years to pay back – if you manage to get a well-paid job … That was financial adviser, Michael Dennis. The news is not all bad for students, however. Some schools have taken part in reward schemes in which they actually pay their students. St. Luke's School in Bristol has given eleven thousand pounds to its A-level students for getting good exam results. Before their exams, the school gave each student target grades to try and achieve. Now the results have arrived, St. Luke's sixth form college has given five hundred pounds to every student who got into university and students get prizes of twenty pounds for achieving each target grade. Caroline Clarke, Head of Sixth-form Education, had to say …

C: The results this year show the success of the scheme. Unlike many schemes, this one rewards every student for doing well, not just the best students in the year.

P: I asked various people what they thought of the scheme. Yesterday, I spoke to a parent of a student at the school and asked her how she felt about the reward scheme.

PA: Well … I'm not sure really. I don't think they should pay students … I mean, young people should work hard for exams because they want to do well … not because they'll earn some money! I think people think about money too much.

P: Later, I spoke to Mike Bell, Head Teacher at St. Luke's. He told me that more students had got places at university this year than ever before. He also said the students were working much harder than before and his school would continue with the scheme next year. Holly, a student at St. Luke's, said she was really pleased that her school had taken part in the scheme. She told me it was a great idea … and that it had made her work much harder. She also said that she was really excited because she had earned over five hundred pounds. When I asked what she was going to do with the money, she told me she was going to buy a new laptop computer, which now she could afford to buy.

H: Yeah, with the five hundred pounds, I can afford a new computer, which is great news … as I really need one for my studies. At my school, most of us thought the reward scheme was really good. Some of us weren't sure at first, but in the end, certainly we all agreed that the scheme had made us work harder.

P: Finally, we heard this week about another reward scheme … this time in the US. With holidays coming up soon, one school in Florida has set up a homework scheme using the internet. Students who do more than twelve hours of practice exercises on the specially-designed internet site during the school holidays, will get prizes: children aged six to ten get a bicycle, those aged eleven to fourteen get a hundred dollars and those aged fifteen to eighteen get MP3 players. Some people feel that reward schemes like this are controversial but with prizes like those, I'm sure the students will study as hard as they can! … Well, that's it for today. I hope you can tune in for next week's *Money in Education* summary. And now … over to Fiona in the weather studio …

Track 2.40

W1 = Woman W2 = Woman 2

W1: So, let's find four things we've got in common … erm … what about going shopping? Do you like going shopping?

W2: Ermm … well, I'm not very keen on shopping in general, but … I like clothes shopping.

W1: Yes, me too. I really like looking for interesting clothes … you know, something a bit unusual …

W2: Mmmm … I like looking for interesting, cheap clothes. Lots of clothes are so expensive, but if you look hard enough, you can usually find some bargains.

W1: Yes, it's always good to find bargains! OK … well, I think that's two things we've got in common: We both like shopping … clothes shopping, I mean. And both of us like looking for bargains.

W2: How do you usually pay for things when you go shopping? I pay in cash. Actually, I always pay in cash because I haven't got a credit card or anything.

W1: Yes, that's the same for me. I haven't got a credit card either.

W2: OK … So, neither of us has got a credit card – that's number three … ermm …

W1: And … number four is … we both pay in cash when we go shopping. Yeah … that's four things we've got in common.

Track 2.41

We asked fifty students various questions about their attitudes to money and the results are as follows:

Firstly, forty percent of people said they would basically describe themselves as a 'saver'. Forty-five percent said they were a 'spender' and fifteen percent weren't sure or said they were a bit of both.

For the second question, we asked about lending and borrowing money. Two-thirds of people said they would lend fifty pounds to a friend. However, the majority of those people said they would be worried about doing so, in case it spoilt their friendship.

The third question was about credit cards. Eight out of ten people said they used a credit card regularly. And only a minority of those people paid off their bill completely at the end of each month.

Question four was about shopping habits …

The ActiveBook component features the Students' Book pages in digital format and includes integrated audio and video as well as interactive exercises for students to do in class or at home. The ActiveTeach component will help you get the most out of the course with its range of interactive whiteboard software tools and extra resources.

ActiveBook

Students' Book pages and interactive activities

Audio bank (Class CD material)

Video clips

Interactive video activities

Phonetic chart and dictionary

Video clips to play on DVD player

ActiveTeach

Students' Book pages and interactive activities

Interactive whiteboard tools with save functionality

Audio bank (Class CD material)

Video clips

Interactive video activities

Phonetic chart and dictionary

Extra resources for the teacher:
- class photocopiables
- video photocopiables
- printable audio and video scripts
- editable tests

Video clips to play on DVD player

Pearson Education Limited
Edinburgh Gate
Harlow
Essex CM20 2JE
England
and Associated Companies throughout the world.

www.pearsonelt.com

First published 2011
Fifth impression 2014

ISBNs:
New Total English Pre-Intermediate Teacher's Book and
Teacher's Resource Disc Pack
9781408267288

Set in Meta Plus Book-Roman
Printed in Malaysia (CTP-PPSB)

Cover image: *Front*: Photolibrary.com: George Hammerstein